ENRICHED LEARNING PROJECTS

A Practical Pathway to 21st Century Skills

JAMES BELLANCA

Solution Tree | Press

a division of

Solution Tree

555 North Morton Street
Bloomington, IN 47404
800.733.6786 (toll free) / 812.336.7700
FAX: 812.336.7790

email: info@solution-tree.com
solution-tree.com

Visit **go.solution-tree.com/instruction** to download the reproducibles in this book.

Printed in the United States of America

14 13 12 11 2 3 4 5

Library of Congress Cataloging-in-Publication Data

Bellanca, James A., 1937-

Enriched learning projects : a practical pathway to 21st century skills / James Bellanca.

p. cm.

Includes bibliographical references and index.

ISBN 978-1-934009-74-1 (perfect bound) -- ISBN 978-1-935249-34-4 (library binding) 1. Project method in teaching--United States. 2. Curriculum enrichment--United States. 3. Education (Secondary)--United States. I. Title.

LB1027.43.B45 2010

371.3'6--dc22

2009045804

Solution Tree
Jeffrey C. Jones, CEO & President

Solution Tree Press
President: Douglas M. Rife
Publisher: Robert D. Clouse
Vice President of Production: Gretchen Knapp
Managing Production Editor: Caroline Wise
Senior Production Editor: Edward Levy
Copy Editor: Rachel Rosolina
Proofreader: Sarah Payne-Mills
Text Designer and Compositor: Amy Shock
Cover Designer: Orlando Angel

With great appreciation and love to my father, Leonard, and my mother, Mary, who inspired and supported all that I, my brothers and sister, and my four children have accomplished. Their lives have made us all think harder and learn from each and every experience we have.

Acknowledgments

I would like to thank Phil Harris, executive director of the Association for Educational Communications and Technology, for his suggestions and guidance regarding this book; Bob Pearlman for writing the preface; my daughter, Kate Bellanca, for her assistance and guidance with writing and completing the citations; Gretchen Knapp, Robb Clouse, and the more than helpful editorial staff at Solution Tree Press; Arline Paul, my long-time friend and colleague, for her input and critique of the text; the alumni of the Center for Self-Directed Learning for reminding me of the spirit and joy inherent in the project way; and the many dedicated and creative teachers who taught me how to take that project way.

* * *

Solution Tree Press would like to thank the following reviewers:

John Barell
Professor Emeritus
Montclair State University
Consultant
More Curious Minds
New York

Charlotte Danielson
Educational Consultant
Princeton, New Jersey

Robert Delisle
Dean of the School of Education
Antioch University Seattle
Seattle, Washington

Robin Fogarty
President
Robin Fogarty & Associates, Ltd.
Chicago

Beverly Gulley
Dean, School of Education
Saint Xavier University
Chicago

Peggy Hall
Principal
Washington District Elementary School
Buckhannon, West Virginia

Carrie Kuhn
Sixth-Grade Teacher
Graland Country Day School
Denver, Colorado

Thom Markham
President and Consultant
New Century Schools
Novato, California

Kerry Rice
Assistant Professor
Boise State University
Boise, Idaho

Jim Winter
Founder and President
Wavelength, Inc.
Chicago

David Ross
Director of Professional Development
The Buck Institute for Education
Novato, California

Visit **go.solution-tree.com/instruction** to download the reproducibles in this book.

Table of Contents

Titles in italics indicate reproducible pages.

CHAPTER 7
Creating a Collaborative Classroom Culture . . . 119

CHAPTER 8
Assessing Enriched Projects 147

CHAPTER 9
An Enriched Project Sampler 169

About the Author

James Bellanca is founder and CEO of International Renewal Institute, Inc., and founder of the educational publishing company Skylight. His extensive experience as a classroom teacher, alternative school director, professional developer, and intermediate service center consultant has given him a wide scope of knowledge. Known for his cutting-edge program design and implementation of research-rich, standards-aligned, professional learning programs for educators, Jim has worked with educational leaders in districts across the United States to design programs that promote critical thinking and collaboration to increase academic performance among all children, including high-risk student populations.

In addition to his other accomplishments, Jim has designed alternative school programs; an intermediate service center that pioneered practical professional development programs; a statewide, strategy-based set of courses for teachers; Illinois' largest and most dynamic field-based master's degree program (in partnership with three universities); and a nonprofit service agency dedicated to the development of a 21st century enriched learning school model based on full integration of the Feuerstein method across all areas of curriculum and instruction. He is the editor, with Ron Brandt, of *21st Century Skills* (Solution Tree Press, 2010) and serves as the executive director of the Illinois Consortium for 21st Century Skills.

Foreword

by Bob Pearlman

"High school is boring," says Chicago Mayor Richard Daley in a front-page headline in the September 18, 2003, *Chicago Tribune.* "Students are apathetic," a rural school district administrator from central Louisiana told me recently.

We are now fifteen to twenty years into the standards movement. State after state has enacted a system of content standards and testing in core subjects. Schooling has gotten more boring, and limited, with its focus on content, core subjects, basic skills, and content testing. The unfortunate result of this limited assessment and accountability system has been to identify, and shame, the same schools everyone knew were failing previously. And the latest results from the National Assessment of Educational Progress (October 2009) shows that there was more overall student progress in the six years prior to the No Child Left Behind law than in the six years following the passage of this law.

Standards—what students should know and be able to do—should have worked to enable, not impede, innovative learning approaches, as James Bellanca points out in this wonderful teacher's guide, *Enriched Learning Projects: A Practical Pathway to 21st Century Skills.* All the early 1990s work by the math, science, and other subject-matter associations aspired to just that. However, once the states took control, they turned standards into fodder for basic skills accountability only.

Project-based learning has a long history over the past century. Traditional education, or teacher-directed whole-group learning, holds sway, but project-based learning keeps coming back. And each time it does, it is implemented with more rigor—with stronger methodology, practice, innovative tools, and assessment.

Bellanca has devoted a career to helping teachers acquire the skills to be effective in the classroom. He is the author of numerous books—on cooperative and collaborative learning, graphic organizers, and other instructional strategies—and the publisher of many teacher "how to" books.

Bellanca recounts his own personal history as a project-based learning teacher long before he moved into a career as a writer and publisher of practical education books. Most compelling was his time at the Center for Self-Directed Learning, a small school-within-a-school in Illinois, from 1974 to 1984. There, the teachers—known as "learning facilitators"—fostered student self-assessment, student portfolios, and the exhibition of "products" for evidence of student mastery.

Every decade brings its own fresh insights and powerful new tools and methods. New e-tools began to emerge in the 1980s, standards emerged in the 1990s, and in the 2000s, 21st century skills emerged. These skills go beyond content knowledge to include communication, collaboration, critical thinking, creativity, technology, global awareness, cross-cultural skills, and more, as identified by the Partnership for 21st Century Skills (2002).

Bellanca knows that teachers want to be effective with their students. Nothing pleases them more than seeing their students learn and demonstrate their learning. Bellanca incorporates all the best new tools and methodological improvements in this worthy teacher's guide.

From 2001–2009 I traveled the United States helping local education, civic, and business leaders envision a new, more powerful 21st century learning model, that of New Technology High School. The New Tech model features 100 percent project-based learning, one-on-one computing, and assessment of 21st century skills. Whether I went to East Los Angeles, rural central Louisiana, or rural, suburban, or urban Indiana, I heard the same refrain: "We need to prepare our students to be knowledge workers and citizens of the future. That means 21st century skills. That's why we need project-based learning."

I personally have had two distinct passions regarding project-based learning: (1) to help individual teachers change their classroom practice to project-based learning, and (2) to engage students and give them 21st century skills.

During most of my career I have dealt with helping individual teachers. In the late 1970s and early 1980s I pioneered in using personal computers in education and helped teachers to leverage these new tools to change instruction. At the Autodesk Foundation, from 1996–2000, our team developed a national network of project-based learning practitioners. Two thousand people attended our year 2000 Kids Who Know and Do Annual Conference of Project-Based Learning.

But then my second passion also became possible, and starting in 2001 we assembled a school development team, the New Technology Foundation, based in Napa, California, to assist communities nationally in launching new 21st century high schools.

James Bellanca addresses both my passions—classroom practice and 21st century skills. He writes, "I have designed *Enriched Learning Projects* to be a useful tool for teachers who appreciate the value and benefit of learning experiences based in projects, who want the best learning for their students, and who value 21st century learning" (page xx).

Project-based learning is hard to do well. To be effective, it requires the design of projects that meet and bring to life both state standards and 21st century skills. It requires appropriate benchmarks, interim and final assessments, and significant teacher facilitation. An effective project gets better over time, refined through both execution in the classroom and scaffolding activities.

Project-based learning is getting better and stronger in many countries. In the past, it has not always been implemented effectively, and this has caused new practitioners to rename or rebrand it to emphasize the superior practices and quality of the newer approaches. In Australia they call it *rich tasks*. At Ninestiles School in Birmingham, England, it's called *reality-based learning.* At Homewood School in Kent, England, it is *total learning.*

Bellanca rightly calls his project-based learning *enriched learning.* He really upgrades the methodology and practice of project-based learning, which in the past has often focused on the experiential. He doesn't abandon this goal; instead he gives the teacher reader new practices and methods to ensure student success. His important new approaches include the use of digital tools and teacher's mediation skills to support student critical thinking and problem solving

Enriched Learning Projects is an outstanding companion to the Buck Institute of Education's *Project Based Learning Handbook* (Markham, Larmer, & Ravitz, 2003). This handbook effectively guides teachers through project planning, assessment, and implementation. Bellanca does this and more. His book is an intellectual dialogue direct with you, as a teacher, showing you not only how to design, assess, and implement projects, but also how to directly support your students with mind tools and mediation of critical thinking.

Bellanca identifies five attributes of the enriched learning model: 1) it is research-based; 2) it uses technology as a tool to promote students' learning efficiency; 3) it involves self-assessment (students' thinking about their thinking); 4) it involves learning *from* doing; and 5) it intentionally includes 21st century skill development. He then shows how to design an enriched learning project through backwards design. He brings readers up to date on new technology tools that support students and on teacher implementation of enriched learning projects.

But where he really makes a contribution to the field is in those areas that he has long studied. In chapter 4, "Which Instructional Strategies Count Most?" Bellanca articulates the three phases of enriched learning projects:

1. Gather information
2. Make sense
3. Communicate results

Bellanca shows high-yield strategies that assist students in doing research, in making sense of their findings, and in showing their new understanding. These include the use of graphic organizers, such as KWL (what we *know*, what we *want* to know, what we *learned*), concept maps, fishbone charts, sequence charts, problem-solving charts, and written summaries.

Teachers, in Bellanca's view, are mediators of quality thinking. Bellanca translates Reuven Feuerstein's work to education and identifies the six essential cognitive functions that are most necessary for the success of projects. He shows teachers how to use questioning and suggestions—what he calls mediation skills—to help students keep focus, be flexible, and make connections.

Bellanca also stresses practices that we have found highly effective in the roll-out of New Tech schools nationally. One is the establishment of a collaborative classroom culture to support a project-based learning environment, and a second is an emphasis on student self-assessment. "Projects give you an opportunity to shift the primary responsibility for learning and its assessment onto the students' shoulders," he writes. "Although not a quick and easy task, this shift is possible and desirable. Making the shift so that students take the lead in assessing what and how they are learning enables you to enrich their learning" (page 152).

Finally, Bellanca reclaims the standards movement and shows that the enriched learning project model is the best way for students to learn, and master, the standards. He points out that most state standards go beyond content and call for students to explain, verify, analyze, make generalizations, predict, forecast, estimate, and draw conclusions—mental operations that fit under the generic label of critical thinking.

Most implementation of standards in the United States has stressed rote learning and neglected the thinking operations identified in the standards. Bellanca advises teachers that "by aligning your project with the process element of the standards, you can focus students on explicit development of those critical and creative thinking skills embedded in the standards" (page 117).

Bob Pearlman is a 21st Century School Development consultant. He is the former director of strategic planning for the New Technology Foundation and former president of the Autodesk Foundation (email: bobpearlman@mindspring.com).

REFERENCES

Markham, T., Larmer, J., & Ravitz, J. (2003). *Project based learning handbook: A guide to standards-focused project-based learning for middle and high school students.* Novato, CA: Buck Institute for Education.

National Center for Education Statistics. (2009). *The nation's report card.* Accessed at http://nces.ed.gov/nationsreportcard on October 26, 2009.

Partnership for 21st Century Skills. (2002). *Learning for the 21st century.* Accessed at www.21stcenturyskills.org/images/stories/otherdocs/p21up_Report.pdf on October 27, 2009.

Preface

I had my first experiences with project-based learning in the first grade. My class built a sandbox village out of wooden blocks that showed our town. We started with our school, our church, the town hall, the movie theater, and our homes. After we colored and sketched windows on the first set of blocks, we added the grocery store, the drugstore, and the synagogue. Finally, we marked the streets we used on our walks to school.

I didn't know it then, but that first-grade sandbox village would put me on a path that I would never regret. Like Dorothy on her trip along the yellow brick road, as I passed through my years in school I would discover through project-based learning many exciting challenges.

Grade school was filled with projects. I remember making a diorama of Fort Ticonderoga in the second grade and soap sculptures of Egyptian monuments in the third, as well as attending annual performances about stories we'd read. Later I participated in a dig for dinosaurs, clay modeling, science treasure hunts, making collages, painting murals, and the eighth-grade science fair.

In high school, I remember well the mock legislature, more science fairs, an anti-drinking and driving campaign, a mock court, museum field trips, and a movie production—as well as the peak adventure, a trip to New York City. In college, I recall the math photo album, the biology experiments, a miniproduction of *Oedipus Rex,* journals, and a short story about my friends.

In my novice teaching years, I thought of my mentors. I marveled at how they taught me to weave projects into each unit. Drawing on my own past experiences to create projects for my students, I had my freshman English classes build miniature Globe Theatres, act out scenes from *Romeo and Juliet*, and welcome poet Gwendolyn Brooks for a poetry day. My Latin classes dressed for a debate in the style of the Roman senate. We built a replica of the senate chamber and hung posters around the school. Parents and other classes came to cheer and boo the debate, which ended in the assassination of Julius Caesar.

In the following years, I learned from colleagues whose students traveled to Paris and Moscow, built a miniature computer, made a photo display of Chicago's historic skyscraper architecture, designed culture collages, wrote and passed an Illinois law, tutored children, worked in a soup kitchen, presented plays to senior citizens, campaigned for local candidates, and completed many other projects within the curriculum.

Projects are the sharpest pictures in my school memory bank. For many years, I believed that my love of project-based learning was just a personal preference. But over and over, former students have reminded me about the projects I challenged them to complete. Most comment on how they, too, recall their projects as peak experiences. Some talk about how a project motivated them to follow a career in medicine, music, art, law, and, yes, teaching.

When I am asked to justify my enthusiasm for project-based learning, I always start with my own experiences. I go on to note that my attachment to this method of learning and teaching is not just because I liked and learned from the hands-on experiences. I emphasize, as I do in this book, that there is much more to projects as learning experiences than just "doing stuff" that keeps the hands busy. The best projects in my school years were well-planned learning experiences from which students learned by doing. Such projects were *experiences* during which the teacher stayed with us, commenting on our work, helping us over the humps that stumped us—always encouraging us to examine the how and why of each project.

By the time I first integrated this mode of learning into my own classes, there was still very little research in education on best practices. Even in the 1970s and 1980s, when I learned to take advantage of cooperative learning, thinking skills, and other learning strategies that seemed to enrich students' project work, there was little research that said, "This is going to help the students learn better or faster."

In the 1990s, however, when Howard Gardner's (1991) theory of multiple intelligences illuminated the many reasons for the success of projects and explained why projects were such a motivational way of learning for so many students, it became clearer and clearer to me how project-based learning could expand teachers' repertoires. Well-planned projects take into account and intentionally develop the many diverse talents, styles, and intelligences in a classroom. In projects that include the high-yield instructional strategies identified by research, teachers are able to better engage the increasing number of students who are failing in the traditional one-dimensional mode of direct instruction. In classrooms where teachers seriously include multiple intelligences in their projects, students are happy to escape the mindless hours of repetitive skill drill on boring worksheets. I have designed *Enriched Learning Projects* to be a useful tool for teachers who appreciate the value and benefits of learning experiences based in projects, who want the best learning for their students, and who value 21st century learning. My insights about how to create projects that maximize student learning—about what the standards require and what students need for a lifetime of projects—are gleaned from my many years as a student, teacher, teacher colleague, and teacher developer. Whether you are a novice or seasoned veteran in using projects, I hope you will find in this book a bounty of fruitful ideas for designing project-based learning experiences that bring maximum benefit to your students as they become enriched 21st century learners.

Introduction

What Is an Enriched Learning Project?

The enriched learning project is a new model of instruction. It is a flexible, project-based learning model that enables teachers to enrich middle and upper grade students' learning experiences by integrating standards-aligned content with 21st century skills in a project framework. Teachers modify the basic project framework by selecting the high-yield instructional strategies, digital tools, and best assessment practices that are most likely to increase student achievement, critical and creative thinking, collaboration and communication, and technology use in the project and for lifelong learning.

An enriched learning project provides teachers with the option of using this model as a way of teaching that differs from direct instruction and other stand-and-deliver models. Teachers may design any lesson or unit of any length as an enriched learning project geared to producing standards-aligned outcomes not only for content, but also for critical thinking, collaboration, and communication. Enriched learning projects have the special value of helping teachers to integrate these 21st century outcomes in a single learning experience.

An important attribute of the enriched learning project is the intentional use of high-yield instructional strategies to promote high achievement (Marzano, Pickering, & Pollock, 2001). A second enriching attribute is the intentional integration of an ever-increasing number of digital tools, especially free, open-source websites. Even teachers who are not high-tech wizards can choose from among an ever-increasing number of digital tools. Although these e-tools will enhance student learning in this model of instruction, they are not required—teachers can create highly effective projects without them. Similarly, teachers do not have to restrict instruction to high-yield, best-practice strategies. But research shows that such practices are important contributors to higher achievement, and teachers committed to developing each student to capacity cannot avoid considering the inclusion of these enriching tools and strategies.

The Objectives of This Book

What students learn must prepare them for the challenges they will face in higher education and the work world. The objectives of this book are therefore:

- To enrich student learning of standards-based curricula in a 21st century learning environment
- To infuse the project model of instruction with those research-strong strategies and tactics that give students the best chance for higher achievement
- To enrich instruction with the use of appropriate electronic tools that better enable collaboration, communication, critical and creative thinking, and problem solving by all students
- To enable teachers to mediate, through purposeful reflection, the processes of critical and creative thinking, problem solving, collaboration, and using technology
- To facilitate the integration of new tools and strategies from the enriched learning project model by showing how to design enriched learning experiences that empower students to gather information, make sense of new concepts and communicate new understandings, and assess how well they are learning in preparation for the demands of their 21st century lives

Whether you choose to use one project in a school year, one per semester, or one per unit, or whether you want to transform your instruction so that enriched learning projects are a daily occurrence, this book can help you translate standards-based content to the enriched learning project model. This model therefore offers you many choices. For each enriched learning project, you will determine its length, scope, and complexity. You must feel comfortable with the changes you are making to add this model to your repertoire—even if they sometimes stretch your comfort zone.

In my work in the field, I regularly hear a number of questions from teachers concerned about using this model.

What About Accountability?

Some feel that the accountability climate works against teachers' inclusion of project-based learning in their instructional repertoires. This is especially true when a school district dictates scripted instruction in early reading and mathematics, or eats up valuable instructional time with additional days and weeks of test practice and test taking, or when a principal declares, "Thinking? We don't have time for thinking!" However, as I learned in my review of the research on project-based learning, the studies do more than tell us that it works. A wealth of information not only supports the value of the project-based learning approach for both high achievers and low performers alike, but also identifies what teachers can do specifically to make sure that project-based learning experiences are fruitful for all students (Thomas & Mergendollar, 2000).

Will Projects Allow Me to Teach the Standards?

Many teachers think the standards require them to teach to the test with direct instruction. Projects don't do that, they claim. This response is especially strong in those districts that try to "teacher-proof" instruction with heavily scripted lessons in which teachers and some district administrators kill student motivation with "skill and drill."

However, in my work with schools starting project-based learning, I have found that when teachers are encouraged to start with their districts' learning standards and integrate best instructional strategies and tactics throughout the project, they more readily provide students with both mind-engaging projects and the best chance to learn the required content defined in even the most rigorous and inflexible standards. They discover that students will engage with the same material more deeply and faster in the enriched project model. In fact, the literature on student performance shows that when students learn *from* how they do projects, by reflecting on their performance and by taking in intensive feedback from their teacher, they are much more likely to perform better in their daily work and on their standards-based tests (Barron et al., 1998). In addition, when projects intentionally develop students' thinking and problem-solving skills, students are more likely to develop learning skills and habits that will expand their motivation for learning, make them more efficient and effective thinkers, and—as I have heard from my students—prepare them for a lifetime of problem solving in challenging careers (David, 2008).

Isn't It Complicated?

Another reason I frequently hear teachers give for not using project-based learning is that the project mode of learning is too complex or advanced for their students. Nothing could be further from the truth. In fact, this response clearly reveals low expectations. Students can do well in this mode of learning from the earliest grades, provided teachers prepare the projects to match the grade-level standards. Students of all ages love projects. Like fish in water, they immerse themselves in the hands-on tasks, especially if the tasks are well planned to challenge their thinking and problem-solving skills.

Recently, preK to grade 5 teachers in rural Washington District Elementary School in Buckhannon, West Virginia, learned the value of planning a project during a one-day professional learning experience. Even though they were under strict instruction by their county to focus on scripted lessons with highly defined schedules, they were able to see the benefits of the project approach.

Their investigation of enriched project learning started in collaborative teams, where they gathered information about 21st century skills and their own state's reading standards. After they made sense of these two pieces of information—by finding the similarities that bound the skills and the standards—they created simple newsprint sketches to communicate what they had learned. Next, they analyzed what they had done using the criteria for effective project learning experiences. With this analysis, they saw how they could create simple, manageable project experiences from any material they were required to teach. In fact, they immediately went to a task that ended with reading-centered projects that would challenge their students' critical thinking, build student collaboration, and align learning outcomes with the state reading standards for each grade. As homework, they took their plans to their classrooms so they could try out what they had planned. One Buckhannon teacher concluded:

> I learned that a project is no more than a different way of teaching the same required material. What I like better is the way so much is packed into a single project. I don't have to have different lessons on the content or critical thinking. I can use the cooperative learning and the critical thinking pieces to engage my kids as I was engaged.

Of course, some upper grade teachers would argue that elementary school teachers do not face the "content coverage" demands that they experience. Secondary teachers especially don't feel they have time to use projects. For such teachers, projects are frivolous fun and games that detract from their daily lectures.

However, these arguments in defense of covering required material ring true neither with many middle school teachers with whom I have worked, nor with my own experience as a high school English teacher who obtained some of his deepest understandings of the "content" by challenging students to investigate literature in an enriched project. I can attest that projects prove to be a benefit in helping students understand the core concepts of the standards-based curriculum much more deeply than when they do little more than take notes on teacher lectures and memorize the teacher's analysis of the text. Throughout this book, I have selected some of the best examples I know of such enriched projects. Some are easy starters, such as the Buckhannon sample, and others become more complicated as teachers fold technology into their designs.

Are the Students Prepared? Am I?

The research reinforces teachers' common sense on this point (Thomas, 2000). Certainly, students seldom come to project-based learning experiences with the skills and tools necessary to be self-directed and responsible about the management of project time and effort. And many teachers feel they themselves do not have the preparation that will allow them to exit their comfort zones and take the risks needed for project use. However, the same studies also point out that teachers can compensate for students' inexperience by using projects as a means as well as an end. Well-structured projects include time for teachers to help students learn from their experiences and use new tools that will teach students how to complete projects skillfully.

Once these fears are dispelled, all that then remains is for school districts to encourage and support the use of project-based learning by preparing administrators and teachers in the "how-to." When teachers see the easy adjustments that they must make, the concern about prior knowledge dissipates.

What About Administrative Support?

Finally, many teachers speak of the lack of administrative support as a reason for not using more project-based learning experiences. It is true that such support must go beyond a principal saying OK. Explicit permission is necessary, but it is not sufficient. Parents have reported to me that while some teachers make project work very exciting and beneficial, others merely go through the motions of meeting the administration's expectations—especially in the many environments where going against the principal's wishes is inadvisable.

Principals need to work collaboratively with teachers to make a plan for integrating project learning into the school year. How much time should they allocate? When? Where? And why? Project team leaders must address the benefits to students, parents, and the teachers themselves. The best place to start is a faculty-driven investigation project, one that includes the building administrators, gives everyone a taste of the project-learning experience, and contributes to the creation of a strengthened learning community—a planning process in which all participants learn and that results in a specific, detailed plan with measurable outcomes, a timeline and budget for intensive teacher development, and a means to assess the results. To introduce project-based learning with less support invites understandable resistance on all fronts.

Finding the Time

I recommend that you start slowly and design a small, simple project. Instead of creating a brand-new project as an add-on to insert into the curriculum, rework an existing lesson or unit that lends itself to students making a product, such as acting a scene from a play, creating a PowerPoint presentation, or telling a digital story. If you are a language arts teacher, it is easiest if you can select the first project from the reading standards for that year. If you are a middle or secondary teacher of math, select the content from your next math unit, and identify the relevant standards. When you begin your preparation, remember to remind yourself over and over, "Take it easy," "Keep it simple," "I don't have to design a skyscraper as my first product—a simple doghouse will do." Use the samples and suggested resources included in the book as a guide.

Projects that integrate multiple disciplines such as art, science, social studies, and language arts in a single project can come later. They will not require you to take time away from instruction in math and reading. In fact, by integrating several disciplines around one big idea, you will actually shorten the full coverage time that you would need if you were to approach each discipline separately. For instance, if you are a middle grade teacher, you could select the big idea *The Westward Expansion.* You would instruct your students to read the text on this topic and would add whatever other instruction you generally use (perhaps a video or a novel), so that students can gather the information they need. Then you would ask the students to make a poster or build a web page or collage that communicates what they have learned. Students could work at home to complete the final product before presenting it to the class. As you become as tech savvy as your students, you can integrate more complex tools and media into the project.

Even the little extra time devoted to a concept map or a shareware presentation as a sample product will necessitate a change in your schedule. To create this time, you can look at other lessons or units in the curriculum and decide how to modify them so they each take a little less time. At most, the project will extend the study of the westward expansion by two or three days out of the year. When you are ready to teach several standards in one project, you will create additional time for other lessons or projects. The important thing to know about time use, however, is that if you focus on the learning outcomes, some projects will take more time and some less. Your biggest challenge, and the greatest benefit of project-based learning, is the increased student engagement. The challenge will often come from the students not wanting to stop working on the project!

After you have completed your first successful enriched project, you can plan additional projects for later in the year. Students will become more committed to project learning as you increase the amount of time for projects and provide instruction on how they are to learn from them. This instruction not only helps students complete better initial projects, it also helps them become more efficient when completing future projects—which in turn creates additional time. Like a snowplow moving highway drifts, first projects help students clear away learning blocks, so that they arrive safely and on time at the learning destination.

Chapter Organization

Any book on enriched project-based learning would fall short if it did not provide many examples. Throughout, I have provided examples from real classrooms as well as sample blank forms for use in project planning. I have also outlined four project descriptions. Each has its own strategy variations, which are aligned with a master project outline. You can use these examples either as they are presented or as a model for constructing your own unique projects.

Enriched Learning Projects is organized into nine chapters, plus an appendix containing supplemental resources.

Chapter 1 discusses how instruction must change in the 21st century to match the emerging work and learning demands that students will face. Using technology, students will have the opportunity to learn in new ways. Enriched learning projects will allow teachers to integrate the new skill expectations so that students are better prepared to work and learn in the 21st century.

Chapter 2 prepares teachers to plan enriched learning projects by using *backwards planning*, which favors outcomes (ends) over activities (means). A project template and a model rubric provide a guide through the five-step backwards-design process. You can use this rubric in the following ways:

- Duplicate it and use it as a page mark. As an advance organizer, review the benchmarks before you read a chapter.
- When you review one of the sample projects in the book or online, use the rubric to assess the sample.
- When you are replicating a project design or designing your own, use the rubric to assess the final draft before you implement it.
- After implementing a project, use the rubric to assess your design and practice.

Chapter 3 identifies the many technology tools that teachers can incorporate into learning projects so that students have richer learning experiences. E-tool use is aligned with the national technology standards to ensure that students are achieving 21st century outcomes.

Chapter 4 identifies which instructional strategies incorporated into projects are most likely to enrich student learning and raise achievement levels. The discussion focuses on what research says about incorporating best practices into each of the three phases of learning.

Chapter 5 describes how teachers can nurture quality thinking by attending to six cognitive functions that are core to the development of more efficient critical thinkers and problem solving. Each of the functions is defined and connected to the development of life-long learning patterns.

Chapter 6 shows the importance of critical thinking within enriched projects. This chapter focuses on four thinking skills that serve as frameworks that facilitate problem solving and inquiry in the daily curriculum as well as on how teachers can help students use these frameworks to deepen thinking and advance mastery of required content.

Chapter 7 reinforces the what, why, and how of creating a collaborative classroom so that students become more able to complete their learning tasks and accomplish the project outcomes. Special attention is given to showing how high-yield strategies contribute to the making of the collaborative community by building strong student relationships.

Chapter 8 brings assessment to the foreground of the enriched project. Emphasis is placed on the alignment of assessment with the content standards and with the important 21st century skills that you are highlighting.

Chapter 9 presents four sample projects that teachers can review prior to planning their own enriched learning projects. These project samples align with grade-level and content standards drawn from different states.

There are many alternative ways to use this book. You can read it cover to cover, use the table of contents as a needs assessment to determine which chapters will best add to your knowledge base, follow the Master Project Planner (pages 194–195) and fill in the information you want to remember or use, make an assessment guide and review your current projects, or simply use the book as a reference guide.

Enriched Learning Projects is filled with opportunities for collaboration. Discuss the content with colleagues, give it to someone who can use it, join a peer group and plan an enriched learning project, or give it to your principal and ask for his or her assessment.

Throughout, you will find references to online resources, including tutorials that will allow you to study a new tool before you introduce it in the classroom. In addition, visit **go.solution-tree.com/instruction** to find additional examples and links to online and offline resources to help you plan.

Chapter 1

A New Paradigm for Instruction

> Tomorrow belongs to the people who prepare for it today.
>
> —African proverb

The purpose of this chapter is to establish the need for planning projects as a vehicle for preparing all middle and upper grade students for learning in the 21st century. After identifying how the 21st century will very likely differ from the 20th, this chapter discusses why schools must adapt to its changing learning and working demands. A review of the Partnership for 21st Century Skills' vision of the new century is followed by a definition of the enriched learning project model of instruction, as well as discussion of its methods and value for all middle and upper grade classrooms. The chapter concludes with a description of the book's purpose, goals, and contents related to constructing an enriched learning project model.

All My Life, I Taught Myself

"What was your school like?" I asked my mom.

For a moment she didn't respond. Her ninety-nine-year-old eyes twinkled. I knew her mind was racing as fast as it did when she took on *Who Wants to Be a Millionaire?* She never lost. She was a paper billionaire. My daughter called her "the smartest woman in the world."

"Well, I can say it was a lot easier than what you and your kids had to do. I remember the test we had to take for eighth-grade graduation. I had to know all the states and their capitals and, of course, my multiplication tables and long division. I learned to type by the sixth grade. That made your grandmother happy. She was worried I would have to work in the dress mill. This way I could be a secretary."

"That was it?" I asked.

"Mostly. We had to be able to read, too, but that wasn't on the test. You just had to read the test questions. I read all my life since I was four. I taught myself. Most of what I learned I got outside of school. I read and read. My father used to take my book away after I went to bed. We just had oil lamps when I was really young, and he said I would go blind."

A New Century

When it comes time to ask questions about the future of education, teachers have many. One key question that middle and upper grade teachers often ask is, "How do I adjust my teaching so my students can succeed in this fast-changing, technology-rich, information-bloated global economy? I thought I used to know what was important to know. Not anymore. Where is the time for anything new? Where is the place?"

This big question is followed by many others:

- "How do I develop my students' critical and creative thinking skills, their problem-solving skills, and their skills for collaborating and communicating when I am charged with developing daily instruction in an ever-expanding, standards-aligned curriculum heavy with important content?"
- "How do I help my students develop their ability to read more and more complex materials, deepen their mathematical thinking, and enrich their science knowledge without sacrificing the arts, history, and knowledge of global society?"
- "How do I squeeze technology into this jam-packed daily schedule?"

The middle and upper grade curriculum that you and your peers have inherited from the 20th century is filled with more subject matter and skill requirements than you are able to cram into a daily schedule. Breadth outbids depth. Test time increases; instruction time decreases. As new information develops, the textbooks thicken; abandonment, even of the selective kind, seldom happens. No time slot goes unfilled. And now comes a call from forward-thinking advocates to resurrect critical thinking, collaboration, communication, and leadership, among the many skills deemed necessary for advanced learning and living in the global information society. Who was it that said, "Lions and tigers and bears—Oh my!"?

The Partnership for 21st Century Skills

The Partnership for 21st Century Skills (www.21stcenturyskills.org) is a leading voice advocating changes in how teachers prepare their students in the coming decades. The Partnership, comprised of educational leaders from more than a dozen states and by business leaders and national professional organization officers, is joined by other groups asking for instruction that better prepares students for the more complex life and work of an information-heavy technological age. This instruction, the Partnership notes, should incorporate creative and critical thinking, problem solving, technology, communication, and collaboration skills across a curriculum framed by 21st century standards balanced with 21st century content. This array of skills and the supports required to teach them is illustrated in figure 1.1.

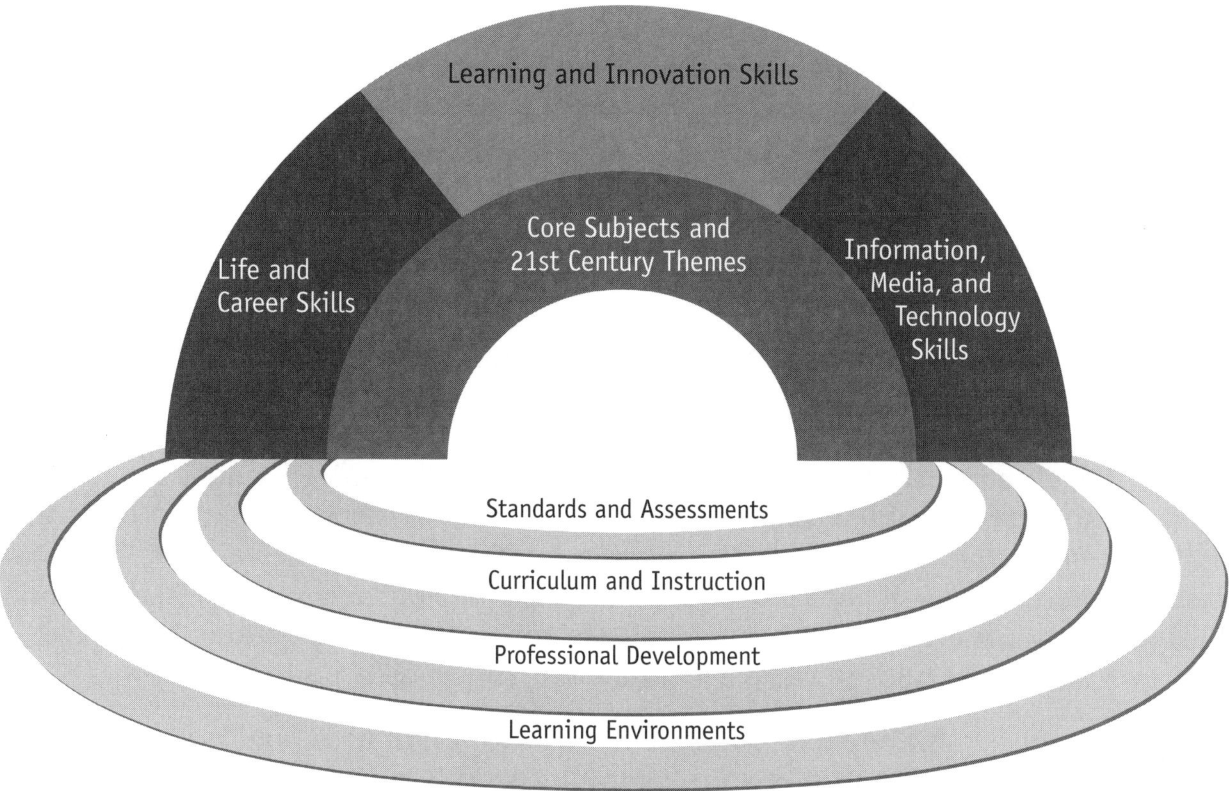

Figure 1.1: 21st century student outcomes and support systems.

Reprinted with the permission of the Partnership for 21st Century Skills.

Replacing the Factory School

Life and work in the 21st century, the Partnership predicts, will require knowledge, skills, outcomes, standards, and support systems that many schools do not yet provide. The factory model of schooling, with its assembly line for producing multiple copies of a single product, may have met the educational needs of the 20th century; however, it falls far short of the needs of the 21st century global society. Just as past decades brought changing requirements for the automobile, the home, and recreation, the 21st century schoolhouse will need to be transformed into a new model of 21st century curriculum, instruction, and assessment.

The Partnership's call for the promotion of critical thinking, problem solving, and collaboration as the heart of a 21st century school transformation is not novel. In the heyday of Greek education, Socrates peppered his students with question after question. He wanted them to think deeply about the most serious issues of their time in politics, ethics, education, law, and more.

In the late 19th century, John Dewey's student Carleton Washburne initiated the progressive movement at the University of Chicago. Washburne introduced the concept of experiential education, which included a method called "project-based learning," into formal teacher training programs. On and off throughout the 20th century, right down to the present, Washburne's disciples fought against the mass education theories of Frederick Taylor's followers. Taylor, best known for his advocacy of scientific management, was an early champion of time and management studies, with the goal of creating more efficient workplaces. Educational advocates took up his mantra and applied it to public schools, especially those in large urban centers.

Taylor's followers in education adopted his scientific management theories. They believed his efficiency-in-the-workplace practices could be carried over to the schoolhouse. In this way, they hypothesized, these rapidly expanding urban areas could provide a quality education that guaranteed all children would master the 3Rs. These were the skills, they believed, that children would need most for working in the manufacturing world. These basics skills were also measurable. Without measurement, Taylor asked, how could educators be held accountable? How would they show that they were doing their job of preparing skilled workers? How could anyone know that children were learning what they were taught?

Brief interludes from the factory model of curriculum, instruction, and evaluation occurred during the Sputnik era and again in the 1970s. Progressives resurrected the call for critical thinking, cooperative learning, and problem solving within daily instruction. Projects were restored to acceptability, especially in elementary schools. However, with the arrival of No Child Left Behind legislation, these "higher order" skills—now called 21st century skills—were relegated, along with project-based learning, to the classroom closet. Taylor's emphasis on scientific research to back up scientific management reappeared, stronger than ever. The age of accountability had arrived.

Hope in the Middle

At the dawn of the 21st century, America's dream of an equitable education for all prepared the stage for teaching and learning approaches that join the best attributes of both the progressives and the scientific managers. With the right models of teaching, there is no reason for educators to be limited in their responses to raised levels of accountability. With the help of quickly emerging technology, it is more possible than ever for all students to master the basics in their early education while receiving challenging instruction to develop the fourth R: *reasoning*. To accomplish this melding of apparent opposites, much will have to occur. For one thing, we will have to avoid burdening teachers with unfunded fads that will fail to accomplish the objectives for improved teaching and learning in the 21st century school.

Choosing a New Paradigm for Instruction

Foremost among the alternatives for meeting the challenges posed by the Partnership for 21st Century Skills is provision for a model of instruction that integrates the development of 21st century skills with 21st century content. For many, this requires a paradigm shift. This shift rests on the understanding that the continuation of the factory model, which separates curriculum and instruction into an uncountable and already excessive number of little boxes, will not solve the problem of the overstuffed schoolhouse. As the Malvina Reynolds song goes:

> Little boxes on the hillside, little boxes made of ticky-tacky
> Little boxes on the hillside, little boxes all the same

If schools continue to follow a factory model in which curriculum is broken into isolated boxes, and what students learn is "English is not math, math is not science, science is not social studies, and so forth," then 21st century skills will simply become more little boxes. Critical thinking and creative thinking will become separate topics to be mastered and tested, but not necessarily used; communication and collaboration will become separate courses; and problem solving will be another separate elective—another little box. Each skill will have a separate syllabus added to the day or taught in summer school. Students will have more worksheets, possibly electrified by shallow e-tutorials that are more fun and games than productive practice. Digital tests will examine their crammed heads each week and again at the year's end, with the results filed away in a giant electronic file with impenetrable access to the data.

School leaders can help teachers take students on a different pathway as the 21st century unfolds. It will require a new paradigm for teaching and learning. Educational leaders can facilitate a change to a new model of instruction—a model that will not only allow for the integration of 21st century skills into existing standards-based curriculum, but will also improve the quality of instruction by enabling students to connect skills, content, and outcomes into coherent wholes rather than separate boxes.

To accomplish this synthesis of scientific management and progressive education, school leaders have at least two choices. The first choice, rooted in the whole-school reforms of the 1990s, calls for new models of instruction that redesign not only curriculum, instruction, and assessment, but also the physical environment of the school. Like the attempts made on a smaller scale by the alternative school movement, which restructured physical space to match more open teaching and learning styles, the most recent whole-school models call for a redesign of school buildings.

The new advocates of whole-school reform want architecture to reflect the goals and practices of the new models, which are usually technology rich and project centered. Already, New Tech High Schools—a charter model financially supported by local business executives and funded by foundations and venture capitalists—feature multiple types of space and high-speed Internet access. At these schools, students work on technology-rich projects alone or in groups.

A second choice, rooted in the effective-practice research of the 1990s, seeks to reform instruction within existing schools. This choice is more evolutionary than the revolutionary flavor of the whole-school reformers (Bob Pearlman, personal communication, June 2009). Many of today's advocates of change within existing school walls favor the integration of progressive policies and practices that will help teachers accomplish the 21st century goals, even if their schools cannot afford the substantial physical changes to school buildings called for by the whole-school reformers. In this choice, teachers are more likely to add project-based learning to a repertoire of instructional models integrated with other models.

The history of change in U.S. schools has not favored either whole-school reform or individual teacher improvement. In the moderate adaptations of pure progressivism and rigid scientific management, educational leaders have adapted the best of each theory. They have focused on a pragmatic integration of the most helpful practices for improving the quality of teaching and learning. Thus, both choices have contributed elements that make sense in the evolving U.S. school. Both choices favor teaching practices that give more attention to the individual students, more attention to how students think and learn, and more adaptation of the school environment to what and how they learn. Today, proponents of both theories accept the demands for increased accountability in a standards-guided education and both allow for some degree of attention to critical and creative thinking, collaboration, and communication, and for the use of technology and projects as valued teaching and learning tools.

A Lesson From History

There is no reason to deny the validity of the Partnership's projection that more attention needs to be paid to the skills they have identified as important for learning, living, and working in the 21st century. The important question is how to best do so. After examining the possibilities, a logical and sensible answer is found in the enriched learning project model of instruction. To get a clearer picture of why this model is an important answer, it may help to look at a brief history of project-based learning.

Project-based learning was formalized as an education method by John Dewey and his followers. The projects that the early progressives advocated were designed to give learning experiences that would replace the more passive approaches in use at that time. In their view, for learning purposes, planting seeds in a garden was superior to reading about the life cycle of a plant in a book. Once students planted the seeds, watered the small plants, and then harvested the crops, they would better understand the process. This was Dewey's idea of "learning by doing" (Dewey, 1916).

Dewey's learning-by-doing concept succeeded for some time in elementary schools. Today, a progressive public school, Crow Island Elementary School in Winnetka, Illinois—created by Washburne—makes extensive use of projects. Students grow plants from seeds, create pioneer villages in a living tableau, investigate historic events, and learn science through hands-on projects for an annual all-school science fair.

In one botany project, Crow Island first-grade students learn to takes notes on what they see as if they are observing botanists. They sketch the changes in a plant's structure and make inferences based on what occurred in the emergence of the mature plant. The teacher then leads a discussion of the observations and helps the students draw their own conclusions. By the end of the lesson, the students are able to present their new understanding of plant growth, including the meaning of key concepts such as photosynthesis, to the entire class.

Dewey's concept of a project began with the hands-on or experiential nature of the activity. The intent was for students to learn by completing tasks that helped them draw their own conclusions from observations and inquiry. From the start, teachers structured the activity as a complete experience, not part of another lesson. Thus, project learning became a new method of instruction that required students to *do* tasks, alone or in groups. It was learning by *doing*, not learning by hearing or seeing or reading.

According to Dewey, this active engagement of the hands increases the engagement of the mind. Motivated by the opportunity to be engaged in the task, students develop a deeper understanding of the concepts. In Dewey's view, that deeper understanding not only leads to increased recall, but also to increased ability to explain the importance of a concept and to transfer its understanding to other related concepts. This, he believed, was learning at its best (Dewey, 1938).

The Post-War Years

Over the years, project-based learning has had its ups and downs, depending on the dominant learning theory of the time. What and how students ought to learn has been a major debate, often colored by the dominant political philosophy. Thus, during the Sputnik era and the very liberal post-Vietnam days, elementary teachers and some middle grade teachers readily adopted the project approach. Textbook publishers joined the bandwagon. Alternative high schools-within-schools, found in Chicago and Winnetka, Illinois; New York; Portland; Ann Arbor; Brookline, Massachusetts; and other cities encouraged projects as well as internships, small group investigations, community service, and other instructional innovations.

Alternative high school faculty members in the 1970s were not known for using research-based instructional strategies. The research push had not yet begun. Most alternative school teachers invented their own high-engagement tactics on the spot or adjusted elementary school methods for their more sophisticated older students. It wasn't until the late 1980s, well after the alternative movement gave way to the "basics," that researchers began to identify best practices. Ironically, the highly dedicated and creative alternative school faculties who invented alternative instructional methods to facilitate student learning introduced their upper grade students to many instructional tactics that are being resurrected today, often in conjunction with the digital tools currently being developed. These small schools, in which teachers risked trying new techniques, such as journals, portfolios, community groups, self-assessments, learning contracts, and other progressive methods, sprouted and grew.

With the arrival of the 21st century, technology tool development sprang forward in leaps and bounds, mostly outside of schools. Young people began networking (Facebook, LinkedIn), writing on wikis, listening to podcasts, and blogging. Well before even the most technologically sophisticated teachers began to experiment with these e-tools in their classrooms, students had figured out how to use these tools to collaborate with their friends. Their successes, reinforced by professional organizations such as the Association for Educational Communications and Technology (AECT; www.aect.org), the International Society for Technology Education (ISTE; www.iste.org), and the Partnership for 21st Century Skills, and propelled forward by Barack Obama's electronically dynamic presidential campaign in 2008, have sparked an increased interest in how technology can enrich teaching and learning. Today, *enriched* is an adjective that distinguishes learning through projects with the assistance of e-tools, use of research-supported best practices for promoting thinking and collaboration, and emphasis on self-directed assessment in high school projects. These projects can be far more complex than the simple experiential projects that Dewey advocated for elementary students.

Discovering how to enrich project learning for upper grade students can be compared to learning how to cook more nutritious and appealing meals for a table of food critics. Novice cooks are happy to put a meal on the table that is hot, liked by the family, salted correctly, and has a mixture of food types that meet the various nutrition standards. As novice cooks become more experienced, read cookbooks, watch master chefs on TV, listen to feedback, and experiment with new recipes, they learn how to refine nutritional content, prepare alternative organic foods, and add special seasonings to suit the tastes at the table. Eventually, some amateur cooks may progress to master-chef status. These master chefs are able to prepare meals from cultures other than their own, holiday feasts for large groups, and specialized dishes that require very specific preparation. Some may become so skilled at enriching the meals they serve that they become professional cooks, ready to face the critics' taste buds.

Since Dewey's day, cognitive psychologists such as Jean Piaget, Lev Vygotsky, and Reuven Feuerstein have deepened educators' understanding of learning. Brain researchers have added their insights. Educational researchers such as Robert Marzano, Roger Johnson, David Johnson, and Thomas Good have identified which classroom practices are most likely to increase student achievement. As a result, today's teachers have a better opportunity to provide project-based learning experiences that are supported by research.

The enriched learning project model encourages each school to devise its own plan for making the changes that expand teachers' professional repertoires. Some may encourage each teacher to do one enriched learning project per year; others may elect to push for projects in only certain classes, such as science or English and language arts. Still others—and this is already happening in many charter schools (www.envisionprojects.org) and new technology high schools (www.newtech foundation.org)—will revise their instructional program so it is centered on student projects. Every day, students at these project-centered schools learn from doing complex problems in lessons that both align with state standards *and* produce high-yield outcomes.

Digital Tools and Project-Based Learning

Just as the limited curriculum of the 20th century no longer suffices to meet the changing demands of the new millennium, neither do many of the instructional methods. Digital tools not readily available ten or twenty years ago promise to enrich learning today in ways never dreamed of before. Some of these changes make teaching a more difficult profession; others promise new pathways to better learning for all students.

The enriched learning project model of instruction can help all teachers evolve their ways of teaching and transform their classrooms to meet the new challenges. Teachers do not have to work in a specially constructed school environment with the latest electronic hook-ups to take advantage of this model. To use it, school leaders will not be required to transform their school environments, change schedules, or modify the curriculum; instead, they need only add the model to teachers' existing instructional repertoires and include the basic e-tools, one by one, to the teachers' instructional toolboxes.

The Benefits of the Enriched Learning Model

Students and teachers derive seven interconnected benefits from the use of this model.

1. Enriched learning projects allow teachers to see immediate and strong gains in classroom management, in student interest and engagement, and in observable student behaviors in collaboration, thinking, and problem solving.

2. Enriched learning projects bring about substantial increases in achievement for all students via the planned use of the strongest research-supported instructional strategies and digital tools.
3. Enriched learning projects allow for an increase in the ways student performance is assessed and reported. It places the primary responsibility for assessment of learning on the student.
4. Enriched learning projects enable teachers to integrate multiple 21st century skills without taking any allotted instructional time away from curriculum content.
5. Enriched learning projects enable teachers to shift from textbook coverage to an "understanding by design" workflow that focuses on knowledge and performance improvements via a project pathway (McTighe & Wiggins, 2008).
6. Enriched learning projects facilitate an expanded use of technology in the classroom as a support for improving the learning of all students and their preparation for higher education and the 21st century work world.
7. Enriched learning projects allow principals and district leaders to focus on a cohesive, technology-rich instructional approach and provide support for the improvement and assessment of that approach.

What Gets Enriched?

In this model, you are the creator of your own script. The enrichment is brought about by tactics and e-tools that, as noted by researchers, have the highest effect on student achievement. In this model, you are encouraged to give preference in your decisions about what tools and tactics to select that provide the best chance of promoting the highest achievement of the project's academic goals. By doing so, you enable students to learn the standards-aligned content faster and with greater depth than if you select strategies that research has shown to have less effect on achievement.

By purposefully selecting high-yield strategies and embedding them in your project, you give students important achievement advantages (Marzano, Pickering, & Pollock, 2001). You help them learn the content and develop the skills targeted in a project more effectively and efficiently. The effectiveness comes from the strategy that produces the achievement results you want. The efficiency comes from the students' learning how to use e-tools and learning-to-learn tactics more skillfully, not only for use in the immediate project tasks, but also for a lifetime of productive learning. In addition, because of your intentional use of these strategies, you win the students' engagement in the project. Through this reciprocal engagement, you make the project more relevant to their needs. This relevance in turn deepens their understanding of the meaning of the core concepts by linking those concepts to their personal values. In the project model, you will see how readily all students are engaged, improve what and how they learn, make substantial progress toward higher achievement, and find their leaning to be more meaningful and more relevant.

Consider, for example, the project use of an e-tool such as a concept map, also known as a cmap (http://cmap.ihmc.us). Some of your students may already be familiar with this graphic organizer. The cmap, a free, online version of the concept map, tutors students in how to use the concept map as a digital tool. They can copy it into their e-journals and work with a peer to chart the characters in a book, events in history, or species in a genus. In your project, you might teach them how to use this e-tool to trace a family history or interconnect all the characters in a complex story such as *The Odyssey*. Once they have shown they can do a simple start-up task with the cmap, they are ready to do more complex tasks with more complex topics. Perhaps they will graduate to tracing the family roots of a president, examining the origins of a scientific idea, or making a map of the connections between Monet and his Impressionist friends.

Five Attributes of the Enriched Learning Model

The enriched learning project model is distinguished from traditional projects by five attributes:

1. **Research-based**—When teachers use research-based instructional strategies to enrich student learning in a project, they are using the first attribute that sets enriched learning projects apart from those projects that simply make a product—it is research-based. Because enriched learning projects are designed to help students become more efficient and effective learners, you select those strategies that, according to research such as that provided by Marzano and the Mid-continent Research for Education and Learning (McREL) team (Marzano, Pickering, & Pollock, 2001), give you the best chances to raise student achievement.

2. **Purposeful use of technology**—The second attribute is the purposeful use of technology as tools to promote students' learning efficiency. Although the research on e-tools' effects on achievement is still in the formative stage, even without a well-documented meta-analysis, tactical studies strongly suggest how large the impact might be. The website Instructional Technology Research Online (www2.gsu.edu/~wwwitr/) contains a huge repository of articles written about instructional technology and its impact in the classroom. It is important to recall that prior to 1985, the instructional strategies that are now recognized universally as best practices were in the same formative stage.

3. **The priority of self-assessment**—A third attribute or distinguishing quality that sets the enriched learning project model apart from more traditional

projects is its emphasis on the priority of self-assessment. Assessment is the practice of providing helpful, informative feedback so that learners can improve what and how they are learning. Assessment is usually thought of as the responsibility of teachers, who give corrective feedback to students. In the enriched learning model, students have the primary responsibility for improving how they learn via assessment. Throughout the project, the teacher provides opportunities for students to assess their own grasp of the content, their own development of critical thinking skills, and their own development of collaborative talents, including improved use of e-tools. After students write reflections about how they are progressing, detailing what they think they have learned, the teachers help them analyze their reflections, provide additional feedback, and translate the assessment into a grade.

4. **Learning *from* doing**—A fourth distinct characteristic carries you beyond Dewey's concept of learning by doing, so that students learn *from* doing. Establishing the high expectation that students must look back and learn from what and how they are doing during an activity or project facilitates students' thinking about their thinking and reflecting on their work. This metacognitive element reinforces how they are learning in all aspects of the project. Enriched learning projects extend students' reflections so that they learn from doing research, solve loosely structured problems, complete tasks that promote complex decision making, use critical and creative thinking, and collaborate with e-tools.
5. **21st century skill development**—A fifth characteristic that makes enriched learning projects different from ordinary projects is the intentional inclusion of 21st century skill development in the formal project outcome. Students should know how to think, cooperate, and collaborate more skillfully as a result of your project. Don't leave these skills to chance or assume that, because students are engaged in tasks that require complex or rigorous thinking, such involvement will necessarily develop 21st century skills. Instead, purposefully enrich your students' learning by teaching these skills and integrating their development for the benefit of mastering the content of your coursework.

Enriched learning projects are not a revolution. They are the next step in the evolution of project-based learning. In this step, we adapt Dewey's belief that students learn best by doing to the needs of your 21st century students. Included among these needs are (1) how to handle increasingly greater volumes of information and (2) how to be more effective in learning increasingly more difficult types of information.

Summary

This is an opportune time for upper grade teachers to add the enriched learning project model of instruction to their repertoires. Although many elementary teachers have used projects to engage students for decades, upper grade teachers who use this model are scarce. However, with the emergence of well-researched instructional strategies and the development of digital tools, upper grade teachers now have teaching tactics and e-tools available that will make the use of projects more beneficial. By carefully designing projects that enrich the learning of your students, you and your colleagues will have the opportunity to better prepare students to master the required content of your course and to develop their 21st century skills.

Chapter 2

Planning Your Enriched Learning Project

By failing to prepare, you are preparing to fail.

—Benjamin Franklin

The purpose of this chapter is to introduce a "results-first" planning process for enriched learning projects. The rationale and steps for planning a project and adapting the understanding by design planning method (McTighe & Wiggins, 2008), are discussed. After outlining the five steps of the results-first process, examples and analogies are provided to illuminate each step. A template, My Notes for a Project Plan (page 34 and online at **go.solution-tree.com/instruction**), as well as a rubric to assess your plan are included to facilitate note taking for each step.

The Project Lady

They called her the "project lady." Arline Paul was the most popular multiday substitute at New Trier East High School in Illinois. After her retirement, she returned year after year by popular demand and because of her love of teaching. Although she sometimes received calls from the English, science, and business chairs, she restricted her substitute days to her own field, history. Arline's reputation preceded her. If she walked through a classroom door, students knew that the next few days would be hard-working project days from the project lady. The students loved her, and the teachers preferred her for these multiday stints.

Although she was always well prepped by the chair or the absent teacher, Arline started every new assignment with the same tactic and the same question: a think-pair-share with "What are you learning about this week?" After the students came up with their answers ("Their variations never ceased to amaze me!" she often said), she asked individual students for their answers and wrote them on a web sketched on the blackboard.

Next, Arline, standing tall at 4'10" with a twinkle in her eye, announced, "Get yourselves in groups of four and come up with a summary that includes all these ideas and tells me what the points of conflict are at this time and place in history." After she listened to the answers, she smiled and said, "That's good. You have been doing really great thinking.

continued →

Mr. Gregory would be proud. Now, let's go to work. We are going to do a project. For this project, you are going to take three days with your three partners to find out some answers to one of the conflicts you told me about. Take this group over here. They told me that the Sunnis and Shiites have fought because of long-time disagreements about their religion. I want this group to take this problem, find out what the specific differences have been, and then come up with a solution. If you were the Iraqi governor general, what would you decide to do that is morally OK to stop the conflict? You will have three days to get your information together. We are meeting in the library. Friday you can figure out what you are going to say to the rest of us. Starting on Monday, each group will have ten minutes to present their findings. You can tell and you *must* show. You have to have visuals that we can all see that will help your presentation. By Wednesday, we'll be all finished. You each are going to write Mr. Gregory a one-page letter telling him what you did and what you learned from this project. On Thursday, when Mr. Gregory returns, he will receive my report about your great work. Now, let's go to work."

Those who knew Arline from her preretirement days as a world history teacher knew her plan. When they returned to class, the teachers could expect a pile of student assessments, her report, and a classroom full of students asking when the project lady would return. "I've always thought projects were the best way to teach," Arline would tell her colleagues. "By the time students do their research and present their ideas in a really visual way, they can recall more facts or show better insights than I could ever talk to them about. My projects are simple, but they get the kids involved. They never forget what they learned in projects, big or little. If you know what you want them to learn when you start, it's easy to get them learning."

To read an example of one of Arline Paul's projects, go to page 183.

The End Is the Beginning

When presenting a project to your students, the quickest way to grab their attention is to describe the final product they will make or problem they will solve. Quickest, however, is not necessarily best. When it comes to introducing a well-designed project, it will help your cause and students' learning if you focus their attention on what they will know and do as a result of completing all the project tasks.

As with cooking a good meal, careful preparation is a key. You don't want a meal that looks good but is short on taste. Just as careful meal preparation most often starts with a recipe that ensures the look and taste will be sensational, careful project preparation will help you ensure that the project will challenge, interest, and help your students achieve the project goals as much as it will encourage them to enjoy their work.

When starting a project, especially if you are a novice with the enriched learning project model, it is essential that you think first about the standards-aligned result. What do you want your students to understand and be able to do when they are finished? For instance, in a simple study of ancient Greece in a world cultures course, you might choose to excite the students by focusing on the end product—a class web page that will introduce parents and other students to the wonders of ancient Greece. The web page may link to other products such as slideshows, a video stream, or podcasts. However, the final product is not the most important result.

When planning an enriched learning project, you must keep in mind that the most important results are the learning outcomes, not what the students make. What will students understand about ancient Greece and its citizens' contributions? What skills will the students develop as they research the topic and make the final product? Here are some possible outcomes of the ancient Greece project:

- Students will understand how and why ancient Greece blossomed as a great civilization.
- Students will understand what its citizens contributed to its economic, political, and artistic successes.
- Students will show increased skills for finding, accessing, and recording information from Internet sites.
- Students will show increased skill in analyzing and selecting data relevant to telling a story about one citizen's contributions to ancient Greece's importance.
- Students will show new design skills for making a single web page that communicates their stories.

The Five Steps of Backwards Design

In *Understanding by Design* (2008), Jay McTighe and Grant Wiggins made the concept of *backwards planning* popular (fig. 2.1). When using this approach to design projects, it is important to remember that the primary goal is understanding. As with other elements in enriched learning projects, the end results are not just a fun-to-make product, such as a website, a slide presentation, or a physical performance such as a dance or play; the product result must show that your students understand key concepts selected from the curriculum or that they have developed an important 21st century skill. The more explicitly the final results show increased knowledge and skills as dictated by standards, the better.

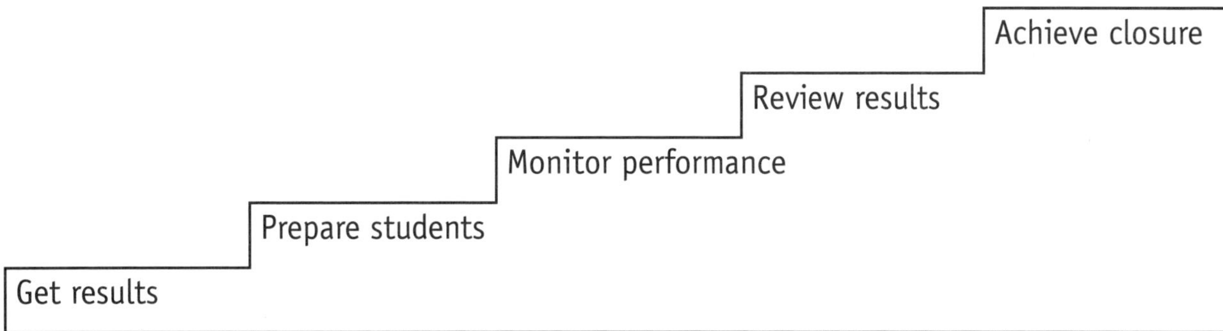

Figure 2.1: Understanding by design—a five-step process.

Step One: Get Results

To identify the desired results, you may start with the lesson you used last year on the same topic. For instance, suppose last year at this time your unit covered circles. You used a direct instruction lesson in the tradition of Madeline Hunter (1982). On the first day, in your anticipatory set, you asked the students to explain what they knew about taking measurements of a circle. When no one volunteered, you answered the question by moving directly to an explanation of the two key terms and showed examples on the board regarding their measurement. You then demonstrated how to measure circumference and radius.

You gave each student a worksheet with practice problems. You checked for students' understanding of the terms by using a thumbs-up signal. Finally, you proceeded to guided practice on the worksheets. Time elapsed was twenty minutes.

Reviewing this lesson, you noticed that you had identified what students were supposed to know: the definition of the terms, the formulas for measurement, and the evidence that they could put the formulas to good use. These were the benchmarks for the measurement of a circle. You recalled how disappointed you were with the unit test scores. "Hopefully," you thought, "the results will be better this year if I have them do more measuring."

If you aren't clear on a unit's learning standards, identify the standards and benchmarks for your first project. Finding your state's standards and benchmarks or national standards and benchmarks for your curriculum by going online is easy. You can use your browser to enter "state standards [your state] [your grade] [your subject]" or "[national professional organization] [your subject]." For instance, entering "Iowa reading standards, grade 11" brings up the following:

> Students in grade 11 read a variety of previously published fiction (for example, narrative), nonfiction (for example, general science and social science, history, essay, memoir, general interest, informational), and poetry. This standard expects students to not only understand the literal meaning of grade-appropriate text, but also to interpret meaning through complex processes of analysis, inference, and generalization. To read grade-appropriate text with comprehension, students in grade 11 must demonstrate the processes of:
>
> - Factual understanding
>   - ☐ Understand stated information
>   - ☐ Determine the literal meaning of words or phrases
> - Inference and Interpretation
>   - ☐ Draw conclusions
>   - ☐ Infer traits, feelings, and motives of characters
> - Infer relationships
> - Interpret information in new contexts
> - Interpret nonliteral language

- Analysis and generalization
    - ☐ Make generalizations and interpret nonliteral language
    - ☐ Determine the main idea of a text
    - ☐ Identify the author's viewpoint or purpose
    - ☐ Distinguish among facts, opinions, assumptions, observations, conclusions
    - ☐ Recognize literary or argumentative techniques
    - ☐ Analyze the style or structure of a text

At this level, the content and process dimensions of reading comprehension emphasize in equal proportions critical thinking through factual understanding, inference and interpretation, and analysis and generalization of grade-appropriate text. (Iowa Department of Education, n.d.)

This sample standard from Iowa is extremely comprehensive. For a project that would not exceed four or five weeks, you would edit this standard by selecting those benchmarks your project will address. If you were a teacher in Iowa, these reading standards would help you decide which critical thinking skills you want your project to develop (such as *infer* or *analyze*), as well as what content. Since this standard doesn't designate which texts to use, you would have the choice to build these benchmarks around fiction or nonfiction.

Step Two: Prepare Students

Once you have identified what the project will help your students know and do, you are ready to decide how to build their interest. As in a preview for the Super Bowl or Academy Awards, you can build that interest well before the project's first official day by interspersing advance organizers in the closing weeks of the previous unit or project.

David Ausubel (1963), a pioneer in the identification of best practices via research, studied how advance organizers affect student achievement. An effective advance organizer helps students draw on their prior knowledge about a topic they will be studying or a skill they will be developing. At the same time, the organizer can pique students' interest and encourage them to think more deeply about the topic or skill they will be studying. Advance organizers come in many forms: for example, questions, graphic organizers, visual presentations, banner ads, slides, bulletin board displays, and role-plays (Bellanca, 2008).

A Sample Advance Organizer

In preparation for a project in which your students will investigate how to reduce corruption in local government, you might use this sequence of activities as advance organizers.

Day 1: Pop Question With Think-Pair-Share—After reading to the class a news article from the local paper about the arrest of a city official, ask, "What do you think should happen to this official if he is found guilty?" (Allow five minutes for discussion.)

continued →

Day 2: Pop Question With Think-Pair-Share—Ask, "How serious do you think corruption is in our local government?" (Allow five minutes for discussion.) Follow up with a homework assignment to ask parents the same question.

(Allow one to three days to pass.)

Day 5: Pop Question With Web Task—Using groups of six, have students make a web showing parents' answers to the corruption question. Have each group present to the class. Announce that the class will be starting a three-week project on Monday. Explain the project rationale and the final product(s).

Step Three: Monitor Performance

In this third step, you select the means that move students to the desired project results. Included in this section are your selection of the research-strong tactics for advancing student work, deepening their understanding, developing their skills, and making their products. In addition, in this step you identify the e-tools that students will use to collaborate with their peers. Finally, you assemble any materials needed for making the products.

Instructional Elements to Consider in Step Three

When deciding which instructional elements will most help your students accomplish the projects' objectives, there are ten elements to consider as you prepare your plan. If you take your notes on the template (page 34), you will be ready to transfer your ideas into a sequenced project schedule, as follows:

1. **The result**—What product (such as a website or short story) will mark the end of the project? What 21st century knowledge and skill results will it show? What is the connection of the project to the content, process (such as critical or creative thinking, or collaboration), and technology know-and-do standards for your state and course?
2. **Timeline**—How many class periods or hours outside of class time do you estimate are needed (for example, nineteen class periods and over twenty hours outside class)?
3. **Authentic issue**—What is the launch question or authentic problem? How will you select the issue or problem?
4. **Advance organizer**—How will you build the students' anticipation for the project, piquing their interest and organizing their mindsets in advance?
5. **Difficulty level for students**—How rigorous is the content? What do your students know about learning in a project?

6. **Purpose**—Why this particular project? What is the value proposition for students? How will students benefit? What is the connection of the project to the standards?

7. **Digital tools**—Which e-tools do you have in your classroom? Which e-tools will you need to prepare students to use (such as email, website construction, blogs, and so on)? How will these tools enrich students' learning in the project (practice in visual design, getting and receiving feedback, verbal communication)? How will you enhance students' collaborative skills? How will you build a community of learners (for example, through shared work roles in groups or interactive peer feedback on blogs)?

8. **Instructional strategies**—Which high-yield instructional strategies will you select to enrich student learning (such as advance organizers, feedback directed to objectives, questions and cues, and so on)? Which of the following research-strong tactics will you use to enrich instruction in each of the following three learning phases (see page 58):

    a. Gathering information (matrix spreadsheet to distinguish attributes, cmap to identify related parts)

    b. Making sense of the information (sequence of analysis questions for teams to make sense of matrix in relation to launch question)

    c. Communicating the results (website with team presentation to class)

9. **Project results**—How are the standards connected to specific know-and-do outcomes that you will expect students to master or develop (such as, "Students will understand the relationship among the family members in the story")? What assessment tools will you use to determine how students are performing (for example, individual blogs, tags, e-portfolios, action guides, project rubric, observation checklists, individual conferences during project, grading rubric for final project, and so on)?

10. **Equipment and materials**—What equipment will students need (for example, one computer per team, one printer per four teams, Internet access, web-making program, spreadsheet program, email access, blogging software, individual e-portfolios)?

Putting Your Plans in Order

After you have your lists gathered and checked twice, you are ready to plan your project schedule. Use your online calendar to construct the project schedule. Sequence tasks by day. What is it that students will do on Monday? Tuesday? Wednesday? What tactics and e-tools will they use? It will help if your calendar includes a day for a project overview. This is the day for the project's formal introduction. Handing out calendar copies for inclusion in students' journals or posting a calendar online is a task for this first day, as is discussing goals and expectations.

You can distribute written copies of the project's purpose, goals, and objectives and performance expectations for learning the content; developing critical thinking, collaborative, and technology skills; and producing the products. If you have sample products from previous years' projects, show these to the class.

Following is a shared timeline that starts with the advance organizer and ends with your project's formal closure to help everyone see how the project events and elements are connected. Note that the timeline goes through the three phases of learning: gather information, make sense of it, and communicate the results.

1. Prepare students with an advance organizer (the week before project starts).
2. Identify the results and provide a project overview (one day and setup).
3. Prepare students with technology tools (one day).
4. Initiate phase one, gathering information, with students starting their online research.
5. Monitor phase one; observe as students research the key issue online (four days).
6. Review research summaries (one week out-of-class prep and one day in-class share).
7. Monitor phase one; observe as students assess their research summaries (one-half day).
8. Begin phase two, making sense; teach instructional strategies for helping students understand the material they gathered in phase one.
9. Monitor phase-two team discussions; observe discussions by collaborative teams using tools for learning (two and one-half days).
10. Monitor phase-two assessments; observe student teams assessing how well they understand the material (one-half day).
11. Monitor phase three; observe as students prepare the project product (five days).
12. Review the project products (three days).
13. Administer final assessment of know and do (one day).
14. Provide closure (one day).

After you make your timeline, post it on a bulletin board, make a paper handout, or post an online calendar of events on a class blog. Please note: the times required will vary by the size and complexity of each project.

Step Four: Review Results

The next step in your plan calls for you to align the assessment of students' collaborative and cognitive work through the three phases of learning and at the project's end. Here, you will have the opportunity to think about the mix and match of various assessment tactics that will best enable students to learn *from* their doing.

In an enriched learning project, the responsibility for assessment and the providing of corrective feedback starts with the students. For students who are novices at thinking about what they are learning and how they can improve, it is sometimes difficult to be self-analytical. That is why you can best facilitate their reflections by providing "I learned . . ." stems they can answer in a confidential e-journal, available only to your eyes and theirs. Encourage students to complete such stems at least once a week to start. A single complete sentence will suffice for the first entries; however, as the weeks progress, it is beneficial to encourage longer and longer responses, focusing especially on content. "Today, I learned how the character of Bigger was developed" is a first response, while "Today, I discovered how the character of Bigger was influenced by the people in his life. For instance, . . ." is what you should see later in the process. Following is a sample student reflection:

> Today, I was pleased with the detail I brought to my comparative analysis of Bigger's love and hate relationships. Yes, I had gathered the facts to compare. But better yet, I focused on the attributes that defined each element. For instance, . . .

Stems are powerful reflective tools. Your students can expand their insight with stems that focus on the 21st century skills each is developing. For instance, when you align the stems with the critical thinking skills that are targeted by the standards in your project, you not only secure their thoughts and personal assessments on content or product results, you also motivate the students to examine their thinking and collaborative skills.

Stem completions can lead students into deeper reflections when you provide them with multilevel questions. Consider the use of the three-part question sequence *what, so what, now what* demonstrated in the following:

1. "What did you learn new today about Bigger's motivation?"
2. "So what are the implications suggested by your new insights?"
3. "Now what will you say differently about his character?"

Stem-and-question sequences are especially helpful for students in assessing *how* they are gathering information (phase one). This means that they are going beyond assessing the *quantity* of information collected from a story or nonfiction essay. The students are now concentrating on the *quality* of the information-gathering process: "What did I do well when I was analyzing the text style?" "When I continue that analysis in the next chapter, what will I do differently?" "I need some help to analyze the causal connections in the text, because . . ."

The same simple stem tactics can initiate powerful assessments of the students' collaborative work. When you are asking students to share their e-journal entries with you, by the time you arrive at the second learning phase, it is appropriate for you to initiate a dialogue with the student. By starting with the "I need some help" statement, you can feel free to provide your feedback, opinion, advice, or whatever opens and expands the dialogue.

The most effective way to review students' cognitive and collaborative performances—how they are using the thinking skills and cognitive functions as they work on project tasks—is to add a second dimension to their journal entries. Invite students to set individual goals, preferably on a weekly basis, that focus on one or more 21st century skills. A goal might read, "This week, I intend to check my reasoning strategies. How carefully and precisely am I drawing correct inferences about Bigger's traits and motives?" Each day, the student makes an entry indicating to what degree a goal was accomplished and what might be done to improve. Students can use the reproducible Journal Checklist (page 38 and online at **go.solution-tree.com/instruction**). At the end of the week, the student writes a progress-summary paragraph. Each week, you have the opportunity to read four or five of these summaries and provide feedback.

Step Five: Closure

To complete an enriched learning project plan, it will help to identify the following five closure elements for the project's final day:

1. **Final check for understanding and skill outcomes**—Start the final class period by presenting a summary of project events. You can do this using a simple slide presentation, a photomontage, or a video projection. As you depict each project phase, spark review with such questions as "What were you thinking here?" or "What did you learn about ________," or "What did you learn to do better with ________?" Remember to distribute the opportunity to answer around the class, and allow time for complete answers (ten minutes).
2. **Building forward bridges**—Instruct students to write a short summary about one knowledge outcome and one skill outcome. At the conclusion of each, encourage them to tell you one or two ways they will bridge what they have learned to future studies. If they have email, invite them to send the statements to your email address or to the class blog. Otherwise, use note cards (ten minutes).
3. **Summative assessment**—Ask students to do a human wiki. Select one volunteer to start with the stem "What I liked about this project was . . ." Invite

other students in turn to add to the first statement. After four or five have added, change the stem to "What I learned in this project will help me . . ." Continue with other students adding on until everyone has had a chance to add or pass. Conclude with your addition (ten minutes).

4. **Accolades**—Ask students to thank their teammates for specific contributions to the project as if they were at the Academy Awards. After team accolades, encourage students who wish to give all-class accolades. Conclude with your list (five minutes).
5. **A look at the future**—Use the remaining time for an advance organizer about the next unit or project.

Your Enriched Learning Project Rubric

Your reflections on the project's success are important. By reflecting, you can identify what you did well as you worked with your students, what you want to change in the project, and how you will make those changes.

The Rubric for Assessing Your Enriched Learning Project Plan (pages 35–37 and online at **go.solution-tree.com/instruction**) may help you think about your project and keep focused on the most important elements that can enrich your students' learning experiences. Keep this rubric saved in your documents or in a desktop folder so that you can check it before, during, and after the project. Reflect again on what you are doing well, what you want to change, and what help you might need from colleagues to remove a glitch or solve a problem during implementation.

Summary

As the 19th-century poet Robert Burns eloquently noted, "The best-laid schemes o' mice an' men go oft awry." That truism applies to enriched learning projects as well. On the other hand, as Benjamin Franklin suggests, failing to plan is a fast track to failure. Reuven Feuerstein (1980), who includes goal-directed planning in his list of important cognitive functions, teaches that careful planning helps us to make order out of chaos and to proceed in a systematic way toward a goal. In this chapter, you reviewed how to start your project plans by proceeding backward for a clear goal. In enriched learning projects, the goal is always what students will know and do better at the project's end. Following the five-step model adapted from *Understanding by Design* (McTighe & Wiggins, 2008), you received suggestions on how to identify best instructional practices and e-tools that demonstrated the "how to."

In the following chapters, you will read in much more depth about other e-tools and high-yield learning tactics to use for enriching your students' learning experiences.

My Notes for a Project Plan

Your project may be entirely your own creation or an adaptation of a project from this book or one of the recommended online sites. The rubric on pages 35–37 can help you see what key elements you may have missed. (In your first projects, you may wish to abbreviate the rubric so you can add the enriching elements gradually, a few per project.)

Project title:
What is the product?
How much time do we need?
How will I prepare students?
What is the level of difficulty?
What is the value of this project to students?
What e-tools will we use?
What instructional strategies will I use?
How will I review and assess results?
What equipment will we need?

Rubric for Assessing Your Enriched Learning Project Plan

	Not Yet Ready	One Starter Step	Effective Performance	Enriched Performance
Content Mastery	No standards	One content standard	Multiple content standards	Multiple, integrated content and technology standards
	No launch question	Launch question aligned with standard	Launch question aligned with standards and big idea	Launch question aligned with standards, big idea, tasks, and assessments
	Information gathering only	Two phases used to deepen understanding	Three phases connected to outcomes for transfer of concepts	Three phases aligned to promote deep understanding of outcomes
Critical Thinking	No cognitive framework for project	Use of inquiry or problem-solving framework	Cognitive framework focused on deep development of one high-yield thinking skill	Cognitive framework aligned with standards to promote the thinking skill as a way to master content
	No intentional mediation of cognitive functions	Ad-hoc focus on one to three cognitive functions	Intentional focus on improvement of one to three cognitive functions	Improvement of selected functions aligned with outcomes
Collaboration	Little or no purposeful collaboration planned	One to three e-tools promoting collaboration in or outside classroom	Collaboration and communication in classroom fostered by e-tool tasks	E-tool use aligned with outcomes to promote communication in and out of classroom

Rubric for Assessing Your Enriched Learning Project Plan

	Not Yet Ready	One Starter Step	Effective Performance	Enriched Performance
Collaboration (continued)	No attention to building of classroom learning community	Students prepared with one to three learning tactics to improve task collaboration and communication in classroom	Students prepared to use a sequence of learning structures to develop a classroom learning community	Learning structures aligned with outcomes, with students prepared to build a learning community
Product	Finished product stands alone	Research informs product completion	Product responds to the essential question; developed through attention to all three phases of learning	Final product aligns with outcome, answers the essential question, and provides evidence of deep understanding of the big idea
	No intentional thinking or problem solving by students required for product making	Evidence of intentional development of two to three thinking or problem-solving skills	Evidence of intentional development of three 21st century skills in addition to critical thinking and problem-solving skills	Strong alignment of 21st century skills in the promotion of deeper understanding of content
	Students working to copy prior product	Students replicating prior product	Students making innovative adaptations to prior product	Students inventing a new product
Assessment	No alignment of parts with final outcomes	Outcomes aligned with standards; other parts not in complete alignment	All elements aligned with content outcomes and standards	All elements aligned with content and process outcomes and standards, including critical thinking and collaboration

Rubric for Assessing Your Enriched Learning Project Plan

	Not Yet Ready	One Starter Step	Effective Performance	Enriched Performance
Assessment (continued)	No student reflection required	Reflection used for formative assessment of content	Reflection used for formative assessment of content mastery, critical thinking, and collaboration	Reflection used for formative assessment of all three elements, followed by teacher feedback
	Teacher-set outcomes; grades resulting in content only	Teacher-set outcomes; opportunities provided for students to set individual goals for content	Teacher-set outcomes; opportunities provided for students to set individual or team goals for content mastery, critical thinking, and collaboration	Outcomes for project set by teacher and students, with students setting individual goals in all three elements
Enriching Technology Tools	No technology included in project	Students allowed to select technology tools from their existing skill base	New e-tools and their proper use added to repertoire of students, who assesses development within project	Students challenged to integrate new tools that align with project goals by teacher, who assesses outcomes
Enriching Strategies	No selection of high-yield strategies	One to three tasks encased in a high-yield strategy	Multiple high-yield strategies used to enrich learning of all content	High-yield strategies integrated in all phases of the project and aligned to enrich highest achievement through intentional development of students' learning habits

Journal Checklist

Name: ________________________________ Date: ________________

Topic: ________________________________ Completed by: ____________

In this journal entry, I . . .

- ☐ Wrote my goal.
- ☐ Selected how to measure my goal.
- ☐ Targeted the concept to ____________________.
- ☐ Listed my self-reflection questions.
- ☐ Named my task strategies.
- ☐ Set a timeline.
- ☐ Named my resources.

Teacher Comments:

Chapter 3

Technology Tools for Enriched Learning Projects

> The contribution of technology is that it makes possible projects that are both very difficult and very engaging.
>
> —Seymour Papert

Technology tools can contribute greatly to the enrichment of students' learning in projects. This chapter selects e-tools that have special potential for helping students to learn, think, and collaborate more skillfully in the enriched format. It also provides an introduction to the technology standards before moving on to a series of design questions that guide the selection of appropriate e-tools for each of the three phases of learning in an enriched learning project. Keep the template My Notes for a Project Plan (page 34) handy as you read this chapter.

Teens in the Digital Age

"Listen to this," Tom Wright announced, and immediately began to read aloud an article from the morning paper. The other teachers in the faculty room had no choice but to hear his booming voice. "It's from a MacArthur Foundation report. 'Results from the most extensive U.S. study on teens and their use of digital media show that America's youth are developing important social and technical skills online—often in ways adults do not understand or value. It might surprise parents to learn that it is not a waste of time for their teens to hang out online,' said Mizuko Ito, University of California, Irvine, researcher and the report's lead author. 'There are myths about kids spending time online—that it is dangerous or making them lazy. But we found that spending time online is essential for young people to pick up the social and technical skills they need to be competent citizens in the digital age.'"

"So what?" interrupted Charlene Davis, a seasoned English teacher, in her most sarcastic voice. "What has that got to do with anything? It sounds like an excuse for all that texting the kids are doing in class."

"I don't think so," Bill Gregory, another veteran English teacher, responded. "They have to be learning something just considering all the time they spend."

continued →

"That's what the article implies," said Tom. "Listen to this: 'This study creates a baseline for our understanding of how young people are participating with digital media and what that means for their learning,' said Connie Yowell, PhD, director of education at the MacArthur Foundation. It concludes that learning today is becoming increasingly peer-based and networked, and this is important to consider as we begin to reimagine education in the 21st century."

"Well," huffed Charlene, "that is her opinion."

"I think not just her opinion," Tom responded. "The Foundation spent $50 million on this 2009 study of digital media and youth. There were lots of serious researchers involved, twenty-eight over three years, it says here. I think we have to think seriously about these results."

A technology tool is a piece of hardware (computer, printer, cell phone, camera, and so on), software (Microsoft Office with its application tools such as PowerPoint, Excel, Word, Paint, or tags), or Internet sites like the following that enable you and your students to enrich your learning experiences:

- Global School Network (www.globalschoolnet.org)
- NoteStar (www.notestar4teachers.org)
- Tellecollaborate (http://nschubert.home.mchsi.com)
- Fire and Ice (www.elluminate.com/fire_ice/index.jsp)

These are tools that the MacArthur study suggested teachers think about. Note: visit **go.solution-tree.com/instruction** for live links to these and other URLs mentioned in this book.

Just as dentists have many new digital tools for their clinical work, you and your students have many e-tools to help you in yours. Like the novice dentist who starts his or her career with mastery of a few dental tools, you and your students can start classroom projects by learning to use the basic technology or e-tools. Some of those learning tools are located on your computer when you purchase it. As you gain experience with your electronic tools, you can add new ones by bookmarking favorite websites, mastering clipart or photo exchange, making file folders, and researching ways to expand your teaching or classroom management repertoires.

Students can find new ways to adapt e-tools as well. Some new e-tools may help them do their learning tasks more efficiently. They may master a spreadsheet, join social networks, or listen to podcasts. They may collaborate with peers in a small group or take a course via Moodle (http://moodle.org).

Like dentists who master new tools to improve their dental practice, you and your students can use new e-tools in your teaching and learning.

E-Tools to Jumpstart Project Learning

E-tools raise the level of challenge and engagement in project-based learning. They give projects four distinct advantages over projects that don't incorporate e-tools:

1. **E-tools make it easier for you to manage classroom projects and organize tasks**—Various websites assist you in tracking student contributions, giving individual and whole-class feedback, maintaining schedules, encouraging students to talk with each other online, filing student folders for quick recall, filing project portfolios, and translating assessment data into grades.
2. **E-tools help you intensify student engagement in your projects**—As a project challenges your students with more rigorous content, it will promote their critical thinking, communication, and collaboration. It will guide their problem solving and encourage them to invent creative solutions with tools and applications to help them organize their thinking processes more efficiently.
3. **Projects are a strong vehicle that enables you to more easily integrate technology with your course content, especially if your content is standards-aligned**—Some advocates of technology in 21st century skill development advocate technology instruction for its own sake. Yes, you may have to prepare mini-lessons that will instruct students on how to bridge the use of the tool into their assignments, but you do want to keep technology in its place as a tool. If some students choose to make technology study a career, that is a bonus outcome. Most students, however, are in your classroom to learn specific content and to develop critical thinking skills most appropriate to your content. For your classroom, e-tools are usually a means to improve learning, not the end product.
4. **E-tools can transform students into more efficient learners as they master the e-tools**—You improve students' learning efficiencies in two ways. First, you give them the chance within the project to master e-tools for scheduling, tabulating data, thinking critically, planning, and communicating the ideas they are constructing. Second, you allot time to help them sharpen important cognitive functions such as impulse control, precision, accuracy, and logical reasoning.

Just as you can jumpstart a dead car battery easier with one of the new powerful, portable battery packs than you can with the old-fashioned cables or a call to your local car service, you can jumpstart your projects with a small collection of powerful e-tools. You *can* organize projects that increase student engagement without such e-tools as whiteboards, Google docs, podcasts, and blogs. However, with the addition of such basic e-tools as email, tutorial websites, and software-embedded programs such as PowerPoint and Excel, you can organize and keep track of project performance with less effort and time. When you add free tutorial Web 2.0 sites that prepare students to work on projects, such as http://electronicportfolios.org, http://edublogs.org, or http://scriblink.com, you accelerate and improve what and how students are learning.

Once you start your investigation of how to enrich students' learning with electronic tools embedded in the project model and make notes, you will quickly understand that your students will not just be doing a project as a fun activity or time filler. And they won't just be doing a well-designed conventional project. The enriched learning project model will be far more engaging than most tech-less projects your students may have finished in other classes.

To begin, you will need to select e-tools that are most valuable for transforming project learning into an enriched learning experience that dramatically improves students' achievement, as well as their 21st century skills. It will not matter what subject you teach: English, mathematics, science, social studies, art, music, or career skills. It will also not matter if your students have special needs, are learning English, or come to school needing a free or reduced lunch.

Blogs

A blog (from *weblog*) is a website that operates as an electronic journal. You can maintain an all-class blog, students can maintain small team blogs, or you can set up an all-class blog while students each have their own. You can design an all-class blog so that you can talk to students and they can respond to you. Eventually, you can make the blog open to still pictures or video. The all-class blog can facilitate discussions that respond to a question you post, student commentary, and your feedback to the entire class. As an electronic journal, the blog allows for reflections and self-assessments and maintains a history of the class project.

If students have project blogs, you can post a reflection or assessment question on your blog and they respond on their own. In this way, you can better maintain their privacy as you provide individual feedback. You can also create special assignments for students to include in these electronic journals.

Podcasts

A podcast is a series of audio or video digital media files that are distributed over the Internet by syndicated download through web feeds to portable media players and personal computers. You can make a podcast that goes to each student's computer. Your podcasts might include project instructions, all-class feedback on project events, or motivational announcements to start each day. You might schedule each work team to give an update on its project on a different day or allow teams to create their own motivational messages. In phase three, communicate the results, you might schedule each team for a fifteen-minute summary that introduces their final product. Students can also find free podcast download sites for background music or free screencast sites for videos to stream.

Whiteboards

A whiteboard is any glossy surface, most commonly colored white, on which you can make nonpermanent markings. The original whiteboards operated as chalkboards, except with the use of special markers. Eventually, whiteboards were developed with connections to computers so that the content shown could be composed on the computer. Recent developments include a free Web 2.0 site (http://scriblink.com), which allows drawings done on a computer screen to be networked to other computers, and interactive SMART Boards (www.smarttech.com) that can be used with hundreds of activities.

Interactive whiteboards have several functions that help with project communication. At the beginning of the day, you can post a work plan, set up a conference schedule for the groups, make all-class announcements, or send feedback to all the computers in the classroom. Teachers have used smart whiteboards to review a common math problem, review grammar and punctuation in small groups, make slide presentations as a project product, show timelines, and promote intergroup collaboration.

Tags

A tag is a keyword or specific term assigned to one or more pieces of information. Internet bookmarks and computer file names are common tags. A tag helps describe how single items, such as like documents, are connected to each other and allows for speedy searching for related information or documents.

In projects, students make tags for research items that they want to keep linked. Many current Web 2.0 services use tags to help students navigate common themes. You can use tags on your blog instead of categorizing the material. When you want students to create indexes, they can tag single posts that link to other related posts.

Twitter

Twitter is a social-networking and micro-blogging service that allows its users to send and read other users' updates, known as tweets, which are text-based posts of up to 140 characters. Each day during a project you could post a tweet reminder for the students. Tweets are also an easy tool for encouraging students to make succinct responses to stems that you might call for in the middle of a class period: "Right now, I think our project . . ." "Today, I learned that . . ." or "The five most important questions I asked this week were . . ." You can control who receives a tweet, including parents or students at other sites around the world who might have an interest in brief project updates, or engage students in a wiki tweet contest, in which they use Twitter to summarize a story.

E-Portfolios

An electronic portfolio, also known as an e-portfolio or digital portfolio, is a collection of electronic evidence assembled and managed by the students, usually on the web. Such electronic evidence may include text, electronic files, images, multimedia, blog entries, and hyperlinks, assembled as individual student commentary, self-assessments, reflections, and project products. E-portfolios demonstrate what students are doing and how they are progressing with their projects. With the online connection to your blog, which can have its own e-portfolio for storing student responses and project work, you can gather evidence of students' achievement in all three learning dimensions: content mastery, critical thinking, and collaboration.

Social Networks

A social network is an electronic social structure comprised of individuals or organizations who have shared values, visions or functions, or a common purpose. Research has shown that social networks operate on many levels, from families up to the level of nations, and play a critical role in determining the way problems are solved, organizations are run, and the degree to which individuals succeed in achieving their goals.

In a project, you build the social network around your students. The stronger the bonds of interdependence, the more productive the student members will be in their projects (Johnson & Johnson, 2009). You can use the network to facilitate interdependent problem solving among the student teams that give feedback to each other, encourage students to coach each other across team boundaries, and manage the development of team projects. By limiting social networking to students in your classroom, you set up the safety net needed to block out unwanted visitors while still encouraging students to do the online collaborating they value so highly.

Moodle

Moodle (http://moodle.org) is a free, open-source e-learning software platform, also known as a course management system, learning management system, or virtual learning environment. Moodle is designed to help you create online courses with opportunities for rich interaction among your students. You can set up a classroom Moodle to tutor students in how to use an e-tool or one that students themselves can use to Moodle their project results for classmates.

Web 2.0

Web 2.0, a recent development in web services, is associated with applications that facilitate information sharing, user-centered design, and collaboration. Most

Web 2.0 sites are open source, provide free access, and encourage free use of their service. Many of the sites provide free tutorials so that you and your students can learn how to use the service for projects. When a tool is new to you, such as constructing a blog, it is helpful to use an online tutorial for yourself first and then use it to prepare your students.

The following sites provide free services. You can add these services to your list of project e-tools.

- **Blogs**: http://edublogs.org, http://21classes.com
- **Podcasts**: www.about.com
- **Whiteboards**: http://scriblink.com
- **Tags**: http://delicious.com
- **Twitter**: www.twitter.com
- **E-portfolios**: http://electronicportfolios.org
- **Social networks**: http://globalschoolnet.org, www.epals.com
- **Calendars**: www.google.com/calendar
- **Surveys and spreadsheets**: http://zohopolls.com, www.google.com/docs
- **Projects**: www.thinkquest.org, www.iearn.org
- **Note taking**: www.notestar.4teachers.org
- **Webwork (rubrics, think tank)**: http://poster.4teachers.org
- **Photo and image sharing**: www.flickr.com

You can further enrich project learning when you have students take advantage of more advanced e-tools, many of which are on Web 2.0 sites and are applicable to each of the three learning phases—gather information, make sense of it, and communicate the results (fig. 4.2, page 58). Projects that integrate technology in any or all of the learning phases will engage students more deeply in their inquiry or problem-solving tasks, add a powerful new dimension to the enrichment of the teaching and learning process, and free your time for the one-on-one coaching that creates the most differentiated classrooms.

In addition to making coaching easier and allowing you to spend more time with your students, many of these web tools give you the ability to talk with parents and share tips, lesson plans, and resources with your colleagues in the same building or anywhere around the world. Beyond that, the tools give you and your students the ability to "show and tell" about project artifacts (www.flickr.com), plan cross-country and cross-nation projects (www.epals.com), participate in international project competitions (www.thinkquest.com), and easily find resources and share documents (www.google.com/docs).

Getting Ready: The Technology Standards

As you prepare to enrich your project with the e-tools that make the most sense to you, review the technology standards that you judge to be relevant to your project's goals. The development of content standards to guide you in selecting the most important concepts and procedures was one of the important contributions of late 20th-century reforms. National professional organizations such as the National Council of Teachers of Mathematics (www.nctm.org), the American Association for the Advancement of Science (www.aaas.org), the International Reading Association (www.reading.org), and the National Council of Teachers of English (www.ncte.org) led the way in defining what content was most important for students to know and do. To this information, the International Society for Technology in Education has added the National Education Technology Standards (www.iste.org/nets). Not only will these standards guide you in understanding what 21st century students need to know and do with technology, they reinforce the value of using technology to foster project-learning experiences that align with rigorous content standards.

As your students may have experienced even before they entered kindergarten, computers are like a flower attracting bees. There is a powerful "pollen scent" emanating from the many technology tools that students mastered before they boarded their first school bus. Because of students' early interest in computers, be it role-playing with a toy cell phone, playing Transformer games, watching siblings on MySpace, listening to a podcast, or watching a streamed movie—uses that make computers as friendly and ubiquitous as basic eating utensils—many students come to today's classrooms well-versed in using the computer and Internet. At times when some students revolt against reading from a book, writing with pen and pencil, or doing hand calculations, computers and e-tools such as Kindle, Plastic Logic, or Excel spreadsheets make it far easier to involve them in difficult learning tasks and move them to higher planes of learning—especially with project-based learning.

Students using technology appear to be more at ease in gathering new knowledge that they can easily transform into their own modes of expression without encountering the blocks and barriers that come with traditional learning. Not having to circle right answer after right answer on a sleep-inducing worksheet helps! What helps more is the chance to use various media to create products that integrate the knowledge they have gathered through their online research or invented through their own windows to the world.

With a variety of e-tools at their command, your students can respond to new information in ways that excite them and keep them interested in what they are doing. You need only encourage them to make use of their innovative thinking skills—to generate new ideas, explore complex problems, analyze trends, and forecast possibilities.

As helpful as e-tools can be, the glitziest hardware, the most compelling software, and the most magical Internet sites are not enough to ensure that all students learn effectively. However, when you make it possible for students to get away from the drag of such e-tools as electronic drill sheets and set up an investigation or problem-solving framework for their learning, you dramatically increase the learning pull.

When you can give your students the opportunity to learn their lessons via technology projects, you kill several birds with a single stone. First, the e-tools make many of the learning tasks needed to meet the content requirements easier; second, at the same time, students have a chance to develop their critical and creative thinking skills; and third, they will move toward achieving the 21st century educational technology standards.

National Educational Technology Standards for Students (NETS-S)

The fourth of the six National Educational Technology Standards—critical thinking, problem solving, and decision making (National Educational Technology Standards: NETS for Students, 2007)—calls for students to use critical thinking skills so they can plan and discuss research, manage projects, solve problems, and make informed decisions using appropriate digital tools. This standard guides your project plan development, as do the other five for students and the matching standards for teachers (International Society for Technology in Education, 2007; National Educational Technology Standards: NETS for Teachers, 2008).

There are four benchmarks (a through d) for the fourth student standard that are especially apropos when preparing to address student learning through the project model. Students should:

a. Identify and define authentic problems and significant questions for investigation.
b. Manage activities to develop a solution or complete a project.
c. Collect and analyze data to identify solutions and make informed decisions.
d. Use multiple processes and diverse perspectives to explore alternative solutions. (International Society for Technology in Education, 2007)

In this standard, a completed project is identified as an end result. Its only shortcoming is that it does not make explicit reference to a project's content. The standard implies that identified solutions and completed projects are the desired end results. As a teacher trying to instruct students in a possibly unfamiliar method of learning, the enriched project method, you will have to integrate your own content standards.

National Educational Technology Standards for Teachers (NETS-T)

Teaching and learning are often described as two sides of the same coin. It is very difficult to separate one from the other. In high-quality classrooms, teaching always informs learning and vice versa. It is an interactive process. When using the project model of instruction, the teacher standards allow you to view your project construction from both sides. Each of the five teacher standards provides you with benchmarks against which you can mark the quality of your instructional performance with the project model:

1. Facilitate and inspire student learning and creativity
2. Design and develop digital-age learning experiences and assessments
3. Model digital-age working and learning
4. Promote and model digital citizenship and responsibility
5. Engage in professional growth and leadership (National Educational Technology Standards: NETS for Teachers, 2008)

Bridging the Standards to Enriched Project-Based Learning Experiences

As you did with the content standards, you can use the backwards design model (McTighe & Wiggins, 2008) for project-based learning experiences. If you are using the investigation mode (NETS-S 4.a) as called for by the student standard, your first task is to plug your desired technology outcomes into the content outcomes you have already selected. As you review your plan, you will add in the e-tools and the desired skills needed.

As an example, consider a project that will help students understand the causes of air pollution. In the project, you expect students to demonstrate specific research skills and end with a media show projected from their desktop stations. Start by forming collaborative groups of three that highlight roles and responsibilities in each phase (NETS-S-b). Then analyze data with Google doc spreadsheets (NET-S-c). Finally, use a blog for capturing e-journal entries and Photo Story 3 for Windows to create slideshows (NETS-S-d).

You should also construct rubrics that will guide students as they do their research and complete the show with an alignment of strategy to the standards. And in some cases, you may want students to use a specific tool that most of them haven't yet mastered. In these cases, you will have to plan time in the project schedule for introducing this tool's proper use. Otherwise, after a quick check for understanding that allows you to note who can and who cannot use the tool, pair the knowers with nonknowers for a peer-tutoring session. In such a pairing, it is important that you check to make sure the student tutors are indeed teaching their partners and not just taking over and doing the whole task themselves.

Making Connections Outside School Walls

Not only can students use their e-tools to research information on worldwide sites, they can also make connections with students in other schools, states, and nations to seek different points of view for their projects or to talk with experts on the other side of the globe. In addition to stretching the boundaries of their project research and hearing divergent viewpoints, your students can enter into long-term conversations, compare and contrast ideas from different cultural viewpoints, and share project results beyond school walls.

Voiceover Internet protocol connections such as Skype (www.skype.com) allow them to soar beyond the classroom walls and to build long-term relationships with peers in other cultures by establishing audio and video access to other classrooms. Organizations such as Fire and Ice (www.elluminate.com/fire_ice), e-Pals (www.epals.com), Classroom Connect (www.classroom.com), the International Education and Resource Network (http://iearn.org), and the Global School Network (www.globalschoolnet.org) help you with the logistics.

An expanded data search outside your classroom walls not only enables your students to gather information from sources that are physically removed, but also encourages them to talk with and build relationships with their peers in other communities and nations. These sites also maintain project registries where you can register your projects and see samples from other teachers. Some additional registries are the European Schoolnet Project Database (www.eun.org), the Education Place Project Registry (www.eduplace.com), and the Oz Projects Registry (www.ozprojects.edu.au). Friendship Through Education (http://friendshipthrougheducation.org) provides a list of organizations that will connect you and your students to ongoing international Internet projects.

Free Search Tools

To initiate your students' research in phase one, gather information, you can rely on the many free information-gathering search tools easily found online. Free and low-cost software is readily available for download on classroom computers. You can also teach students how to use file folders to store their information according to topics and subtopics. They can use the notebook feature to make note cards and store assessment rubrics. They can add summaries of material read and store graphic organizers, PowerPoint presentations, or other facts and figures they gather during their research. To connect like information, students can tag topics. Beyond keeping simple files on their desktops, students can take advantage of secure file- and picture-sharing sites such as www.google.com/docs and www.glidedigital.com.

Using these file-sharing sites, you can easily control access and check the entries with your own access to students' folders. At any time, you can examine folders for content, check for sentence structure, punctuation, relevance, accuracy, logic, or whatever other skill or cognitive function you are stressing in a project. Given the access you will have to the students' folders, you don't have to wait until a final due date to see if they are adding to their project folders and doing so correctly. After any check, you can leave notes for each student or give feedback to the entire class on a common observation. To address other safety and security concerns you have about student-to-student conversations beyond your classroom, use the tutorials on the global networking sites already mentioned.

E-Tools to Promote Thinking

As noted earlier, the fourth National Educational Technology Standard for students highlights critical and creative thinking, problem solving, and decision making. These and other cognitive operations require instructional strategies that show students "how to." If you assume that all students will know how to *analyze* data to make informed decisions, *create* models, and *form* new concepts, you are likely to end up with superficial thinking results. For these macrothinking operations, students need to develop such skills as causal analysis, sequential analysis, temporal analysis, comparing and contrasting, distinguishing, differentiating, and challenging assumptions to use with the content they are studying. In addition, students thinking critically in a project will benefit by being challenged to develop cognitive functions that help them learn to take their time and think slowly, precisely, and accurately.

By thinking strategically about how to improve students' thinking skills, you will feel more and more comfortable designing technology tasks that help your students make sense of the information they have found. For instance, they might view online newscasts and websites (such as BBC News, the PBS Newshour, Human Rights Watch, and Friends of Tibet) that take an in-depth look at the impact of China's incursion into Tibet from different points of view; they should also assess the accuracy and validity of these different points of view and compare what they learn from distance correspondence with interviews of Tibetans living in the United States and the magazine articles they select from the local libraries and online resources. Following are criteria they can use for assessing information:

- Accurately interprets evidence, statements, graphics, and questions
- Identifies the salient argument's (reasons and claims) pros and cons
- Thoughtfully analyzes and evaluates major alternative points of view
- Draws warranted, judicious, nonfallacious conclusions
- Justifies key results and procedures, explains assumptions and reasons
- Fair-mindedly follows where evidence and reason lead

You can further assist your students by providing them with a rubric that will guide the quality of their critical thinking. This two-column rubric (table 3.1) adapted from Washington State University's Critical and Integrative Thinking Rubric, illustrates how to provide students with detailed criteria for critical thinking.

Table 3.1: Criteria for Critical Thinking

Emerging	Mastering
1. Identifies and summarizes the problem or question at issue or the source's position	
Emerging	**Mastering**
Does not identify and summarize the problem, is confused, or identifies a different and inappropriate problem Does not identify or is confused by the issue, or represents the issue inaccurately	Identifies the main problem and subsidiary, embedded, or implicit aspects of the problem, and identifies them clearly, addressing their relationships to each other Identifies not only the basics of the issue, but recognizes nuances of the issue
2. Identifies and presents the *student's own* hypothesis, perspective, and position as it relates to the analysis of the issue	
Emerging	**Mastering**
Addresses a single source or view of the argument and fails to clarify the established or presented position relative to one's own; fails to establish other critical distinctions.	Identifies appropriately one's own position on the issue, drawing support from experience, and information not available from assigned sources.
3. Identifies and considers *other* salient perspectives and positions that are important to the analysis	
Emerging	**Mastering**
Deals only with a single perspective and fails to discuss other possible perspectives, especially those salient to the issue	Addresses perspectives noted previously, and additional diverse perspectives drawn from outside information
4. Identifies and assesses the key assumptions	
Emerging	**Mastering**
Does not surface the assumptions and ethical issues that underlie the issue, or does so superficially	Identifies and questions the validity of the assumptions and addresses the ethical dimensions that underlie the issue
5. Identifies and assesses the quality of supporting data or evidence and provides additional data or evidence related to the issue	
Emerging	**Mastering**
Merely repeats information provided, taking it as truth, or denies evidence without adequate justification; confuses associations and correlations with cause and effect Does not distinguish between fact, opinion, and value judgments	Examines the evidence and source of evidence; questions its accuracy, precision, relevance, and completeness Observes cause and effect and addresses existing or potential consequences Clearly distinguishes between fact and opinion, and acknowledges value judgments
6. Identifies and considers the influence of the context on the issue	
Emerging	**Mastering**
Discusses the problem only in egocentric or sociocentric terms Does not present the problem as having connections to other contexts—cultural, political, and so on	Analyzes the issue with a clear sense of scope and context, including an assessment of the audience of the analysis Considers other pertinent contexts

continued →

7. Identifies and assesses conclusions, implications, and consequences	
Emerging	**Mastering**
Fails to identify conclusions, implications, and consequences of the issue or the key relationships between the other elements of the problem, such as context, implications, assumptions, or data and evidence	Identifies and discusses conclusions, implications, and consequences considering context, assumptions, data, and evidence Objectively reflects upon their own assertions

Adapted from Critical Thinking Materials Resource Guide, © *Washington State University (WSU) Office of Assessment and Innovation, Office of General Education, and the Writing Center. Used with permission.*

Tech Standards and E-Tools for Making Products

Many educators who are only casually familiar with project learning often confuse the final product with the project. These teachers may consider the two early phases of gathering information and making sense to be extraneous or just a warm-up. In fact, many projects from past eras skipped the first two learning phases. In the lower grades, many projects are no more than the making of an object such as a diorama or a collage that has no explicit connection to any content, process, or technology standards. Some of these were mere time-filling activities. Others are serious endeavors but focus entirely on the final product rather than the learning that comes from moving from inception to the final result.

Memory of a Science Project

I recall my science fair project in the eighth grade. I was trying to invent a new car battery that would never wear out. I contacted battery companies and requested literature on the makeup of their batteries. I interviewed a neighbor, a scientist at the DuPont Experimental Station outside of Wilmington, Delaware. I learned as much as I could about the current batteries and about metals and acids that might last longer. My neighbor found me samples of the most promising metals and acids. In my basement, I set up a lab and conducted my tests. When I finished, I had found a metal–acid composition that lasted twice as long as the standard battery.

After I wrote my conclusions in a report, I had to make a poster to advertise my discovery. I spent another few days after school getting this ready, and then took it to school for the science fair. After the judging, I was surprised that I earned a blue ribbon and an A.

Reflecting back on that project, it is clear that my memories were built around the grade and the blue ribbon that was hung on my poster. I never was asked what I had learned. When I look back, I don't think I even thought about what I learned from doing the research or making the poster, but I did enjoy my project.

Neither the grade nor the final product is the most important result of an enriched project-based learning experience. In enriched learning projects, the results you most desire are the concepts that students have formed and the skills they have developed as a result of the entire three-phase experience. Final products, be they an informational website, a book of poetry, a newscast, a dance performance, a slideshow, or a new car battery that lasts forever, are only the means to show what the students learned as they completed the inquiry or solved the critical problem.

Phase three, communicate the results, is also more than an afterthought or attachment to the prior phases. In phase three, students continue to develop their 21st century skills as they create a way to best communicate or express what they learned through the first two phases. This output phase (Feuerstein, Falik, & Feuerstein, 2006a) is an integral component of the whole learning process.

In enriched learning projects, you are encouraged to include two or more media requirements for communicating the answers found in the investigation or the solution uncovered. It is best for students if you require them to select an e-tool for the first medium. However, it is important that the second medium require speaking or writing tasks that allow students to meet the traditional content standards for communication (table 3.2).

Table 3.2: E-Tools and Corresponding Traditional Media

E-Tool	Traditional Media
Slide presentation	Music video
Blog or online journal	Public service announcement
Wiki biography	Interactive still production
Podcast	Webcam production
Website	Multimedia ad
Online newsletters	Skype conversation

The end of a project is a perfect opportunity for students to summarize the knowledge gained from the project in an essay or a formal talk. Ask students to use brochures, panel discussions, a mock newsletter or magazine article, a debate or mock interview, a short story, or a poem to express what they learned via e-tools. Streamed text, videos, slideshows, and PowerPoint presentations are but a few of the media available. These products, which facilitate the verbal-linguistic intelligence, can be used in addition to live productions or nontechnological media, such as a one-scene drama or dance performance, a mural, guidebook, musical composition, or sculpture.

My All-Time Favorite

After a year of studying tragic heroes such as Oedipus, Macbeth, Willy Loman, and George Milton, in *Of Mice and Men,* I asked my twelfth-grade literature students to create a sculpture that would represent their idea of a modern tragic hero. I also asked them to write a three-to five-page essay about a current news figure or TV main character (male or female) who matched their idea. On the day they showed their sculptures, each would have to explain his or her idea and link the sculpture and the modern figure to the launch question, "Who is a tragic hero?" After the presentation, I encouraged the other students to ask the presenter what he or she had learned about the study by doing this project. Of all the projects I assigned over the years, this was the most fun, most revealing, and most inspiring to the students.

Summary

When preparing for a project learning experience that will enrich students' learning with e-tools, review the e-tools that will fit the project goals and align with both technology and content standards. After you have identified the e-tools that you want to use, think about which technology standards these tools will most advance. If students are unfamiliar with the e-tools, allow time to prepare students for using the tools.

Chapter 4

Which Instructional Strategies Count Most?

What's the use of running if you are not running on the right road?

—German proverb

This chapter's purpose is to identify the research-supported instructional strategies that are most likely to increase student achievement in a project. In the early 1970s, there was limited definitive research on what methods of instruction had the most impact on student achievement. By the early 1990s, educational researchers had compiled sufficient data so that teachers could answer the question, "What works best in the classroom?" with the results of metastudies. The most prominent of these studies came from a federal laboratory, McREL (Marzano, Pickering, & Pollock, 2001). It identified nine categories of instructional tactics that had the greatest effect on student achievement. In order to build on the processes of identifying similarities and differences and hypothesis testing discussed as enriched learning frameworks, this chapter examines the other best instructional practices identified by McREL. Use the research about these strategies as the best indicators to ensure that your instruction for a project is on the right road.

A Big Idea

Ann and Elise were set with their plan.

"What's first?" Mrs. Minsk asked.

Ann, the more talkative twin, answered. "We decided to investigate the starvation in Somalia. So far, we have only read a couple of news stories. Our first step is to gather as much information as we can."

"I see," the teacher responded. "I think you've taken on a very large project."

"Yes, but remember you said our idea needed to be a big one. We thought that this was very important," said Elise.

"I agree with that. But you may also have to narrow it down."

continued →

"That's OK," answered Ann. "Our plan will let us do that. We've built that in, and we plan to divide up the research."

"What question are you using to start your investigation?" asked Mrs. Minsk.

"We are going to start with 'Is the starvation in Somalia being caused on purpose?'" Ann responded.

"You have already decided there is starvation?"

"Yes," said Elise. "In our prestudy, we gathered that data, and we think the evidence is strong. We are making our search narrower by focusing on this question, but we still have more questions to ask."

High-Yield Instructional Strategies to Enrich Learning in Projects

Some critics of education argue what you do has little or no effect on students. For decades they have tried to create the teacher-proof classroom. Either they don't know about or choose to ignore the research, especially that conducted since 1970, which says otherwise. Foremost among these reports is the meta-analysis conducted by Marzano, Pickering, and Pollock (2001) at McREL in the 1990s. This meta-analysis of what works best in classroom instruction is a high-water mark. In their report, Robert Marzano and his team highlighted the nine instructional strategies that provided the greatest effect in terms of student achievement. These high-yield strategies not only have a significant impact on student achievement, but they can also can be instrumental in developing students' thinking in an enriched learning project (Marzano, Pickering, & Pollock, 2001, p. 7):

1. Identifying similarities and differences
2. Summarizing and note taking
3. Reinforcing effort and providing recognition
4. Homework and practice
5. Nonlinguistic representations
6. Cooperative learning
7. Setting objectives and providing feedback
8. Generating and testing hypotheses
9. Questions, cues, and advance organizers

More Than a "Wing and a Prayer"

What is a high-yield instructional strategy? The label *instructional strategy* applies most accurately to a category of effective teaching methods that are purposefully implanted in a lesson in order to help students achieve the lesson's goal or outcome. Strategies are called high-yield (or high effect) because research indicates that they have the strongest positive effect on student achievement. These strategies build the most power into students' learning experiences. They contradict the notion that learning and thinking just happen—that the mere exposure of students to rigorous content or sophisticated digital tools is all that students need to develop their thinking and learning skills.

In their meta-analysis of the categories, Marzano and his colleagues (Marzano, Pickering, & Pollock, 2001) included specific methods or tactics that were effective in each category. For instance, under the generic category of cooperative learning, you will find such tactics as think-pair-share (TPS), write-pair-share (WPS), and four corners (fig. 4.1). The "house of cooperative learning" contains a variety of effective tactics. Select the ones that will give your students the best chance to increase their understanding or skill development and are most appropriate to where you are in the project. Whether one climbs in the TPS window or enters through the door is less important than choosing the right strategies.

Figure 4.1: The house of cooperative learning.

Three Phases of Learning: What Works

In a well-designed enriched learning project, you can divide students' learning experiences into three distinct phases (fig. 4.2). Although these phases often overlap or require students to fill in gaps and reconsider prior work, the three phases help you separate the main cognitive tasks that comprise the cycle of learning. In the first phase, students conduct research or gather the relevant information from their past experiences as well as from new resources. In the second phase, students make sense of the gathered information. They analyze data, assess its value, and make connections (such as cause and effect, time, similarities and differences, and so on). In the third phase, they decide how to show their new understandings (for example, through a multimedia presentation, dance, essay, or digital story).

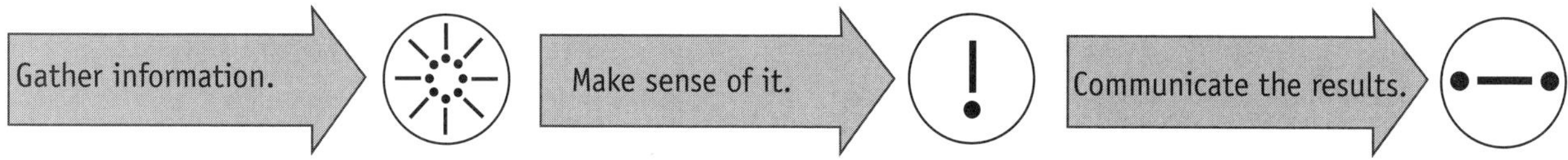

Figure 4.2: Three phases of learning.

An essential characteristic of an enriched learning project is your purposeful or intentional selection of instructional tactics from the high-yield strategies. Certainly you will have in your repertoire what works best for you. You cannot just throw away these tactics simply because they were not validated by a funded, formal research study that said, "Yes, this meets the gold standard." The same must be said of tactics that colleagues provided and you found in your experience to be a help in motivating students, developing their thinking, or advancing their achievement. However, as you add tactics to your repertoire for use in the three phases of enriched learning projects, it is important that you consider how these well-studied tactics can help your students.

Phase One: Gather Information

Two high-yield strategies are especially helpful in the first phase of the learning process: (1) questions and (2) graphic organizers.

Questions

Educational researchers have identified what you can do to address the following difficulties students have with question-asking skills:

- Students often have difficulty generating essential questions that will help them understand a central concept (Torp & Sage, 1996).
- Students have difficulty framing questions to guide their inquiry (Torp & Sage, 1996).

- Students have difficulty with open-ended situations (Torp & Sage, 1998).
- Students wander from the set path of their key question (Pohlmann & Pea, 1997).

To counteract the difficulties of generating a strong and effective launch question, it is helpful to schedule a mini-lesson on asking launch questions early in the project schedule. In a one- to two-period lesson, pay special attention to helping students learn the criteria for and guide their practice in the framing of effective launch questions. At the same time, you can prepare them for developing the question-asking skills that are most helpful for refining their initial launch questions (Torp & Sage, 1998).

Sample Lesson Using Launch Questions

Big Idea: Reducing air pollution (or substitute the big idea or problem that you want to use for the first project)

Launch Question: How can we eliminate our carbon footprints?

Criteria for Launch Question:

- Is open ended
- Addresses a significant issue
- Allows for multiple solutions
- Is considered important by the asker

Tasks:

1. Ask students how the sample question meets the criteria.
2. Ask students to frame other sample questions; let students first share in pairs and then share their questions with the class.
3. Ask other pairs to match samples with the criteria.
4. Give your feedback on the quality of the launch questions.
5. Move to the refining questions, and explain how these questions will help them narrow their project's focus.

Refining Questions:

- What is a goal that is possible for us to achieve in this project?
- How will we measure that goal's achievement?
- How will we make sure that our goal is believable?
- What data will we have to supply?
- How precise and accurate is our data?

continued →

Criteria for Refining Questions:

- To what degree do the questions narrow the original big idea?
- To what degree will the questions result in an appropriate solution?

Tasks:

1. Invite pairs to use a Word document headed with the topic of the first project. (Have them save it to a file folder.) They will add your name, the class period, and the big idea for the topic to the document. Invite the students to turn your big idea into a launch question that meets the criteria.
2. Show the sample refining questions, clarify, and invite pairs to prepare their refining questions.
3. Invite several pairs to share their questions by emailing them to you; then project a list of the questions for all students to see. Ask the authors of the questions to discuss with the class how the samples presented do or do not meet the criteria for refining questions.
4. After assessing several questions, ask the pairs to refine them in the Word document and email them to you with the following closing statement completed: "Today, what I learned about launch questions was . . ."
5. Review the documents and return them by email with appropriate corrective feedback. Repeat this mini-lesson with those students who need more guided practice.
6. Each day, select one of the project goals and have students practice questions that cause them to reflect on how well they are doing.

Student Products: Launch questions completed for their first project

Graphic Organizers

When gathering information in response to the refined launch question, students will find that visual tools, including those available as e-tools, are helpful for organizing their research. Graphic organizers are one of the most effective visual or nonlinguistic tactics identified in the effectiveness research. The key is for students to select the best visual tools that will organize the data they are collecting.

It helps to check which organizers students have used in the past. Review how to use those organizers before adding others that may be relevant to this project. As with asking the launch question, taking time out for a direct instruction mini-lesson on the selected graphic will save time throughout a first project and in future projects.

At the beginning of a project, two types of organizers are especially appropriate for the information-gathering process: (1) those that check prior knowledge and experience, and (2) those that gather data from print or online resources. You can find these organizers online at several sites by browsing "graphic organizers." Your students may already have half a dozen organizers on their desktop or in their applications, such as SmartArt in Microsoft Office, or Claris Works.

The most familiar graphic for gathering prior knowledge is Donna Ogle's (1987) KWL (what we *know*, what we *want* to know, what we *learned*). Encourage students to use this or other data collection organizers in interview pairs or trios. In addition to KWL, you can introduce a big foot–little foot chart (fig. 4.3) to check prior knowledge or to interview. You may also can scan organizers to insert in file folders, download templates, or make your own prior knowledge visual using http://teach-nology.com or http://webenglishteacher.com.

There are many choices of available organizers to gather data from online or standard print sources. Graphics helpful for this task include the camera eye, concept map, daisy chart, fact fan, newspaper chart, and three balloons (visit **go.solution-tree.com/instruction**). Let students select the organizers that fit their data gathering. One of best free organizers for digital data, as well as video and other images, is the concept map, or cmap (http://cmap.ihmc.us).

High Polluters	**Low Polluters**
Buses Chemical plant Diesel engines Old cars Firelpaces Garbage dump Grass fires Horses and cows	New cars Gas heaters Cigarettes Charcoal grills Propane buses
Cutting Carbon Emissions	
■ Update buses. ■ Place filters on smokestacks. ■ Promote hybrid cars.	■ Use gas fireplaces. ■ Bury garbage. ■ Ban smoking.

Figure 4.3: Big foot–little foot—comparing carbon footprints.

When you elect to enrich student learning with graphic organizers, you provide students with benefits that go beyond the high-yield reading effects that these tools provide. Extensive research shows that it matters little in which subject areas or with which racial or ethnic groups you use these tools. Achievement increases dramatically for all (Darch, Carnine, & Kammenui, 1986; Herl, O'Neil, Chung, & Schacter, 1999).

When you have students use visual organizers in phase one, you not only build their 21st century skills with a research-supported tactic, you also raise the odds that they will learn more and think more clearly. This happens because graphic organizers promote their efficiency as thinkers. The visual element also helps them organize the data they are collecting so they can apply their critical thinking skills when it comes time to analyze and interpret the information found. Whether students use the organizers with or without e-tools, they will have a rich opportunity to develop their collaboration skills, especially if you prepare the students to use selected organizers in learning pairs or trios in each phase.

Phase Two: Make Sense

In this phase, the basic strategies of asking questions and using graphic organizers are again helpful. However, they have a different purpose: to help students make connections between the details and to understand the concepts.

Ann and Elise

The two girls sat across from Mrs. Minsk. The teacher began, "I am pleased with the amount of reading you have done. And your notes seem very focused on your big question. Are you ready to make sense of what you found out?"

"Yes ma'am," Ann said. "We found out two things. Most of the articles told us that the starvation in Somalia was not done on purpose."

"Well, not directly," Elise added. "The starvation came because of the government's plan to kill off the Muslim population. The government sent in militia to kill the Bantu Muslims. They killed a lot of the men. Some of the other things they did were burn the crops and kill the cattle. That made the starvation worse."

"And you have evidence for this?" Mrs. Minsk asked.

"Yes. As you can see on our notes, we have the articles that give the facts. The news reports are from different papers," said Ann.

"Have you thought about how you are going to organize your information?"

"Not yet," replied Elise. "But we know we have to make sure that the facts support our argument."

"How will you help each other with that?" the teacher asked.

Both thought a moment. Ann spoke first, "We said we would work together on the arguments. We have agreed with our teammates Alice and Henry that we would allow ten minutes every day to go over what we were doing and see if it makes sense to them. If not, we would have to fix it."

"That's a good idea," Mrs. Minsk said. "It's important that you get and give feedback. I would also like you to do the same with one of your parents, if you can."

"Mom will after she puts the baby to bed," volunteered Elise.

"That's good," said Mrs. Minsk. "Be sure to keep your eyes on the key question. That is your end goal."

Questions

After students have collected sufficient data, they need to understand how the facts are related to their launch question. At this point, you can enrich students' learning by enabling them to ask questions that will help them make sense of their data. Such questions raise student thinking out of the swampy water that can drown them in a flood of details and jumbled facts. With effective questions, students develop concepts that clear their vision and enable them to understand.

Questions That Help Make Sense of the Data

Explain why . . .

Explain how . . .

What do you think was the cause of . . . ?

What do you think was the reason for . . . ?

How are ________ and ________ connected to the idea that ________?

What are the advantages of . . . ?

What are the disadvantages of . . . ?

How do you think ________ is like ________?

How do you think ________ is different from ________?

What ideas have you have gathered that you agree with? Why?

What ideas do you disagree with? Why?

Predict what you think will happen when . . .

Make a summary of the key facts that you have gathered.

What is your opinion about . . . ?

How do you support your opinion that . . . ?

How can you document that . . . ?

In enriched learning projects, the questions you ask students are important, especially when you are addressing a team or the whole class. In addition, these questions are important as models for the types of questions you want students to ask not only about the content, but also about the thinking skills they are using.

As with the launch questions, it is helpful if you take time to identify the types of questions that students can ask as they review their information.

For instance, after reading Thomas Friedman's exposé *Hot, Flat, and Crowded*, you might ask a team investigating the role of oil in geopolitics to explain how—and why—Friedman connects oil problems to dictatorships. Why does he do this?

After listening to their answers and asking additional questions that encourage the students to clarify their responses with data from the text, ask them for their opinions about Friedman's argument. Give them time to come back with documented responses. After providing the students with constructive feedback on their answers, invite them to stop and think about the questions you asked in this sequence (such as "What is your opinion about . . ." or "How can you document . . ."). Discuss the value of these questions, and invite them to use similar questions about the ideas Friedman expresses later in the book. You can continue this process throughout the project by coaching the teams in asking these questions and encouraging them to ask questions, like the following, about the thinking they are doing: "Tell me how you went about *comparing* Friedman's thoughts on Iran and Iraq oil policies." "When you *analyzed the differences*, tell me what parts you identified." "What could you do to better *analyze* the data?"

Graphic Organizers

Graphic organizers help students make sense of the data they have gathered. Many of the graphics students used to gather information can also be used in this second phase. Consider, for instance, the newspaper organizer (fig. 4.4). In phase one, students use the five questions in the upper section to collect the facts about what they are reading: who, what, when, where, and how. In the lower section, they prepare a summary of these facts and answer the last question: why. The facts collected on the graphic translate immediately into a sensible summary.

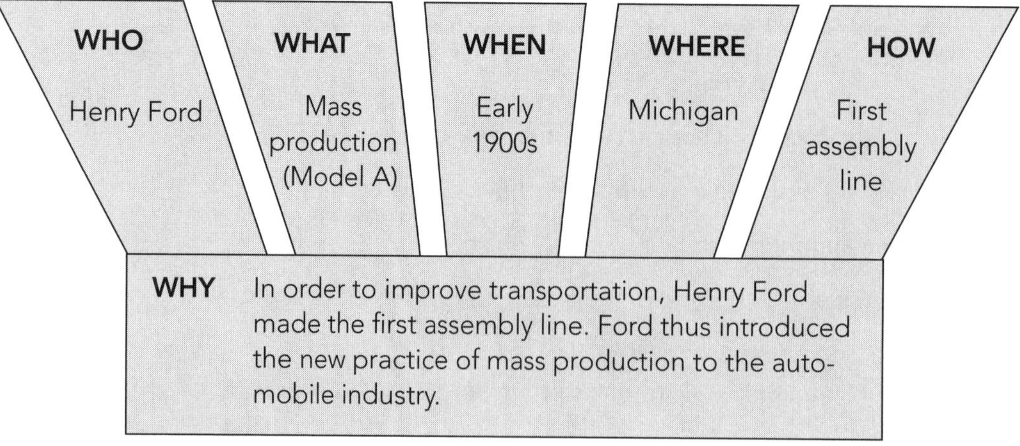

Figure 4.4: A sample newspaper organizer.

A more complex organizer, the fishbone (fig. 4.5) demonstrates cause-and-effect relationships. As students are gathering information from books or websites guided by a launch question, they can use the fishbone to arrange and rearrange the information. For instance, consider the financial crisis of 2008–2009. The "crashed economy" is the result they place in the head of the fish. As they read from different sources, they can identify four to six major causes that economists have identified. These might include housing, banks, government policy, and Wall Street, which go in the major "bones" of the fish. From this point, students have to do more and more precise and accurate thinking as they add the next level of topics, such as the SEC, Lehman Brothers, the president, leveraged buyouts, nationalization, deregulation, Bernie Madoff, and so forth. When the bone is finished, the students will have a visual picture of the cause-and-effect relationships as they perceive them.

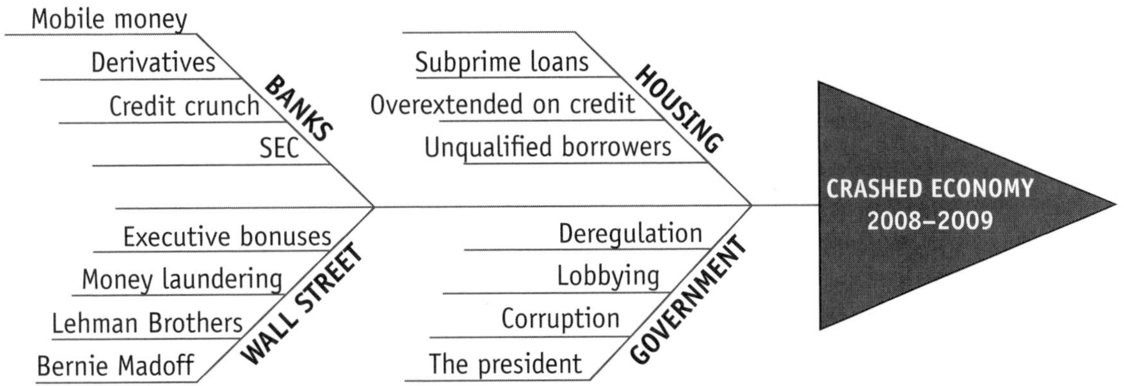

Figure 4.5: A sample fishbone organizer.

Technology provides many other options. Students can translate spreadsheets into matrices for categorizing data. From Microsoft Word, they can select a matrix, a hierarchy, and a cycle organizer or a selection of charts including bar, pie, and line graphs. Here are more possible selections on free sites that provide graphic organizer templates and tutorials that help students make sense:

- Network tree
- Spider map
- Problem-solving map
- Compare and contrast matrix
- Thematic map
- Interaction map

Go to www.teachervision.fen.com for templates of these and other sense-making organizers.

Part Three: Communicate the Results

Ann and Elise, CONTINUED

Ann and Elise breathed a sigh of relief. They had just finished presenting their project to Mrs. Smith, the principal, and three other teachers. They had been selected by their own teacher, Mrs. Minsk, to represent the class. She had judged their project "best in class."

Mrs. Minsk explained her decision to the panel. "First, I thought Ann and Elise had chosen the most sophisticated and serious topic in the class. They wanted to say something about starvation and genocide in Somalia. I thought that for seventh-graders, their insights were very profound. What they decided to do was also interesting. They were going to build a not-for-profit hospital in Darfur for pregnant girls. Volunteer doctors and nurses would come there to work after reading the girls' magazine article. It told the story of the genocide and starvation in Somalia.

"This was the only altruistic project in the class. It was also the best for finding the data to support their case. For their products, they designed and built a simple model of their hospital and made a plan for raising money. What I thought was very special was that they made this a real money-raising effort with the proceeds to go to the Darfur fund. At the parents' association fundraiser, Ann and Elise had a booth that displayed their model. They used PowerPoint presentations and made a brochure about their project to advertise the fundraising.

"Out of all the things the girls did, I thought their journal was the most interesting. They made it like a journal in a travel story. They charted the trip out on a map, which showed all of their decision points, and they discussed what was easy and hard about their project."

In the last phase of an enriched learning project, students communicate what they have learned. What do they know now or know better than they knew before they started? What skills have they developed in technology, thinking, collaborating, communicating, and the many content areas required for graduation? In phase three, students will provide the answers in a product or production. They will communicate the new insights and understandings they formed as they made sense of the information gathered from researching answers to their launch questions. This is the show and tell time for the learning results of their study.

Students' phase-three communication generally takes two forms: (1) a product, performance, or event that expresses what the students have learned about a topic they choose to study, and (2) a record that communicates the thinking and learning behind the making of the product. The focus, as indicated in the discussion on standards, is not on the products or performances, but on what students now know and do, and how they have improved.

Products, performances, and events take multiple forms, as follows:

- **Products**—Collages, models and sculptures, PowerPoint presentations, websites, essays, fiction stories or poems, inventions, video streams, audio streams, network debates
- **Performances**—A dramatic poetry reading (such as Frost's "Stopping by Woods"), a dance, pantomimes, musical performances (from solos to quartets), a play from a story, a one-act drama, a food demonstration, a comedy skit
- **Events**—A charity marathon, art show, garden show, used toy sale, visit to a senior citizens' home, webcast, soup kitchen

Gardner's (1983) theoretical explication of the eight intelligences provides guidance when students are thinking about how they will transform their project ideas into these end pieces. In many projects, such as when a student writes a jazz composition or a group writes a series of poems or short stories, a single intelligence dominates. In other instances, such as when a student creates and performs a modern dance, a team researches the invention of a longer-lasting car battery and prepares a booth display for a science convention, or students direct and stream a multimedia story, you bring multiple intelligences into play. When students plan a charity marathon, a voters' drive, a food kitchen, or a trip to another country as their project, many intelligences are certainly engaged (table 4.1).

Table 4.1: Sample Projects and Products Through the Multiple Intelligences Prism

Written Word (verbal/ linguistic)	Visual (visual/spatial)	Performance (bodily/ kinesthetic)	Musical (musical/ rhythmic	Science, Math, and Technology (mathematical/ logical)
Essay	Movie	Dance	Classical	Math model
Poem	Video stream	Pantomime	Composition	Science model
Drama	Audio stream	Play	Solo musical	Technology invention
Short story	Sculpture	A meal	Solo performance	Poster display
Novel	Mural	Charity event	Choral presentation	Science fair booth
Song	Painting	Circus	Operetta	Ecological map
Blog discussion	Collage	Choral reading	Musical comedy	Business operation
Biography	Diorama	Satirical review		Charitable event
Parable	Architectural model			
Allegory	Slideshow			
	PowerPoint			

Questions

When students are in this final phase of preparing their products and productions, your role is to coach and mediate. As an instructional coach, you help students working alone or in teams to plan and complete their products, performances, and events. In this role, you use your question-asking skills to keep students connected to their learning goals for the content, their collaborations, and their thinking. In addition to asking your questions about what the students are learning, as in the other phases, you enrich their learning further by encouraging them to ask significant questions of their own.

In the role of the mediator, you focus students' attention on the thinking and problem-solving processes they use in applying their new ideas to the product or performance. You mediate their phase-three thinking processes by asking questions about their thinking, giving feedback on your observation of their cognitive functions, and helping them strengthen the quality of their analyzing, reasoning, comparing, hypothesizing, and the other important cognitive operations.

Once students have answered the launch question with an answer that makes sense to them, it is time for them to begin asking the questions that will help them decide how and what they will do to present this information to others. Your first responsibility is to share with them the criteria that will guide their task. You can do this with a rubric. The RubiStar 4 teachers website (http://rubistar.4teachers.org) provides sample criteria for multiple types of products including oral projects, historic role plays, multimedia presentations, web pages, posters, and podcasts. RubiStar also provides templates and tutorials so you can identify your own criteria. A related site, http://pblchecklist.4teachers.org, provides the same services for you to develop criteria-based checklists that your students can use to guide their product creation.

With the criteria made clear, you can challenge students to develop their question-asking skills to transfer their new understandings to the final products. Prepare a slide presentation that you can show to demonstrate to students question-asking skills, and store these in student files. You might make a wiki so that students can add their own questions.

Questions That Communicate Results

What are the most important points I want to communicate in my final product?

Why am I selecting these points?

What is their priority?

What are my options for presenting these ideas?

How will I make my product unique and special?

In what formats am I required to present my ideas (for example, an essay plus a multimedia presentation, a brochure plus a collage, or a website plus an oral report)?

What is my selection?

How does my selection match the criteria (such as content mastery, critical thinking, and collaboration)?

How will I fund the product?

What sequence of events do I need to order the preparation?

What else do I want to include so my product stands out as exceptional?

What is my deadline?

Graphic Organizers

You can use graphic organizers in phase three as the final product. For instance, if students used a concept map or a fishbone chart to make sense of the information from phase one, they could take the information and put it directly into a sequence chart or problem-solving chart. With the information analyzed on the fishbone chart showing how the mortgage industry's use of subprime loans was the major cause of the economic crash in your state, your students' next task would be to prepare a slideshow depicting the cause-and-effect relationship. They would then show the order of events that led from subprime loans to the crash of a local bank (fig. 4.6).

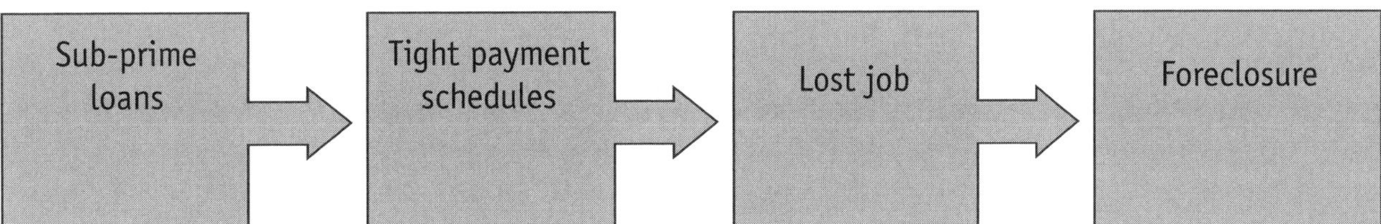

Figure 4.6: A sequence chart.

Students could also use a problem-solving chart to show how they arrived at the selection of the multimedia format for their presentations. You could facilitate their use of this chart by presenting a lesson inserted into your project schedule at the start of phase three.

Sample Tactical Lesson Plan

Title: Thinking About Problem Solving

Dates: March 28–April 7

Class Periods: 1, 3, 5, 6

Selected Tactic(s): E-journals, problem-solving chart

continued →

What I Want to Happen: At the end of the project, I want students to review the decisions they made about the product. With the problem-solving chart, they will have to think about what decisions they made, what consequences they anticipated, and the final outcomes. They can also reflect on what they might have done differently, if anything. In this way, I will have a good sense of how well they are internalizing the problem-solving process.

The Chart: Invite a student to use the projector as he or she fills in the elements of the chart. Model asking, "Why did you choose that?" questions to clarify the student's thinking.

Allotted Time: One class period

Student Products: A completed chart and the comments in the e-journals

How Will I Know the Tactic Is Working? I have a checklist for assessing the charts. It asks how well each student identified the core problems, examined alternatives, and investigated consequences. I will review each of the charts using these criteria. When in doubt, I will ask individual students to comment on their decisions.

Notes: Students will work in their project teams. I must be careful not to let anyone draw me into a team with questions that will have me doing their thinking for them. I did this last semester and I need to watch my tendency to rescue. I want to remember to mediate the cognitive functions I notice are present.

A reproducible Tactical Lesson Plan template (page 74 and online at **go.solution-tree.com/instruction**) will help you insert a tactical lesson plan within a project.

More Strategies That Enrich Learning

In the high-yields research, there are three additional strategies that will enrich your students' learning experiences.

Advance Organizers

Before you begin a project, consider using an advance organizers to stir students' interest and prior knowledge in the project's big idea. David Ausubel (1963) documented the power of the advance organizer for learning large amounts of verbal material. One of the most fruitful ways to use the advance organizer is to block out short amounts of time—two to five minutes—in the week prior to the start of a new project. Use a different tactic each day. On one day, check prior knowledge with a KWL (page 61). On another, ask an open-ended, hypothetical question such as, "What do you think would happen if . . . ?" On a third day, explain to the class the next project, its rationale, and the launch question. If time doesn't allow this slow build-up that stimulates students' thinking about the coming event, a single preview on the last day before the project will suffice. If all else fails, build the advance organizer into the first day of the project's schedule.

A Five-Day Advance Organizer

Project Title: Immigration Reform

Launch Question: How can the United States control the immigration of workers needed for food industry jobs?

Day 1: Read an article to the class about an immigration round up. No commentary. (five minutes)

Day 2: Use a KWL to identify students' prior knowledge about immigration reform. (five minutes)

Day 3: Identify the project and the launch question. Ask students to find a news article to bring to class. (five minutes)

Day 4: Identify the project and the launch question. Ask students to find a second news article to bring to class. (five minutes)

Day 5: Ask students to read articles to each other in small groups. Solicit student questions about the topic. (ten minutes)

Summaries

Another high-yield strategy is student-written summaries. Summarizing involves the cognitive operations of connecting ideas that have a shared meaning. Obviously, summaries fit well at the end of each of the three learning phases. Students can be asked to make summaries at the end of any day or task. And, of course, summaries are an effective way to end the project.

Usually, you will focus summaries on the content. The simplest summaries begin with, "Today, I learned . . ." stems. You can say, "Name three concepts that you learned today" or "Describe to me three discoveries you made in your research today." These more complex stems require students to make a list summary. A complex stem that asks students to compare similarities or to describe differences not only ends in a list summary, it also has the advantage of asking the students to use a similarities and differences strategy. You can create other list summaries with a hypothesis test such as "Make a list of three hypotheses that you are testing this week about [add the topic]" or "What are the three questions that are most likely to help you solve this problem?"

In addition to the list summary, you can prepare students to develop a deductive summary that presents a thesis statement and backs it up with three or four reasons or pieces of evidence, such as: "Macbeth was driven by a lust for power. His wife, Lady Macbeth, wanted him to have the throne. The three witches urged him on. He was convinced that he was indestructible and deserving of the crown."

Short summaries of what students learn in the content are a helpful tool for doing informal checks on their understanding. You can align these checks with the benchmarks that are guiding the students' search for meaning in the project. You can also ask students to use summaries to reflect on what they are learning about critical thinking or collaboration, as in the following example:

> In our team today, we had a breakthrough. It was brought about because we had fallen behind in our work schedule. In our search for the reasons why, we created a fishbone chart. From the discussion in building that chart, three difficulties became clear. First, we were not each pulling our weight. Second, we were rushing. Third, we were not in agreement on the goal. We accepted these reasons, and tomorrow we will discuss what we are going to do differently.

The placement of summaries in an enriched learning project is your decision. You select the place in the project design when making summaries will most benefit students' learning and advance their understanding of the content. You also determine the means. Will students use a section of their e-journal, keep a special file folder on the desktop, use a paper journal, or hand in note cards with the entries?

Note Taking

Another strategy that has a strong effect on student achievement is note taking. In the context of an enriched learning project, phase one is the most likely time that you will use this strategy for their research. However, you may also use it when you conduct a mini-lesson or give a mini-lecture. Many students are not used to taking notes. You can be most helpful if you set up a system for note taking. This may entail teaching the students the outline system of taking notes when you give a mini-lecture or asking them to read a specific article related to the project topic. Many teachers prefer either to teach their students how to use a concept map that they can keep in a notebook or to send them to the cmap tutorial (http://cmap.ihmc.us), so they can learn how to set up an online note-taking system.

So that students are not overwhelmed with notebooks, e-journals, or blogs, two tactics are important. First, select a single system for note taking. Teach the students how you want them to take notes for projects. Second, indicate *when* you want the students to take notes. Make your instructions explicit. "Please pull up your e-journals. Go to the note-taking section. If you are using an outline for your note taking, good. If you are using a newspaper graphic, good. Today, as your team discusses its plan, I want you to take notes on the goals and strategies you are going to use."

Summary

By dividing enriched learning projects into three phases, you help students learn how to complete a successful project. This three-phase breakdown gives your students the required skills for breaking a project into a structured set of inquiry steps

(Torp & Sage, 1998), creates equitable distribution of project work (Brown, 1992), and facilitates time management for debugging the parts of a product before its completion (Guzdial, 1998). Finally, the three-phase approach allows you to show students the different types of thinking, along with the most appropriate instructional strategies and tactics to use in each phase. This gives you the chance to heighten student initiative, provide guidance at critical junctures in the process (Barron et al., 1998), and enrich student learning during the project.

Tactical Lesson Plan

Duplicate this template when you need to make a tactical lesson plan within a project.

Title:
Dates:
Class periods:
Selected tactic(s):
What I want to happen:
The chart:
Allotted time:
Student products:
How will I know the tactic is working?
Notes:

Chapter 5

Nurturing Quality Thinking

> Great oaks from little acorns grow.
>
> —Latin proverb

This chapter shows the value and the methods for improving students' thinking by attending to their cognitive functions. Two of the most renowned cognitive psychologists of the 20th century, Vygotsky and Feuerstein, demonstrated the value of highly developed cognitive functions as the foundation for critical and creative thinking. The elements in the thinking process, cognitive functions, enable students to think and learn more efficiently (Vygotsky, 1979; Feuerstein, Falik, Rand, & Feuerstein, 2006). When students are not thinking well in their projects, teachers can mediate improvements that enrich students' learning. This chapter identifies those cognitive functions that are especially important for producing quality thinking in a project. For each, analysis charts are provided, as well as tactics for classroom use.

I Have to Change Them!

Marilyn Voorhees frowned. It hadn't been her best teaching day. In fact, it was more like the book she was reading with her son about a boy named Alexander and his worst day ever. "It's like they don't think," she told her colleague Dave, a senior teacher at North Town High School. "They are supposed to be high school freshman, and they act like three-year-olds."

"How so?" he asked.

"Well, first off, it's their impulsivity. They just blurt out whatever comes into their heads. Nobody will stop and think. It's like they are in a race. I need their behavior to change if I am going to teach them anything."

Dave smiled as he sipped his coffee. "First, I learned long ago that you have to accept they're ninth-graders. Impulsivity is built into their genes."

Marilyn said, "That I know well . . . in more ways than one. But that doesn't help me change them."

"Do you really think you can?"

"Change them?" Marilyn asked. "Isn't that my job?"

continued →

"Depends," Dave replied. "There are lots of ways to use that word. Personally, I've never been content just changing their observable behavior."

"What do you mean?"

"You have to change how they think," Dave said. "And that is not easy."

"Easy or not, if I want to teach anything, they have to behave differently. How can anyone think with all this shouting out of answers and hand waving?"

Dave smiled. "Some around here would say you have a good problem," he said. "They would want to see at least one student excited to answer."

"So what do you suggest?" Marilyn asked.

"Well, first you have to understand that their impulsivity is not a behavior. Their blurting out is just a sign that they lack control over how they are thinking. You have to get them to control themselves."

"How do I do that?" the young teacher asked.

"You change some of your teaching behaviors. The next time you are going to ask your questions, you need to give them a little preamble. Talk about the importance of thinking before they act, not putting their feet in their mouths. Then tell them that you are not going to call on anybody who blurts out or jumps around hissing, 'Ms. Voorhees! Ms. Voorhees! Ms. Voorhees!' You will have to discipline yourself to wait. Or you can tell them to write out their answers first and then tell them, 'No hands. I will pick who will answer.'"

"That sounds good, but it will never work with these, kids," Marilyn asserted.

"That's what I thought when I first had to do it. Try it first for a week. Stick to your guns and then let's see what happens. It's like drinking coffee without any sweetener—you can't know it's possible until you've tried."

The Basics of Critical Thinking

You have seen students who look out of control. They pay no attention to you or their schoolwork. You see at least one of these students every day. In the worst scenario, these students sap your energy. For them, the classroom is a social center. Laughing with their friends and dissing their enemies is a game. Listening, taking notes, or working on project tasks is not their thing. Even in the best scenario when most students are engaged with their teams, glued to their computers, and working intensely on their project tasks, there are students who exhibit behaviors that work against their optimal learning and distract others. They seem to always miss the point, impulsively wave their hand before you can finish asking a question, or constantly make careless, inaccurate, and imprecise recordings of data.

As Dave pointed out in the previous section, it is shortsighted for a teacher to try and control students' external off-task behaviors. He suggests that Marilyn see the hand waving and blurted answers as outward signs of the students' weak control over how their brains work. Similarly, Dave might suggest that the other behaviors Marilyn sees and hears, such as her students using generic expressions such as *a lot* or *a bunch* instead of precise numbers or other accurate descriptors, indicate she needs to pay attention to the basics of how poorly these students are thinking.

The most basic elements of the thinking process are the cognitive functions (Feuerstein, Rand, Falik, & Feuerstein, 2006). Cognitive functions are like the acorns that grow into a giant oak. When undernourished or undeveloped, neither the oak tree nor the mind matures. The mental immaturity hinders the quality of thinking students use in and out of the classroom. When your students don't focus, are haphazard or random in how they search for data, or can't connect cause and effect—all of which are brain functions that are essential for successful project work—their learning, and ultimately the quality of their projects, suffer. Worse yet, these basic cognitive deficiencies undermine the more complex functions needed for enriched projects: drawing logical conclusions, explaining abstract ideas with details, or writing clear summaries.

Understanding the Brain's Basic Functions

What is a cognitive function? A cognitive function is a micro-operation of the mind. It is the smallest component in the process of thinking, and determines how well or how poorly each of us gathers, makes sense of, and communicates ideas. When students' cognitive functions have not developed, their minds need increased nurturing from you so that, like healthy acorns, their minds can fully develop into strong and mighty oak trees.

Jean Piaget introduced the concept of the brain function as a cognitive function. In his classic work, Piaget (1974) hypothesized these functions as the physical and biological tendencies to organize and adapt experiences into a coherent and meaningful concept. Building on this work, Reuven Feuerstein and his colleagues (2007) identified twenty-six cognitive functions that students must use as they perform the various mental acts that we call thinking. In this chapter, we will take a closer look at what have been called the six core cognitive functions—those in boldface in the following list:

1. **Focus.**
2. Hypothesize.
3. **Make systematic searches.**
4. Internalize concepts.
5. Label accurately.
6. Test strategies.
7. See spatial orientation.

8. Choose the frame of reference.
9. Make temporal orientation.
10. Plan.
11. Conserve constancies.
12. Summarize a concept.
13. **Be precise and accurate.**
14. Express a concept.
15. Integrate information sources.
16. Express a virtual relationship.
17. Discover and define problems.
18. **Think flexibly.**
19. Make relevant information selection.
20. Avoid trial-and-error guesses.
21. Make spontaneous comparisons.
22. **Control impulsive thinking.**
23. **Make connections.**
24. Form and describe categories.
25. Use logical evidence.
26. Widen conceptual field.

Developing the Six Core Cognitive Functions

Of Feuerstein's (1980) twenty-six cognitive functions, the six core functions are especially applicable to the quality of how students learn when thinking about a project. When well developed, these six functions help students think critically as they complete their project tasks.

To the degree that students control the six cognitive functions essential for optimal project success, they can perform the key thinking operations used in project learning. With high-performing functions, students learn from what they are doing in a project more successfully.

In some instances, inefficient use of these critical thinking functions is a one-time event that happens because the individual is overtired or distracted. At other times, the inefficient thinking happens because the individual has not developed the mental operation. When poor thinking occurs because of underdeveloped cognitive functions, learning—and eventually achievement—suffers in many different ways. Certainly, students with less-efficient cognitive functions will have little chance to achieve optimal learning. While they may earnestly try to do their best, they fall short time and time again.

Good and Bad News About Cognitive Functions

Let's review the good news and bad news about cognitive functions. First, the bad news. Deficient or weak cognitive functions tell you that students' minds are not operating well enough for them to meet the cognitive challenges of a high-standards-based learning project.

When your students are not doing the quality thinking required to succeed in these academic-rich learning experiences, especially in the "doing" mode inherent in projects, they learn poorly.

Take, for instance, a student working on a chemistry project. The student has formed a hypothetical theory that a hybrid car battery's life could be extended by using metals different from those common in today's batteries. If the battery life is extended, it might be possible, he thinks, to build a battery that propels a car longer without any gasoline for a week or more—a greener car!

As he tests each of the metals selected, the student neglects to keep a precise or accurate record of each trial test. He jumps impulsively from test to test without double-checking the exact numbers. When he is finished with the tests, he tries to recall the data, but without any systematic record, he gets flummoxed and loses focus. There is no way he can frame a conclusion from the hodgepodge he has made. In short, his weak cognitive functioning in the information-gathering stage (systematic data collection, precision, accuracy, and focus) blocked his ability to perform the important mental operation of forming a valid conclusion in the final stage of learning.

Now switch to the good news. In overseeing the battery project, you face one of those teachable moments that will allow you to improve the quality of this student's thinking. You know that you can help the student think more efficiently. More efficient thinking will give the student a greater chance to interpret his data correctly. By raising questions to mediate the student's thinking about the project, you can coach his impulse control and show him how to avoid trial-and-error guessing, and how to use a system to keep data. Having spotlighted the causes of his lost focus (unsystematic data search, imprecision, and inaccuracy), you provide the conceptual tactics that become his tools for learning. You ask the student:

> What would happen if you kept a notebook with a page assigned to each of the metals you are testing? you ask the student. I suggest that you use a Three Little Whats chart [fig. 5.1, page 80] to categorize your responses. Let me show you how. Let us say that you are going to target being precise and accurate. In the first column, record your observations. "What

did I observe?" Be as precise and accurate with details as you can be. In the second column, record your answers to the "So what?" question: "So what does this detail tell me about the metal?" Finally, in column three, respond to the "Now what?" question: "Now what does this indicate I should do to be more precise and accurate in future observations?"

What?	So What?	Now What?
Metal strip I/black spots on yellow	The speckles and spots indicate differences in chemical reactions.	Check for spots and other color changes precisely.
Difference in my notes	Inaccuracy wrecked my measurements.	Check notes for accuracy.
Inaccurate calculation in column II	The error threw off results.	Double-check calculations. Be accurate.
Measurement of strip II precise	Precise measuring made the comparison reliable.	Keep checking for precise measurements.

Figure 5.1: The three little whats, targeting precision and accuracy.

When you intervene in the work students are doing and help them see the inefficient thinking they are using, you encourage them to use a positive function (in this example, precision and accuracy when working with details). In essence you are telling them, "Sharpen your thinking the way you sharpen your pencils." Your feedback about the quality of thinking is one of the most powerful gifts you can give your students. This detailed feedback, itself precise and accurate, helps them learn how to learn more efficiently. When you add a tool such as the Three Little Whats chart, you do as the Chinese proverb suggests: you don't just give them a fish to eat; you teach them how to fish, and give them a lifetime of meals.

A reproducible Three Little Whats chart is found on page 100 (and online at **go.solution-tree.com/instruction**).

Mediating the Six Core Cognitive Functions

As you moderate students working with their projects, you have unique opportunities to mediate the quality of these six thinking processes. You can stop and observe impulsive thinking or poor reasoning. Then you can take the time to show small teams and individuals better ways to think about the work they are doing. This coaching time is the most important time you can spend during project work. At this moment, you switch from being a giver of information to being a mediator of thinking who is going to bring fundamental change to your students. You don't have to wait for a tutoring session outside of class or after school. In projects, you can capture and use those teachable moments at the precise moment your students are open to change.

What Is Mediation?

Mediation, in this context, is the act of improving the process of thinking. The mediator is a coach who improves the quality of a student's thinking about the subject matter. Being precise is a cognitive function highly important for mathematical thinking. As a mediator, you intervene when you hear imprecise thinking, as in the following demonstration.

Measuring Precisely

"I just noticed that you are calculating the distance between the two walls. Can you show me how you did that again?"

"We used John's foot. We guessed it was about twelve inches. We counted his steps and multiplied."

"Why did you do that?"

"It was the quickest way."

"I want you to remeasure. This time, use your carpenter's tape. Tell me what you get."

A pause.

"Thirteen feet, two inches."

"What is that going to do to your answer?"

"Change it."

"And what will that do to your blueprint?"

"We will be way off . . ."

"So what can you learn about taking measurements?"

"I have to be precise."

Where do you start your mediation? The key to initiating successful change of student thinking during a project begins with identification of deficient or underdeveloped cognitive functions. You will see or hear the behaviors that tell you a student is thinking weakly during a task. In project-based learning experiences, you will most likely see and hear evidence of deficiencies in the six essential functions. These highly predictable thinking errors provide a rich opportunity for you to help students correct functions that inhibit higher cognitive operations.

The examples that follow include tactics you can use to mediate students' thinking and eliminate deficient functionings. Combined with questions you pose to focus students on the undeveloped function, these tactics make it possible for you to avoid telling students about their weak thinking and, instead, encourage them to do the cognitive work.

1. Focus

Focus is a cognitive function that enables learners to pay attention to what they are doing or where they are going. Stories of professional athletes who benefit from the ability to concentrate on an object are legend. Ken Dryden (1983), one of the great National Hockey League goaltenders for the Montreal Canadians, claimed in his biography that he could focus so strongly on a puck that its size enlarged, so he could follow its flight more easily. Baseball players have reported that with focus, they could enlarge a pitched baseball and slow its turning so that they could count the stitches.

While doing project work, focus allows students to keep the project goals clearly in view and pay attention to the immediate task. Their focus shuts out noise and visual distractions. They can concentrate exclusively on the task at hand. For instance, with strong focus, a student who is examining bacteria under a microscope can block out classroom chatter for long periods of time. Knowing what he must finish before the class period, the student gives all of his attention to examining the squiggling bugs on the microscope's slide, recording his data, and checking its accuracy until he is satisfied that he is done. In a second example, members of a student work team getting ready to test an electric cart for fuel efficiency lock in on their specific responsibilities. All of their attention is given to the checklist of tasks prior to the test run. In a third example, all eyes in a classroom focus on the model building that the demonstration team is presenting to them. They are caught up in observing the details that are highlighted.

What are the benefits of maintaining focus when working on a learning project? There are two of special import. First, focus enables students to attend to the work at hand. By blocking out distractions, the students avoid wasting time and effort on side issues that slow their progress. For instance, think of the time saved when a project team planting a garden ignores the basketball game being played in the next lot.

Second, focus enables the students to avoid side discussions and debates, even if they are tangentially related to their current project. Think of an investigative team that is working on the Internet to gather information about hunger in Nigeria. One of the student members finds some interesting facts about the effects of dry winds on the African continent. However, there is nothing in this information that enlightens the Nigerian hunger study. They pass on following the thread, clarify their goal, and concentrate on the precise information they need to add to their study. Table 5.1 demonstrates how to mediate the maintenance of focus.

Table 5.1: Focus—From Deficient to Efficient Functions

Deficient Function		Efficient Function	
Looks like . . .	**Sounds like . . .**	**Looks like . . .**	**Sounds like . . .**
Looking around room	"What are we doing?"	All eyes on the task	"This is the key point."
Side conversations by some team members	"What are we doing?"	All eyes on the speaker	"Let's review our goal."
Star gazing and daydreaming	"I am not sure what to do."	Engaged body with eye contact	"This is our next task."
Unrelated tasks	"Why are we doing this?"	All heads nodding *yes*	"We are on target."
One group member unengaged	"This is boring."	One person speaking at a time	"Tom has the floor for this part."
Add yours		**Add yours**	

How Do You Mediate the Maintenance of Focus?

The most effective mediation makes use of cues, clues, and questions to encourage students to think about their cognitive functions, not give them answers. Mediation is a form of loosely structured problem solving in which the teacher doesn't tell the student the answers but asks questions that communicate, "It is yours to figure out. I will give you the clues to help." Thus, when a student is unable to keep focus on a task or idea long enough to complete it, the teacher mediates with those strategies that communicate the importance and the how to.

Recently, in a classroom in Holly, Michigan, certified mediator Meir Ben Hur worked with a middle school student with special needs who was struggling with learning to focus. Ben Hur's questions and cues guided the student to a self-discovery.

Thomas Learns to Focus

"So, Thomas [a pseudonym]," Ben Hur asked, "What are you working on this week?"

"How to keep focus," the boy said.

"What does that mean?"

continued →

Thomas paused and pursed his lips. "It means I have to concentrate on what I am doing."

"Why?" Ben Hur asked.

"'Cause I have a bad habit of letting myself be distracted. I look around at every noise."

"So what do you do to focus?"

"When I want to look at a noise, I stop myself and say, 'Think.'"

Ben Hur smiled. "That is a good idea. Does it work."

"Yep, it does," said the boy with pride in his voice. "I just keep right on reading. Sometimes, I look hard at the picture on the page or a graph."

"Do you do anything else?"

"Sometimes I count to myself as I look at the words. Sometimes, I just read real hard."

"Are you improving?" Ben Hur asked.

"I am. Yesterday, I counted to twenty before I looked up. I used to get stuck at five."

In addition to coaching with questions and cues, teachers can help students improve focus with different tactics, such as the following:

- **Tactic chart**—On a poster for all to see, students can post instructions for keeping focused during group work, such as "Know your goal," "Concentrate," and "Attention is worth a thousand minutes." Another sign can remind them to use a timekeeper. Periodically, call attention to these, and discuss their value with the class.
- **Invitational interventions**—When you notice students are off task or not concentrating, intervene one-on-one or with the small group. Ask such questions as "What is your task?" "What are you supposed to be attending to?" or "Is there a difficulty that is distracting you?" Your tone should be matter-of-fact rather than sarcastic.
- **Main topic guide**—At the start of a week, send students a message for their file folders. Fill it in with the project goal, the list of main topics or tasks for the week, and the schedule for competed tasks. Encourage the students to review this at the start of each project day.
- **Roles and responsibilities**—Assign teams a *focus keeper*. This person is responsible for calling team members to attention when they get distracted or off task.
- **The camera's eye**—A camera's pictures need to be in focus. Using the image of a camera's eye, start with a think-pair-share in which students bring into focus the project goal, concepts, and facts in response to the big

idea. Discuss the value of separating the goal, the concepts, and the facts into groups as a means of maintaining focus.

2. Make Systematic Searches

Look for My Red Hat

"How will I find you in that big auditorium?" Marie asked her mother.

"I will sit as far to the right as I can. You have to come in on the center aisle. If I wear my red hat, you can start in the back, close to the aisle. I would use a pattern to look for me. Look down each row of seats starting nearest the aisle. If I am not in the first row, start over again in the same spot, and look down the second row. Keep doing that until you see my red hat."

"Sounds like a plan," said Marie. "I think it will work."

How often do students go into a library and just start looking? They forget that the Dewey decimal system tells them where to start their search. They also forget that books are alphabetized by author's last name. If they used these two cues for a systematic search, they could go to the exact section and the exact aisle, and find the first letter of the last name that they are looking to find.

In the first phase of learning, students gather the information that is important for accomplishing a project's goals. Later, in the final phase, as they are preparing to communicate their new understandings or the results of their project study, they have to select the data that will have the strongest impact in their report. With a systematic search, they avoid random trial-and-error glances at topics that would prove to be distractions to their audiences.

What is the benefit of a systematic data search? When the students use a system that matches an existing system, they complete their search for information more rapidly. As in the search for a library book, systematic searches for which they use a search engine such as Google or Yahoo! will speed their way to the information they desire. Even if they start an Internet search with no more than a keyword from their project, they can follow the e-pathway to exactly what they want to know. This is especially true if they define the parameters of their search.

In cases where the information is not available within a framework such as the Dewey decimal system, students must learn to organize their own systematic search process. For this they must define the parameters of the search and set the pattern they will use. For instance, when police are searching for a lost child, the best method is a systematic search plan. "Just fan out" is the least effective way. Instead, teams are formed and assigned a specific search area. Each person on each team receives a designated section to cover step by step. After the first round of searching, new volunteers are assigned to review the first search pattern step by step. As each specific part of the overall search area is covered, it is marked off.

The more systematic these project-based data searches, the more likely students are to find the data they need to form a hypothesis or to establish the proof they need to affirm or deny one. On the other hand, if their search is random, superficial, or dependent on unguided trial and error, it is likely to extend their timelines or divert them into unhelpful sidetracks. Moreover, the unsystematic search is likely to miss important data. Table 5.2 demonstrates how to move students from random trial and error to a systematic search for data.

Table 5.2: Make Systematic Searches—From Deficient to Efficient Functions

Deficient Function		Efficient Function	
Looks like . . .	**Sounds like . . .**	**Looks like . . .**	**Sounds like . . .**
Starting a search at a random point	"I guess I can start here."	A written plan for the search, with starting place identified	"Let's start with the beginning of the song."
Scrolling haphazardly with the browser	"Let's just open any of these sites."	Site and sequence of procedures identified for a search	"Let's use the alpha list to make the order."
Picking a starting point on impulse	"You start here, I'll start there."	Makes and follows a sequence chart that leads to pre-picked outcome	"Let's make a sequential plan and follow it from start to finish."
Using sequential procedures without order	"Who cares? It doesn't matter what comes next."	A search map with traces from start to end location	"I googled a map, and I am following its directions."
An uncategorized list of ideas	"Just do it."	A list of tactics to try in an order	"This is my plan for finding the answer."
Add yours		**Add yours**	

How Do You Mediate the Systematic Search for Data?

It is helpful if you spend some time prior to the two phases that rely on systematic data searches—the first phase when students are initially gathering information and the last when they will gather the most salient information on which to build their reports or other products.

- **Mediating questions:** A direct question such as, "What is your system for doing your research for this project?" followed by clarifying questions such as "What will be your first steps?" and "How will you maintain the system?" are a good start. As students progress through the first phase, have them show you how they are sticking with the system. In phase three, change your questions to, "What is the most important information you have to share? Why? How will you organize it?" Encourage different students to respond. Invite all students to keep a "good ideas for planning" file folder.
- **Sequence charts:** Show students how to make a sequence chart (page 69). Ask groups of four to brainstorm all the information categories they will need to gather and make a list of what they will have to do to get the information. In the chart, invite each pair from the group of four to list the order they will follow. After all have their charts finished, ask a selection of teams to share and defend their rationale. Coach the groups as you walk around the classroom, with a special emphasis on using questions to overcome any unclear thinking.
- **Ladder charts:** Show students how to use the draw features in their software to sketch a ladder that is leaning against a wall. This graphic organizer will help students put the ideas they have formed into a priority order. The most important idea to communicate about their project goes on the top rung, the second most important goes on the next rung down, and so on. Match students in pairs or trios to share their charts and explain their rationale. If time allows, select several students to project their charts on a screen for all to see and explain how and why they selected the top three ideas on their ladders.
- **Identification of irrelevant information:** Prior to phase one, teach students how to distinguish relevant from irrelevant information. Project a current newspaper column to which you have added irrelevant sentences. Let pairs pick out the irrelevant information and explain why. You can settle disputes as a last resort.
- **Student self-assessment checklist:** Distribute the Sample Checklist for a Systematic Search to students to use as a guide when they do their search (page 101 and **go.solution-tree.com/instruction**).

3. Be Precise and Accurate

Iceberg!

"Iceberg ahead, 3.2 miles," noted the first officer.

"Do you have a bearing?" asked the captain.

"Yes, it is 4.6 degrees off the starboard bow."

"OK. Bring us to 8.15 degrees and hold. . . . What is our precise speed?"

"12 knots," answered the first officer.

"Drop that to 5," ordered the captain. "If we are not accurate, we will be closer than I want to be. These Antarctic waters are a bit too cold for a swim."

Precision and accuracy are closely related.

Precision identifies the exactness of a measurement (for example, one-tenth of an inch) that can be repeated over and over. The measurement may also identify the degree of refinement with which a mental operation is performed, such as forecasting the weather conditions for an exact place at an exact time.

Accuracy, on the other hand, indicates the freedom from error of a thought or measurement. It describes the similarity of an attribute in comparison with a standard. For instance, if the standard is nine strikes out of ten, a baseball player is described as accurate when he throws strikes nine out of ten times.

When students are gathering information for a project, accuracy and precision are very important cognitive functions. As they search for answers to their launch question, you want them to find information that is as close to exact as possible. For instance, if a student team is trying to find why a certain species of fish is dying in the local lakes, they must be sure that they have a way to measure pollutants and possible poisons in the water. It will be important that they refine their measurements to get exact counts of the dead fish in any one lake (precision) and balance that against a standard that would help them distinguish between natural die-off and the amount that is occurring (accuracy). The less careful the team is with its calculation, the harder it will be for them to draw a valid and reliable conclusion.

What are the benefits of precise and accurate thinking? The benefits appear in two phases of learning. In the first phase, exact thinking (precision) and refined thinking (accuracy) will determine the quality of the information the students gather. The better the quality, the closer they will be to valid and reliable conclusions drawn from their evidence.

In the final learning phase, the sharpness of students' thinking will determine how accurately and precisely they report the information. Will they be on target?

Or will their report misrepresent the best solution? Throughout the project of a single student who shows a low use of precision or accuracy, or with a whole-class project in which precision and accuracy are important, it helps to intervene on a weekly basis to promote the development of these two closely related cognitive functions. Table 5.3 demonstrates how to move students from inexactness to precise and accurate thinking.

Table 5.3: Be Precise and Accurate—From Deficient to Efficient Functions

Deficient Function		Efficient Function	
Looks like . . .	**Sounds like . . .**	**Looks like . . .**	**Sounds like . . .**
Unchecked measurements	"That's *sorta* right, I think."	A checklist with each step spelled out	"I double checked each answer."
Frequent misspellings, grammar errors, sentence structure errors, and so on	"I didn't proofread it. Why do we have to be so exact?"	No remaining grammar or spelling errors after a step-by-step check	"I used the spellcheck."
Miscalculations in number operations	"I'm just guessing."	Calculations double-checked and correct	"Mary checked my work."
Poor or no outline of concepts and facts	"That's close enough."	Problem displayed proofs	"I reran the numbers."
No proofs shown	"I'm not sure."	Outline of proofs with details shown	"I wanted to be sure the answers were *all* correct."
Wordy problem statement	"I got the big idea, didn't I?"	Tight problem statement	"I went back and eliminated extra words."
Lack of detail	"Facts aren't important."	Three or more facts provided for each example	"I made sure the facts aligned with the idea."
Add yours		**Add yours**	

How Do You Mediate Precision and Accuracy?

When you are mediating precision and accuracy, it helps students when you structure your intervention so that the students assume the control and responsibility for making the needed changes. You play the role of the question asker, the problem poser, or the play director. The students do the thinking and responding so that you can coach, encourage, and help them refine their skill and become more precise and accurate.

- **Asking questions:** As a high-yield strategy that impacts students' learning, the questions you ask before and during a project will go a long way in helping students develop the need for precision and accuracy. Ask students to respond to one question a week and post their responses in their e-journals. If time allows during the week, ask students to share their responses with the class. Consider using questions such as the following:
  - "Tell [show] me how you can be more precise in defining this problem."
  - "How did you check your work?"
  - "How could you refine this information to better align with your goal?"
  - "How do you know that your solution is on target?"
  - "What evidence do you have that proves your accuracy?"
  - "How important is it for you to be more accurate (precise) with this information?"
- **Posing problems:** Prior to starting a project, ask students to brainstorm the barriers or obstacles that could inhibit their success. Ask the students to put the three top barriers on index cards and state each as a problem. In pairs, students will help each other refine the problem statements so that they are as accurate and precise as possible. Ask for volunteers to share with the class and make suggestions for any that need more fine tuning.
- **Using think alouds:** Pair students to review the information they have gathered. One student at a time will review key information gathered and talk about how it is precise and/or accurate. The listening partner may ask only clarifying questions that elicit more details or rationales. On the next day, the students reverse their roles.
- **Using role-plays:** Provide students with a political speech such as the Gettysburg Address. Have study teams analyze it for historic accuracy and then conduct a role-play with the principals debating the accuracy.

4. Think Flexibly

Alex was born with his brain choked by a tangle of blood vessels. As a result, he was mute, half-blind, partially paralyzed, and epileptic. His doctors removed the left hemisphere of his brain. In a few months, he began to talk, and by the age of sixteen, he was communicating fluently, telling jokes, and performing well in school. His brain rearranged its learning pathways to allow the right hemisphere to take over the operation of the excised left brain. Today, Alex is completing his studies in a community college (Feuerstein, Falik, Rand, & Feuerstein, 2006b).

Flexibility is the cognitive function that most reveals the plasticity or adaptability of the brain. With flexibility, students are able to adjust how they think and what they think about with ease. They can even develop new structures that open up new ways of learning. In some fields, such as science or architecture, flexible thinking is an essential function that allows the chemist, physicist, or architect to look at problems from several points of view and then select a solution from many alternative possibilities.

This function, when called for, helps students be better problem solvers, investigators, and project managers by enabling them to think along more diverse channels in search of alternative solutions. In the arts world, flexible thinking becomes a valuable tool for generating different points of view, ways of expression, and use of multiple intelligences.

Many students, however, have difficulty thinking flexibly. Their thinking is described as literal, rigid, or single-tracked. When students think without flexibility, they experience difficulty with problem solving. They see that every problem as having a single, given solution. Finding alternatives is troublesome.

Of course, an excess of flexibility can be troublesome as well. Public officials who are too flexible in their thinking about an important problem are labeled *flip-floppers*. In political campaigns, flip-flopping is a big negative.

Many stories like Alex's are emerging about the brain and its ability to adapt and adjust. At one time, it was believed that the brain developed in certain stages. It could not change after those stages. Now, however, scientists recognize that Alex and others like him who have had parts of the brain removed gain new mental capabilities that take over for the removed parts. This plasticity leads to students being able to grow brain structures that allow them to think in new and different ways (Nelson & Thomas, 2006).

What are the benefits of brain flexibility for students? Obviously, the most fundamental benefit is found in the understanding that the brain can change. It is not fixed. Thus, intelligence is not fixed. Students can develop their brainpower not simply by adding in more information, but also by developing the capability to think faster, in different ways, and more efficiently. Knowing that their brains are not set in concrete provides students with the hope and anticipation that they can learn better than their genetic heritage prescribed.

With the old myth of the fixed intelligence fractured, many students of color and economic deprivation, students of different ethnic heritages, and even those born with special learning challenges can now reach higher and farther than their ancestors were ever taught to believe they could. A second benefit is that students can develop the function of flexible thinking. Table 5.4 demonstrates basic ways to move from rigid thinking to flexible thinking.

Table 5.4: Think Flexibly—From Deficient to Efficient Functions

Deficient Function		Efficient Function	
Looks like . . .	**Sounds like . . .**	**Looks like . . .**	**Sounds like . . .**
Refuses to try a different tactic for problem solving	"That is the only way to do that." "My way or the highway."	Brainstorming on a web	"Is there another way to do this?
Sees only one right answer	"That's not the way I do it!" "That is the wrong way."	Using a concept map in search of multiple ideas	"What else can we try?"
Refuses to look at others' points of view	"I already tried that, and it doesn't work." "That's not correct."	Searching for alternatives	"Let's brainstorm some different possibilities."
Single-minded	"There is only one answer."	Trying out a different way to solve a problem	"Maybe try a different path? What do you guess it might be?"
Accepts only literal interpretation	"Where did you get that idea?" "Don't sidetrack me."	Sketching different paths to a goal	"What predictions can we make?"
Requires a place for all and everything in its place compulsively	"That is not how I was taught to do it. It belongs here, period."	Exploring options	"Let's explore some other possible places to place that shape."
No variations to a template with specific slots for each answer	"I told you what the result will be. There is only one possible answer."	Using a prediction tree organizer	"What if we move these items over here and those over there?"
Add yours		**Add yours**	

How Do You Mediate Flexible Thinking?

Flexibility is one of the most important functions of the problem-solving mind. Feuerstein teaches that the amount of flexibility that a person shows when thinking, the greater that person's intellectual potential. Although the more rigid mind may seem to have the least chance of growing or becoming smarter, Feuerstein has demonstrated that the use of mediation can open that mind and help the person become more flexible and better problem solver. For the classroom, the teacher can include tactics that promote flexible thinking (Feuerstein, Falik, Rand, & Feuerstein, 2006a).

- **Brainstorming:** This is the grandfather of all tactics that stretch students' mental flexibility. Whether you approach brainstorming as a simple list of ideas built by adding one random idea after another or whether you take time throughout the year to add the questions favored in the "creative problem-solving approach" (such as bigger variations, smaller variations, wider, narrower, more simple, more complex), practice of this tactic will take students out of their comfort zone and enable them to think more flexibly. Add a web organizer as the tool for recording the many ideas.
- **Prediction gallery walk:** Make groups of five. At the end of each chapter of a work of fiction, challenge the groups to make predictions about what will happen next. Give each group a sheet of newsprint and markers so they can list the ideas they generate. Post these lists and invite the class to walk in the "gallery" and search for ideas they didn't have on their lists. After the walk, discuss the different ideas they found. End with a discussion of how this walk promotes cognitive flexibility.
- **Creative problem solving:** Present a problem to the class. Draw the problem from the project work they are doing as you walk among the working teams. Post the problem and then ask the teams to each come up with several possible solutions. They then will brainstorm as a team the advantages and disadvantages of each idea before selecting one preferred solution. Record the selected solution from each team for all to see. Discuss the advantages and disadvantages of each before asking about the benefits of creative problem solving in promoting flexibility.
- **Alternative search:** On a projector, brainstorm a list of alternatives. No one may repeat an idea. Students may add a new idea, an alternative to an idea already posted, or pass. After the round is done, ask for discussion of which ideas are the best possible answers (no student can select his or her own idea). After ten minutes of discussion, give each person three votes to use or not use. Calculate the results. End with a discussion of why it was important to list the alternative ideas first before discussing and selecting.

- **Variations on a theme**—Using a projector for all to see, pose a question that relates to students' thinking in the current learning phase of the project (such as gathering information, making sense, or communicating results). Make it a "How would you . . ." question. After allowing students to form their answers, randomly select one student to give his or her response. The person sitting to the right of the speaker will note, "That would help me because . . ." The same person would then answer the original question and the next person would explain, "That would help me because . . ." Continue down each row until all have had a chance. You may want to spread this activity over several days doing just one row of students at a time.

5. Control Impulsive Thinking

Examples of the battle between impulsive behavior and reflective thinking abound in literature. Eliza Doolittle triumphs in *My Fair Lady* ("By George, she's got it!"). Other characters, like the white rabbit from *Alice in Wonderland*, are not so lucky. Impulsive thinkers suffer from the same disequilibrium as Alice's white rabbit. "Hurry up. Hurry up. I am late. I am late," cried the rabbit as he ran willy-nilly around Wonderland. He expected everyone to think and act on the spot. The rabbit would probably hassle people to race through their projects in the same fashion.

Control of impulsive thinking occurs when students intentionally stop to think. This halt may be a reflective moment before speaking, a notation on a 3 x 5-inch index card, an entry into a journal, the making of a plan, or the jotting of ideas on a web organizer. Most important, this purposeful action gives the student time to think before acting.

What is the benefit? When students stop to think, they allow themselves time to formulate answers, review instructions, and assure themselves that the answer they will provide is exact, precise, complete, accurate, and on target. In short, it enables students to check the quality of their ideas so they can be sure they have considered all the criteria that will make their answers or their project work as complete and correct as it needs be. Table 5.5 demonstrates the process of moving a student toward more efficient impulse control.

Table 5.5: Control Impulsive Thinking—From Deficient to Efficient Functions

Deficient Function		Efficient Function	
Looks like . . .	**Sounds like . . .**	**Looks like . . .**	**Sounds like . . .**
Waving hand while blurting out and jumping around seat	"Me, me, I got it!"	Wrinkled brow	"I need to stop and think about this."

Deficient Function		Efficient Function	
Looks like . . .	**Sounds like . . .**	**Looks like . . .**	**Sounds like . . .**
Answering before question is over	Blurted answer	Puts pen down and thinks	"Let me think about what I must do."
Writing before reading all of instructions	"I got it. I know it."	Writes question in journal	"Ummm . . . Let me see . . . "
Completing someone's sentence	"Hurry up, before it's too late."	Outlines the details of the problem in a problem identifier	"Hmm, let me think about that for a minute."
Interrupting a question to answer it	"Let's just get this done."	Makes a web of ideas	"I have to consider all the angles."
Add yours		**Add yours**	

How Do You Mediate Impulse Control?

What can you do to mediate impulse control as students work on their projects? You can apply these tactics at the various phases of learning in the project. Consider each tactic carefully, making sure it is appropriate for the students and the project phase. Some of these interventions are appropriate for individuals, others for small groups or the entire class. Adapt as needed.

- **"Stop and think" signage:** Make an online banner ad or bulletin board for the whole classroom that proclaims the importance of thinking before acting. Discuss with the students why it is important to first stop and think, whether answering a question, reviewing instructions on a task or test, or beginning a team task.
- **Think-pair-share:** Start each day with a short question related to thinking about the project theme or goals. With an email, invite student to think first (or write or make a sketch) and then share responses in pairs. Sample ideas from the pairs one at a time before sending students back to work on their projects.
- **Turning to a neighbor:** At the end of a class period, ask an assessment question about how students used stop and think during the period. Have each send an email to a peer sitting at the next computer station.

- **Response-in-turn:** Poll the class in the middle of a class period. Ask a question or use a lead-in for students to complete. After allowing time to think, select one row of students to respond in turn (for instance, "Today, I needed to slow down and think when . . ." or "Today, a tactic I used to stop and think was . . .").
- **E-journal entries:** At unannounced times through the week, invite students to make a journal entry in which they write about how well they are controlling impulsive thinking. If time allows, call on individuals at random to share their reflections.

6. Make Connections

What's a Metaphor?

"What do you mean it would help if I learned how to 'connect the dots'?" Raul asked.

"There are lots of ways to explain it," replied Ms. Schultz. "Some puzzles are made up of dots. All the dots have a number. If you follow the numbers, they will form a picture."

"That sounds like fun," Raul said. "But it's kid's stuff. What does it have to do with me?"

"Let me give you another example," Ms. Schultz replied. "For instance, there is a game called dots and boxes. Players get points for finding two boxes that share the same side. Players earn added points when they connect those sides with the sides of another box. I'll show you a picture illustrating how these boxes connect. But connecting the dots is also a metaphor," said Ms. Schultz, getting ready to drive home her point.

"What is a metaphor?" Raul asked.

"It is an explicit comparison. For instance, when someone says, 'The mayor connected the dots when he explained the new bus service,' she is using a metaphor that says he pointed out how the bus service would work in different places. For the people listening, it was like connecting the dots."

"So when you want me to connect the dots, you want me to see how different ideas are connected."

"Now you have done it!" said the teacher. "You have connected my examples with ideas. You have connected the dots."

"Connecting the dots" has become jargon in the news industry. Commentators will say, "Now let's connect the dots" before explaining how two events are related or how a political figure's words are related to a current topic of interest: "Now let's connect the dots on the two candidates' positions on the environment." Or "Let's see how the dots connect with the senator's words and the president's policy."

When speaking of connecting the dots, teachers are telling students that it is time to make sense of what they are studying. They are inviting their students to look for the similarities that connect two or more facts, concepts, or opinions or that relate one event to another. The connections take many forms. Some connect events in time; others relate one place to another. In some instances, the relationships are cause and effect. Others are familial relationships: a real family such as the Kennedys or the Bushes, or a categorical family such as mammals, deciduous trees, or General Motors automobiles.

When teachers ask students to connect the dots, they must specify the type of cognitive relationships they want their students to make: temporal, spatial, familial, cause and effect, cultural, or logical. In all cases, teachers are asking students to identify the unifying concept that binds people, places, objects, events, ideas, and so on into a common group.

Making connections is one of the most necessary cognitive functions for life, school, and project-based learning. It is the bridge between those more simple functions that are essential for students who are learning to take control of more complex thinking operations, such as comparing, hypothesizing, and investigating, and more demanding functions that help them refine their use of the operations (the latter group are described in the next chapter).

What are the benefits to students who improve how they make connections and develop their abilities to understand cognitive relationships? Most of the benefits are captured in those "Eureka!" moments in which students report their sudden comprehension with the very simple but powerful statement, "I see what you mean." "I see what you mean" is the summary statement that captures the moment when the student makes connections among disparate points and puts them into a single, connected whole.

Making connections is at the heart and soul of students' discovering meaning in what they are being asked to learn each day in school. When asked, "What does that mean?" they explain what a word or concept means. On the other hand, students may respond with, "I don't know what you mean." This indicates that they cannot connect *a* with *b* or give a definition. Table 5.6 demonstrates how to move students from missing connections to making connections.

Table 5.6: Make Connections—From Deficient to Efficient Functions

Deficient Function		Efficient Function	
Looks like . . .	**Sounds like . . .**	**Looks like . . .**	**Sounds like . . .**
Multiple similar errors	"I don't understand the connection."	Completing graphic organizers that show connections (for example, Venn diagram or concept map)	"These ideas make sense. They connect together when I . . ."

continued →

Deficient Function		Efficient Function	
Looks like . . .	**Sounds like . . .**	**Looks like . . .**	**Sounds like . . .**
Shaking head *no*	"I don't understand why." "What caused that?" "I'm lost." "I don't see the relationship." "How does *a* fit with *b*?" "What's the point?" "This doesn't make any sense."	Completing the fishbone graphic organizer, which shows cause and effect	"The cause [effect] was . . . " "Let me explain why." "Here are the reasons why." "I see the cause-and-effect relationship. This makes sense, because *a* is the cause of *b*."
Random entries in a log or journal	"Here are some ideas. I don't see how they connect."	Written summary or expository essay with key points	"The point is . . . " "The relationship is clear: *a* is like *b* because . . . "
Add yours		**Add yours**	

How Do You Mediate the Making of Connections?

The phrase *connecting the dots* has become a commonplace way to express the idea of making sense or understanding relationships between parts and whole, between facts and concepts. It signifies that a person understands the connection or relationship between ideas or events that he or she thought were unrelated. Sometimes the person connects the unconnected dots to see how one event was the cause of another or what common concept connected two different positions in an argument. In the classroom, teachers mediate the making of connections by challenging students in ways such as the following that force them to work on finding connections:

Asking questions—Questions that ask students to explain why, to predict, to reason, and to hypothesize are especially forceful in helping students make the important connections in the material they are studying. Teachers do not have to ask factual questions first. They can proceed directly to the questions that enable students to connect facts, ideas, and opinions.

Making metaphors—Metaphors lead students directly into spontaneous comparisons. Metaphors invite them to see relationships that are hidden below the surface of objects and ideas that appear very different ("The camera is your eye" or "His brain is his map," or as we have already seen, "Connect the dots"). Invite pairs to make metaphors related to their project work. Insist that they use at least one metaphor when they present what they have learned.

Making analogies—Analogies and similes also lead students to make spontaneous comparisons. The comparisons are explicit (for example, "My love is like a red, red rose" or "Hatred is like a snake that poisons all it bites"). Invite students to start their presentations in phase three with an analogy.

Using concept maps—At the end of each class period, have individuals or teams spend the last five minutes expanding a concept map and indicating how different entries are related to each other. Show the connections with a variety of color-coded lines. Build the map until the project's end, and include it in a team presentation that explains the relationship of the parts and facts to the whole.

Avoiding formal grades—When teachers grade the processes of making connections, they inhibit students' best chance of making the critical connections they need. Grades put boundaries on expansive and original connection making. They tell students "Make the types of connections that will surely get a good grade. Make the connections you think I want to hear. Don't do anything that is not allowed by the rubric." It is more helpful for teachers to provide the prompts that enable students to explore possible connections and to listen and encourage diverse responses in quantity and quality. There will be plenty of opportunity to grade summative responses that show how well students have developed their connection-making capabilities thanks to formative feedback.

Summary

Thinking is the glue that ties the content of the curriculum together. When you take the time to mediate thinking by improving how students' brains operate, it is important that they start with the six project-essential cognitive functions. These are the quality indicators that tell how well students are using the various operations, such as comparing, sequencing, analyzing, predicting, and so forth. These are the functions that teachers, as mediators of quality thinking, should pay most attention to, as they enrich students' opportunities to learn from the project experience. When using tactics that help students assess and improve their cognitive functions, teachers are making high-quality formative assessments. These assessments provide important feedback to the students and should not—at all costs—be contaminated by putting a grade on them.

The Three Little Whats

Ask the students to identify one cognitive function they were working to make more efficient. Ask them to make a list of what they learned to do well to strengthen the function. List these responses under "What."

Ask the students to make a list of the implications of each "what" under "So What." Explain that an "implication' would describe how the improvement might enrich their use of the function in future tasks.

Ask students to list under "Now What" the tactics they will use to continue improvement of the function in future tasks.

Use the lists to conduct a discussion.

Targeted Function:		
What	**So What**	**Now What**

Sample Checklist for a Systematic Search

Name: ______________________________ Date: __________ Class Period: _____

- ☐ Set your goal: what do you want the data to show?
- ☐ Pick a starting point to find the data.
- ☐ Pick an end point for the final step in the search.
- ☐ Brainstorm the information categories.
- ☐ Sequence your steps to find information that will get to the end point.
- ☐ Follow them step by step.
- ☐ Check for the alignment of each step to the plan.
- ☐ Check for the alignment to your goal of the information found.
- ☐ Check for the relevance of your found data.
- ☐ Look for holes in the data you collected.
- ☐ Check for the necessity of your data.
- ☐ Check for the sufficiency of your data.
- ☐ Other: ______________________________

Student Comments:

Teacher Comments:

Chapter 6

Making Critical Thinking Matter

> The function of education is to teach one to think intensively and to think critically.
>
> —Martin Luther King Jr.

Critical thinking is one of the preeminent skills called for by the Partnership for 21st Century Skills. Most state and national content standards contain the process standards for critical and creative thinking. By identifying the thinking process embedded in a content standard, teachers can target the appropriate thinking skills to include in an enriched learning project's instructional plan. Using the three phases of learning, this chapter explains various approaches to help students learn and use these thinking skills in instructional frameworks.

Thinking Mathematically

Geometry and calculus teacher Vernoy Johnson asserted that he never taught mathematics. "I teach thinking," he said. "I teach students how to think mathematically. Sharp thinking is the essence of mathematical thinking and problem solving."

Vernoy's favorite instructional tool was the journal. "Journals allow us to talk to ourselves without anyone believing we are crazy. In a thinker's journal, you can play with numbers or solve complex problems or do whatever you want so that you understand what your world is about in mathematical terms. That means you can also draw your own geometric shapes, quicken your mind, and shape how you think. The best mathematicians were great thinkers."

Vernoy, however, did not believe that thinking was limited to mathematics. He taught his students that thinking is the heart and soul of literature, sociology, science, music, and the visual arts. "Carpenters think," he would say. "Plumbers think. Philosophers and kings think. The challenge to all is the same: how well do we think?"

Factory School Teaching

Some educational leaders strive to reduce the teaching of mathematics, literature, and other subjects to scripted reading instructions. The students sit and listen.

At the end of this supposedly teacher-proof "sit and git," teachers are directed to require that students memorize the facts and figures they have heard by practicing endless hours on repetitive worksheets. In this method of teaching and learning from the industrial age, the more students memorize, the higher their grades. No thinking allowed. The only two choices are to call on rote memory or to miss the correct answer altogether.

Those who fight to keep teaching and learning mired in the curriculum and instructional mode of the 19th-century factory school sell today's teachers and students short. These short-sellers will never agree that the essence of effective teaching and the most successful learning are based on the improvement of students' thinking abilities. The strongest state and national learning standards contrast with this outdated view of school and reinforce the value of students as thinkers. To verify this, you only need to review the math standards provided in figure 6.1, extracted from the Illinois Department of Education (1997). Notice how the verbs used in these standards highlight the thinking processes students are asked to develop as they study the prescribed content of their course work.

Early Elementary	8.B.1	Solve problems involving pattern identification and completion of patterns.
Late Elementary	8.B.2	Analyze a geometric pattern and express the results numerically.
Middle/Junior High School	8.B.3	Use graphing technology and algebraic methods to analyze and predict linear relationships and make generalizations from linear patterns.
Early High School	8.B.4a	Represent algebraic concepts with physical materials, words, diagrams, tables, graphs, equations, and inequalities and use appropriate technology.
	8.B.4b	Use the basic functions of absolute value, square root, linear, quadratic, and step to describe numerical relationships.
Late High School	8.B.5	Use functions including exponential, polynomial, rational, parametric, logarithmic, and trigonometric to describe numerical relationships.

Figure 6.1: Illinois math standards.

Do these standards say, "The students will recall" or "The students will commit facts to memory"? Not at all. Instead, they call for students to *solve problems*, *analyze*, *predict*, *make generalizations*, *represent*, *use*, and *describe*. These are mental operations that fit under the generic label of critical thinking. When whole years of instruction ignore these all-important thinking operations and the vast majority of time is spent on the memorization and recall of facts and formulas, especially by students who are deemed too low performing to think, is it any wonder that so many students cannot comprehend, compose a written argument, think mathematically, or understand the key ideas in the curriculum?

In enriched project-based learning experiences, you have a model of instruction that has the potential to pull your students out of the swamp of low expectations. This model will give you the methods to stretch your students beyond their current academic performance. As you organize your projects, you can energize your students' minds, whether they have been labeled low performing or high performing, to inquire into critical issues and solve tough problems. Simultaneously, you can enable them to comprehend challenging texts, manipulate complex equations, and compose stimulating essays. Moreover, you can counter those naysayers who hold that intelligence, cognitive operations, and high achievement are fixed and immutable from birth (Murray & Herrnstein, 1994). To defy these arguments, you can enrich your projects so that the standards, high-yield instructional frameworks, and well-documented instructional strategies form the heart of instruction designed to produce students who think and learn more skillfully than when they walked into your classroom.

Critical Thinking in the Standards

If all of your students spent twenty-four or more years in school, they would not have sufficient time to meet all the content standards prescribed for them. However, in the enriched learning project model of instruction, you can select those standards that will have the greatest impact on your students' critical and creative thinking while enriching mastery of the prescribed content. It makes common sense to organize your projects under the umbrella of those standards that fit your curricula and for which you want to promote deep understanding, rather than superficial coverage and memorized facts. By starting with the thinking processes that are the driving force for the best enunciated standards, you provide a great impetus for the high achievement and efficient learning that are the hallmarks of enriched learning projects. These projects help you ensure from the start that your students' minds have no limits. With your help, they can become better thinkers than even they ever suspected. The full capacity of their minds is unknown. You have no idea how much thinking a student's mind can make!

Contrast, for example, the common practice of limiting instruction to students' memorization of numerical facts with the National Council of Teachers of Mathe-matics standard, which calls for students preK–12 to "understand patterns, relations, and functions," "represent and analyze mathematical situations," "use mathematical models to represent and understand quantitative relationships," "make generalizations," and "analyze change in various contexts" (National Council of Teachers of Mathematics, n.d.). Note how the standards include words designating cognitive processes, such as *understanding relationships*, *representing*, *generalizing*, and *analyzing*. In like manner, the Common Core Standards for math emphasize high-level cognitive processes like *interpret, estimate, explain,* and *adapt.* For K–12 literacy, the core standards are replete with cognitive commands to *interpret, sustain focus, create logical progressions, delineate, analyze,* and *synthesize* (Common Core Standards, n.d.).

The Operations Bypass

In figure 6.1 (page 104), each stated cognitive operation drives a standard. When it comes to classroom application of these standards, however, there is little if any mention of the complex operations on workbook pages. Instead, instruction often bypasses these operations to focus only on the content nouns, such as *linear relationship, diagrams,* or *trigonometric functions.* In many cases, the scripts pushed into teachers' hands change the standard into a set of procedures that the students will memorize and perform by rote. In this low-expectations situation, teachers can do little more than bypass the thinking operations identified in the standards.

This circumvention of cognitive operations stated in the standards is not unique to mathematics. Math teachers are not the only ones who are pushed to cover content and ignore the thinking elements of the standards. The bypass is common in every state and every academic discipline. In the Texas Standards for Social Studies, knowledge and skills samples from American History Advance Placement also use thinking phrases like *explain why, identify reasons, analyze events, analyze issues, analyze cause and effect,* and *analyze impact* as the driving force at the heart of each expectation statement:

> The student understands the emergence of the United States as a world power between 1898 and 1920. The student is expected to:
>
> (A) *Explain* why significant events and individuals, including the Spanish-American War, U.S. expansionism, Henry Cabot Lodge, Alfred Thayer Mahan, and Theodore Roosevelt, moved the United States into the position of a world power;
>
> (B) *Identify* the reasons for U.S. involvement in World War I, including unrestricted submarine warfare;
>
> (C) *Analyze* significant events such as the battle of Argonne Forest and the impact of significant individuals including John J. Pershing during World War I; and
>
> (D) *Analyze* major issues raised by U.S. involvement in World War I, Wilson's Fourteen Points, and the Treaty of Versailles.
>
> The student understands significant individuals, events, and issues of the 1920s. The student is expected to:
>
> (E) *Analyze* causes and effects of significant issues such as immigration, the Red Scare, Prohibition, and the changing role of women; and
>
> (F) *Analyze* the impact of significant individuals such as Clarence Darrow, William Jennings Bryan, Henry Ford, and Charles A. Lindbergh. (Texas Essential Knowledge and Skills, 2009)

When students read these thinking verbs on their tests, have they had any instruction on how to analyze cause and effect or impact? Where have they learned to distinguish what thinking process they will use for the required cognitive operation? What formal instruction in cognition did they have that will enable them to do this type of thinking with the different cognitive operations? Or are they expected to grasp the thinking processes intuitively? With the emphasis of the 21st century standard to develop critical thinking and problem-solving skills, the bypass seems out of place.

The best students can easily figure out on their own some of the cognitive operations called for in a standard. For instance, consider the operational words *explain* and *identify*. A modest percentage of students, perhaps 20 percent, will know how the operational word *analyze* asks them to think. They will move intuitively to break the big idea into smaller parts. Half of this 20 percent may know how to go further in search of a high-quality analysis. The rest are stuck in the mud of trial and error. At best, they can guess or use random trial and error to do the analysis. Even if the students have memorized Wilson's Fourteen Points mentioned in the Texas standard, most have a slim chance of meeting the standard because they have a shallow understanding of the skills needed to analyze. In like manner, students may have memorized some classroom notes about the causes and effects of immigration or the impact of Lindberg's flight, but such lists will provide little help when it comes time to analyze cause and effect or impact.

Most standards include a thinking operation that drives each content statement. This makes it easier for you to identify which thinking skills to include when enriching student learning in a project. It is helpful to recall that standards are like the banners or flags that identified each Roman legion marching into battle. The soldiers followed their legion's standard wherever they marched. In a like manner, you can follow your state's standards.

When the learning standards delineate both thinking process and content, you can more easily guide your students through their projects. Not only will students feel more motivated to engage in project learning so they can master the prescribed content, they also will have the opportunity to master the secrets of becoming more efficient thinkers. By formally teaching both the prescribed content and the cognitive skills they will need to understand that content, you give your students a double preparation. Table 6.1 (page 108) illustrates which thinking tools are helpful for promoting specific thinking skills.

Promoting Critical Thinking

Just as golf coaches help budding golfers learn new club swings and give feedback on the practice tee, you can take time out of your daily class schedule to initiate explicit instruction about critical thinking skills. In a project, you can follow this explicit instruction with feedback on the quality of their application of the targeted thinking skill. Yes, students could learn the skill in the project without formal instruction. Formal instruction, however, speeds the learning of the thinking skill, ensures that students are using the skill correctly, and enables students to use the skill more effectively in the project.

Table 6.1: Effects of Thinking Tools on Thinking Skills

Tool	Thinking Skill
Instructional frameworks	Hypothesis testing, deducing, comparing
Instructional strategies	Investigating, predicting, sequencing, persuading, summarizing
Asking questions and cueing	Developing abstract thinking and reasoning
Cognitive functions	Reflection, focus, precision, accuracy
Challenge	Seeing relationships, being divergent

One way you can use enriched learning projects to strengthen students' thinking is by explicitly embedding thinking skills. Perhaps your project needs students to make estimates of time and distance travel. You may need to schedule a day or two of time as the project unfolds to teach a mini-lesson about the critical thinking skill called estimation. In that mini-lesson, you might use the direct instruction model to explain the term, model its use, check for understanding, guide practice with simple applications, and coach individuals who might be struggling with the skill.

In each project, you can schedule one or two mini-lessons that focus students on the most important cognitive operations identified by the content standards. In selecting which thinking skills are best for your students, you have several options:

- Select the highest-effect thinking skills—such as hypothesis testing, comparing, and making connections—that research has identified to have the most impact on student achievement (Marzano, Pickering, & Pollock, 2001). Design your projects so that students develop these thinking operations throughout your course.
- Integrate 21st century critical thinking skills, such as investigating, sequencing, predicting, persuading, and summarizing, to help students better understand new and old material as they improve their use of these skills. Target one per project.
- Select the thinking operation called for by the content standards for your project. You can use your browser to locate your relevant state or national standard for the course you are teaching. Identify the cognitive operation by the stated verb in the standard or the appropriate benchmark that will guide your project.

Instructional Frameworks

You can initiate your work with students' cognition by building your standards-based projects on those instructional frameworks that are most likely to have a strong impact on helping students to learn more and think faster, deeper, and more critically. An instructional framework shapes the major pattern of thinking that students will do in a project. Unlike lessons that blindly follow the textbook page by page, these high-yield frameworks organize the flow of a project and facilitate the primary types of thinking that students must do in order to complete it. In addition, when each phase of the project is complete, you will have the opportunity to deepen your students' learning by structuring tasks that require them to reflect on the thinking processes they used and determine how these processes might help them in other learning experiences inside or outside the classroom. By focusing on the mediation of student thinking, you help students focus on the efficiency of their thinking, so they are more effective in their standards-aligned learning efforts. Use the template Selecting Your Instructional Framework (page 118 and online at **go.solution-tree.com/instruction**) to plan your instructional framework.

Mediating the Thinking Experience

You take on the mediator role when you elect to teach students how to fish rather than provide them with a fish to eat at each meal. When you provide students with a meal, you tell students about the content and then ask them to recall what is in their notes. When you teach your students how to fish for a lifetime of meals, you empower students by helping them improve the thinking skills that will make them lifelong, self-directed learners.

In a project, the process of mediating a thinking experience occurs when you focus a good deal of your coaching time on the development and use of critical and creative thinking skills. You step back from the content and ask questions or use instructional tactics that challenge students to understand the *how* and *why* of their thinking. You intentionally ask the students to put the content to the side so they can focus on the thinking process itself, free of the content (Feuerstein, Falik, Rand, & Feuerstein, 2006a). When they have completed the project, you have given them both the fish (the core content) and the tools to go fishing for a lifetime (improved thinking skills). Your mediation will have enabled them to make more extensive transfer of "how to think" to other situations both in and out of the classroom. This is the primary impetus for students learning *from* doing, the hallmark of the most effective projects.

The mediation of the cognitive functions also helps students improve the quality of their thinking. It eradicates bad habits of thinking which make students inefficient in the use of the major operations, or what are more regularly called thinking skills. You can select from at least four research-supported instructional frameworks that promote the most powerful types of student thinking and give students improved methods for thinking through any enriched project-based learning experience. As we have seen, these include:

1. Hypothesis testing
2. Investigating
3. Comparing
4. Connecting parts to whole

By building projects around these thought-developing processes, you put into practice the research on high-yield instruction. The McREL meta-analysis (Marzano, Pickering, & Pollock, 2001) identifies how these cognitively strong instructional strategies can result in the highest achievement yields. In addition, you provoke student interest, one of the keys to motivation, by creating a need for students to find an answer rather than having answers presented to them (Feuerstein, Falik, Feuerstein, & Rand, 2006a). As the framework for an enriched project, the specific, targeted thinking skill becomes the colead in a play with the actress "content."

Think for a moment how this works. Do you think it is possible to learn content—to know, for example, what a deciduous tree is or how it differs from a coniferous tree—without doing any thinking? Of course not. When you define, you have to compare. Comparing is perhaps the most common thinking skill used in school to learn content. Some students compare well; others just don't get it. Still others compare inaccurately or imprecisely (those cognitive functions again!). In a project framework that highlights comparing, you can sharpen students' abilities to make comparisons. You can also help students to make more precise and accurate comparisons.

Now consider whether a thinking skill such as comparing or a function such as being precise could stand alone. Can you see yourself saying to students, "Now I want you to compare. Go for it," or "For the next minute, I want you to compare more precisely"? The blank looks would immediately ask you, "Compare what?"

The moral of the story is that thinking and content must go hand in hand. Projects give you a rich opportunity to create teachable moments during which you can help your students improve their thinking skills as they improve their understanding of the prescribed content. The opposite is also true. In both cases, the result is that more of your students, who are now more efficient at thinking, can apply those skills to help themselves grasp content faster and deeper.

By selecting strategies that have been identified as most proactive in promoting achievement to frame your project, you enrich student learning at still another level. The framework you select depends on what you feel will most help your students become more efficient thinkers and more effective learners. What is most important is that you add to the impact of projects you design by starting with one of these proven thinking skills as your framework for a power-packed learning experience.

Hypothesis Testing

You can initiate enriched projects that test a hypothesis by providing a launch "what if" question about the big idea contained in the standard. The standard you select will be the finish line of the unit you are starting. As a result of answering the "what if," your students will arrive at the finish line with data that will either support or negate the hypothesis, just as scientists know that an answer to their hypothesis may be negative or positive. It is important that students understand they have not failed if they find that the evidence does not support their hypothesis. What matters is that the test was done and that even the negative answer they derived is supportable by evidence. Hypothesis testing is a complex thinking process. Learning about the negation of *their* hypothesis is a more significant learning experience than one that limits them to listening passively to a lecture and memorizing answers to a test that only define the term *hypothesis*.

Testing a Hypothesis Using a Standard

The Project Results: Students will design and build a green building that requires them to introduce and test a hypothesis. As a result, they will show they can gather the necessary data, deduce which data proves the hypothesis, and apply the data in the construction of the green building. Using mathematical modeling, they will show mastery of the concepts of linear measurement, scale drawing, ratio, fractions, angles, and geometric shapes.

The Big Idea: Mathematical Modeling

The Standard: Students will use mathematical models and multiple representations of math concepts to provide a means of presenting, interpreting, communicating, and connecting mathematical relationships.

The Hypothesis: By using multiple representations of math concepts to design a green building, students will understand the concepts used in their model.

The Hypothetical Question: If we use a mathematical modeling process, can we design a green building that saves greater amounts of energy than a nongreen building?

The Content Focus: *Core*—mathematics (geometry); *secondary*—ecology, technological literacy

California Math Standard—Visual representation and transformation of two-to three-dimensional shapes

1. Use scale drawings to represent real objects and spaces.
2. Use the coordinate plane to explore geometric ideas.
3. Use appropriate tools to show geometric relationships. (California Department of Education, n.d.)

Investigating

You can launch students' enriched projects as investigations by providing students with an open-ended launch question that promises an inquiry. This question must challenge them to gather ideas, make sense of the information, and communicate their new understandings resulting from the project. In the spirit of Sherlock Holmes, students will search for data that allows them to deduce the answer to a perplexing problem. In that "megaprocess," students will find themselves using other cognitive operations, such as analyzing data, forming generalizations, and drawing logical conclusions. At the end of the project, you will expect them not only to know the content they have uncovered, but also to show their skill in the process of investigating.

In science, students might investigate the effects of El Niño on their local environment. In social studies, they can investigate the impact of identity-theft laws on their community. In language arts, they might investigate the impact of local TV news coverage on gang control. Very often, investigation projects allow you to structure an interdisciplinary learning experience that involves multiple standards that you can integrate into the inquiry.

An Investigation Using Multiple Standards

The Project Results: Students will investigate the impact of fossil fuels on the quality of life in our community, showing that they can produce evidence that solves a problem.

The Big Idea: The local impact of fossil fuel pollution

The Launch Question: Fossil Fuels—Pollution or Not in Our Town?

The Standards:

1. (Science) Students will *understand* and *apply* scientific concepts, principles, and theories pertaining to their physical setting and living environment.
2. (Language arts) Students will use *standard* English skillfully and with individual style.
3. (Visual arts) Students will be *knowledgeable* about and *make use* of materials and resources available for producing artwork.
4. (Analysis, inquiry, and design) Students will *use* mathematical *analysis,* scientific *inquiry,* and engineering design to *pose questions, seek answers,* and *develop solutions.*

The Content Focus: Core—science; secondary—language arts, visual arts, inquiry

When a set of standards does not supply benchmark or performance indicators, you are free to determine what knowledge and skills you want students to develop through the project. For instance, for this project you may want to include such concepts as pollution and greenhouse gases. You may also want to frame a set of subquestions that ask your students to offset opposing theories about the origin of fossil fuel pollution in the local community. All of these would align their project investigation to the science standard. As you develop the project, you could also design it so that students have to keep journals to summarize what they have learned each week. To match the language arts standard, you would use a rubric to check their standard English usage in these written summaries. For the arts standard, you could assign teams to construct collages from simple art materials such as poster board, paints, and tape. The final standard related to analysis and inquiry would be met by students learning to follow the investigation process as applied to the problem of fossil fuel pollution.

Comparing

Finding similarities and differences between ideas, concepts, processes, events, and objects is inherent in curricula from the first day of kindergarten. When first graders are studying dinosaurs, they are asked to compare the different genera and species in many dimensions: size, shape, color, habitat, eating habits, life span, and so forth. Middle graders are challenged to see the similarities among characters in a short story or among cultures. In math, students learn to identify the attributes of different triangles so they can distinguish one from another.

Comparing may be the most important cognitive operation that students must use day to day in their formal studies. In addition to being asked to make comparisons throughout the curriculum, students must learn to make spontaneous comparisons every day. When they look at two triangles, they make spontaneous comparisons; when they examine two mammals, they make spontaneous comparisons. Any time they are asked to define a term or describe an object, they must compare on the spot.

Most important, it is through spontaneous comparisons that students are able to make generalizations. In the act of comparing two objects, they must look at the specific descriptors (for example, size, shape, and color). When students put these descriptors into a specific configuration, they must be able to say, "That is a triangle" or "That is a square." If they are weak in this essential cognitive function, they will be unable to make sense of what they are studying in a meaningful way.

Enriched learning projects that encourage students to use their comparative thinking can range in size from the very small to the gargantuan. When you use the cognitive operation of comparing as the framework for an enriched learning project, you enable your students to refine the thinking processes inherent in identifying similarities and differences. As a consequence, students will learn to break complex concepts into similar and dissimilar characteristics or attributes. This helps them analyze the simpler components of a more complex problem in search of its solution. At the end, the process enables the students to know and label objects, processes, situations, and, eventually, abstract concepts.

In an enriched learning project, you can spotlight the thinking processes that go into the operation of comparing. By helping students analyze these processes, you empower them to better understand how they are thinking and to better use these processes in other situations.

When starting a comparison-framed project—such as comparing two books, cultures, historic events, physics laws, or mathematical concepts—research shows that it is helpful to start off with a visual tool. Graphic organizers, such as the ever popular Venn diagram, are examples of tools for facilitating the mental operation of comparing.

In the graphic organizer comparison alley, students can see two or more ideas matched for their similarities. Figure 6.2 demonstrates the use of this graphic with two Shakespearean tragedies.

HAMLET					
Dane	Son of king	Indecisive	Incited by ghost	Hatred	Faithful friend
Moor	Son of general	Hubristic Jealous	Incited by servant	Love	Two-faced friend
OTHELLO					

Figure 6.2: Hamlet versus Othello.

The comparison framework allows you to start your project design by extracting what you want students to compare directly from the standards-aligned curriculum. You might begin with a standard that calls for students to show that they can compare literary genres or historic periods. Next you would select the specific item for comparison in the project and match it directly to the standards that you will integrate into the project.

A Comparison Using Multiple Standards

The Project Results: A comparative essay on two novels showing students know how to compare major characters

The Big Idea: The Triumph of the Human Spirit

The Standards:

1. (Literary Analysis) Compare the presentation of a similar theme or topic in a genre to explain how selection of the genre shapes the theme (10:3.2 Reading).
2. (Research) Develop main ideas within the body of a composition through use of accurate and specific evidence (10:1.8 Writing).
3. (Composition) Clarify a position with precise and relevant evidence including facts, expert opinions, and quotations (10:2.5 Persuasion). (California Department of Education, 2003)

The Content Focus: Language arts (reading and writing)

The comparative framework allows for a wide range of topics and the differentiation of the materials according to students' demonstrated reading abilities. For instance, you might have one group of students compare *Lord of the Flies* with *A Separate Peace.* A second group might accept the challenge of comparing the more difficult novels *The Scarlet Letter* and *Big Boy.* Other groups might analyze *Lost* and *Robinson Crusoe.* All three groups in this project would do a comparative analysis of their novels in response to the launch question, "How do the principle characters show the triumph of the human spirit?" The project would conclude with each person writing a comparative essay that meets the investigation standard, as follows:

1. Identify the comparative essay requirements for the end of the project.
2. Target the big idea or theme.
3. Identify the reading materials appropriate to the students' age.
4. Structure the project tasks to fit the comparative framework and align with the standards.
5. Align the investigation with the standard for making an investigation.

Connecting Parts to the Whole

None of the thinking frameworks is more suited to enriched project-based learning and none is more challenging to students than the framework that develops students' ability to connect the dots or see relationships among the concepts, themes, topics, and information they study in a standards-based curriculum. However, from the beginning to the end of a project, the opportunities to facilitate students' making connections within a single content area or in a multidisciplinary study are many.

Working With Standards Across Disciplines

The Project Results: The completion of a visual design for an invention that will make use of technology easier for persons with physical disabilities. The project will show that students can identify a problem, visualize alternative solutions, apply best practices of design, and construct the final tool according to their design.

The Big Idea: Invent a machine to solve a simple problem.

The Standards:

1. (Math, Science, and Technology) As a result of activities in grades 9–12, all students will show development of their abilities in technology design. (National Science Teachers Association, n.d.)
2. (Language Arts) Students deliver polished formal and extemporaneous presentations. (California Department of Education, 2003)
3. (Artistic Perception) Students develop perceptual skills by identifying and using the principles of visual design. (California State Board of Education, 2009)

The Content Focus: Science and technology, language arts, visual arts

A design project will make the development of students' capacities to see and understand relationships and then communicate what they have seen much easier through the demonstration of inventions that solve fun or serious problems. You will also kill many birds with one stone when you ask students to think about the connections they made within the project and what connections they can make to their lives and learning outside the project. You can ask these questions as they work through the project, or at the end of one. Sometimes you may drop by a group and pose a connection question. At other times, you may ask them to write a journal entry and respond to a prompt such as:

- "What was the big idea I learned from completing this project?"
- "What did I do to connect contributing ideas, facts, and other factors with the big idea?"
- "Why is this big idea important? What connection does it have to my other school work? To my life outside of school? To other people?"

Building Your Own Framework

Now that you have the big picture, you may want to develop your own framework following these steps and using the reproducible Selecting Your Instructional Framework (page 118 and online at **go.solution-tree.com/instruction**):

1. Identify your project—what will the students do (for example, operate a soup kitchen at Thanksgiving)?

2. Identify the cognitive operation that will frame the project (for example, comparing).
3. Identify the big idea (for example, "What is empathy?").
4. Identify the standard (for example, "Students will organize and conduct a service event that contributes to the community").
5. Detail framework that students will use (for example, comparing their own lives to the lives of those they serve in the project).
6. Explain the challenge students will face (for example, to be able to step back and review their own situations with those they serve in an empathetic manner).
7. Identify the content areas that students will study in the project (for example, service requirement, sociology, economics, and so on).

Summary

Most projects implicitly promote student thinking. When making a product, students have to decide what part goes where, what to do when a problem arises that hinders completion of their idea, and how to make sure that the project fits their design idea. However, most products do not have an explicit goal to enhance students' thinking and problem-solving skills. If you elect to use the enriched learning project model of instruction, you will be called upon to examine your content standards for the cognitive element and use that element to establish a framework for the project. By aligning your project with the process element of the standards, you can focus students on explicit development of those critical and creative thinking skills embedded in the standards.

Selecting Your Instructional Framework

1. **Identify the project:**
2. **Identify the cognitive operation that will frame the project:**
3. **Name the big idea:**
4. **Identify the standard:**
5. **Detail the framework that students will use:**
6. **Explain the challenge they will face:**
7. **Identify the content areas they will study:**

Chapter 7

Creating a Collaborative Classroom Culture

> The world in which children are now growing up differs dramatically from the world which gave rise to the industrial age school.
>
> —Peter Senge

This chapter explains the value and the methods for developing a community of learners that will enrich students' project-based learning experiences. It begins with an explanation of why creation of a learning community is important to the enriched learning project model of instruction. It then identifies two means that facilitate development of a learning community: digital tools and cooperative learning. After explaining your role in using these tools and tactics, the chapter discusses the five stages of development for a learning community. For each stage, you are presented with examples of research-strong, collaborative-learning tactics embedded in e-tool use. The tactics selected here (as well as others referenced at **go.solution-tree.com/instruction**) are designed for easy integration into a project schedule. Use the reproducible Creating Your Tactical Plan for Collaborative Learning (page 145 and online).

Palatine High

Sally Berman started with collaborative learning in her first-period chemistry class at Palatine High. In that year, first period was her best class. It was a mixed-ability group with two students from special education and seven ELL students in the mix. The class had thirty-two students all together. Since her lab was attached to her classroom, Sally felt comfortable starting with collaborative learning during lab period. Groups of four fit her tables, and she could match pairs in the classroom seats. She marked each lab table with four colors of tape. She assigned a role to each color and rotated the students each week. In that first year, her twenty-third at Palatine High School, she wanted to keep the groups tightly controlled.

By the next year, Sally was feeling more at ease. She had the procedures down, and students were doing a good job, she thought, assessing their lab work and their collaborative group roles. She had added a thinking web to her classroom for reviewing each

continued →

chapter. The groups came up with questions about what they were studying, and she recorded them on the web. Sally loved calling on students by pulling their names out of her magician's hat to answer the questions. She felt this helped break her habit of calling on the same kids all the time without wait time.

Midway into her second year, Sally spread collaborative learning to her other three classes, including the AP group. She also decided to try out journals and team portfolios. A colleague in the English department suggested these two ideas to save grading time. Sally was all for that! She had students divide their chemistry notebooks (a staple in her course) into two parts. They could use the back section of the journals, working forward, for their self-assessments and reflections. Once a week, she would give them questions about their participation in the lab team and their understanding of the week's topic. Then they would share their answers with their lab teammates and give each other feedback. Each team would keep its own portfolio with all the journals and lab reports together. Once a week, she would check two of the teams' portfolios.

At first, some of the students resisted the journals. They wanted Sally to give them the usual grades, based only on lab reports. Sally kept grading the lab reports, but only used comments on the journals. After a while, she started journal conversations. After several quarters' experience with the journals, Sally borrowed another idea from her colleague, Nancy. She introduced some mini-projects. By the end of the year, she had two that she felt were helping make the teams work better together—the vocabulary map and the Möbius hotel contest.

The vocabulary map solved a nagging problem. Sally had each lab team tape eight sheets of 8½ x 11–inch paper into a big square. In the middle, they put a key unit concept such as *Möbius*. After each lab, they would record the key words as they built the unit's concept map (fig. 7.1).

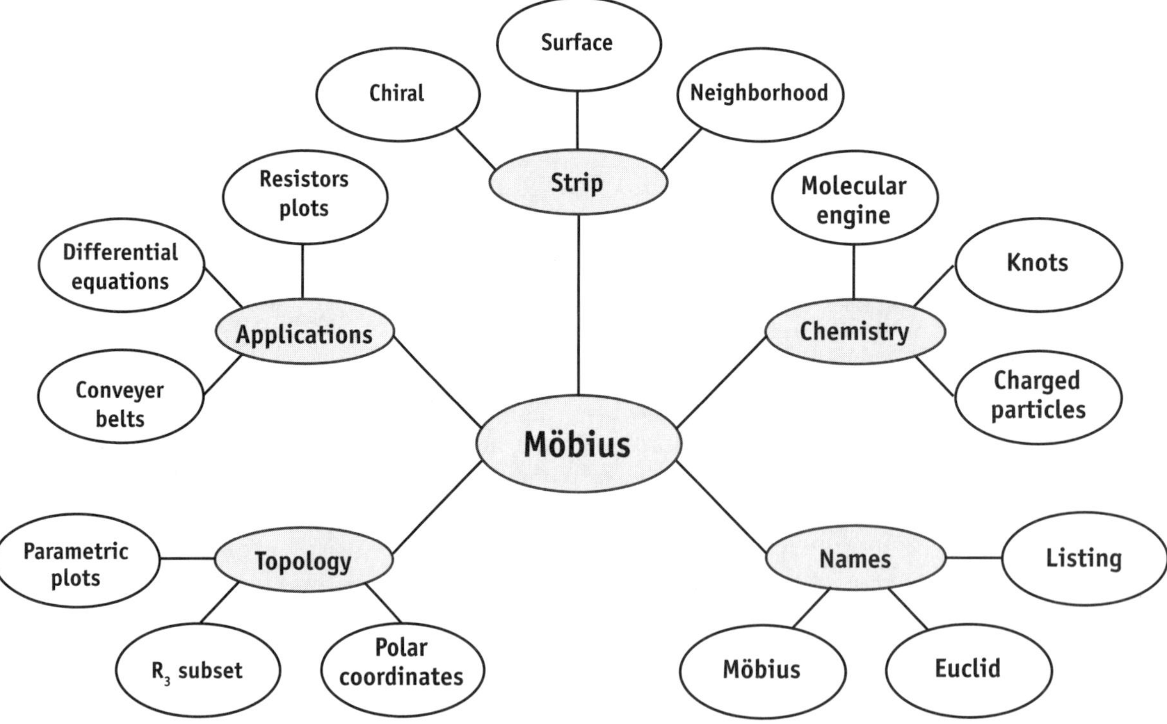

Figure 7.1: A Möbius map.

That year, at the end of her last period class, a team brought her a gift. They had made a shoebox house that they called Möbius Motel. "Inside, it had all sorts of puns on the vocabulary words," Sally shared at her retirement dinner. "These kids couldn't stop laughing at their own bad jokes. That's when I got the idea for the contest. Here I am seven years later, and the showcase outside my room holds all the winners. My all-time favorite is a big white whale—a stuffed one called Möbius Dick. These projects won't go down for their academic rigor, but they sure were a magical way to bond the kids in each class. I couldn't believe that some parents asked for my class because they think the contest is a Palatine tradition."

The industrial age of the early 20th century spawned the urban factory. In these factories, workers sat jammed into cramped workspaces. Mass production dictated that each worker do the same repetitive tasks. In factory-like schools, thirty to fifty students sat at desks often bolted to the floor. Each day, students memorized and recited the alphabet, numbers, the names of each state, the capitals of each state, important dates in world history, and the names of U.S. presidents. On slates, they calculated basic number operations or scribbled one-word answers to factual questions. Each had an individual goal to graduate.

Today's high-tech work environment is very different from the work world that Frederick Taylor advocated for schools and factories, as are many of the new, high-tech schools where students work in teams, supported by sophisticated high-tech tools and engaged in collaborative projects and other learning tasks that challenge them to think critically and solve complex problems. For instance, at High Tech High School in San Diego, students end their coursework by making a video or a physical structure that shows what they understand. In one physics and math project, Pool Hall Junkies, students make a small pool table that is the culmination of their physics study. In the project, they learn about how impulse, momentum, and angles impact motion. The medium is the game of billiards.

New developments in project collaboration are not contained within school walls. Around the globe, e-projects are connecting students of many nations. Their goals are shared. With new advances in learning via technology arriving almost daily, any teacher can easily connect a classroom community with others in their school or around the globe. For instance, Fire and Ice (www.elluminate.com)—an award-winning nonprofit initiative that delivers distance education programs to rural schools in developing nations—uses cost-effective web conferencing technology that excels across low bandwidths and in unstable Internet conditions. Fire and Ice connects schools from remote rural communities in the Southern Hemisphere (the "Fire") with partners in the Northern Hemisphere (the "Ice") and delivers school-to-school collaborative projects. Students from different countries collaborate on topics of social importance, including climate change, peace, and poverty reduction.

In a learning community, there is not just bonding among teams doing work; there is bonding among all students within classrooms and across hemispheres, and this has a strong impact on the quality of the learning that takes place (Johnson

& Johnson, 1983). Just as individual players in a symphony orchestra join to help their instrument section perform as a unit with a common goal and the sections join in a common sound as a total orchestra with a common goal, students in a learning community with or without physical boundaries can collaborate with their learning teams to enrich what and how each of them learns. All the team members, be they in a single space or in many different nations, can contribute to the community spirit that expands every individual's learning potential. They do this by switching out of competitive and individualistic goals to a common goal that brings increased interpersonal connections and higher achievement (Roseth, Johnson, & Johnson, 2008).

When you think about creating a collaborative atmosphere in a learning community, you can compare your challenge to the one that faces NASA space launch teams. In this situation, an individual working alone is insufficient for overcoming the challenges inherent in the monumental task. No matter how much each single person knows or how high the skill level, working as an individual, or even within a group of individuals, will not bring the same degree of success that comes when all the individuals learn to work as a team. To succeed not only in launching the rocket with its precious and perishable astronaut crew, but in bringing them all safely home, every person engaged in the launch must join hearts and minds in a shared effort

The Classroom as a Learning Community

In a fully functioning learning community, a classroom performs like a symphony orchestra making its best music. The conductor raises the baton. The violinists poise their bows above the strings. With a slight twitch of the baton or a bend of the conductor's pinkie finger, the musicians begin in unison. Working together with one page-turner per pair, the players glide through the score. At precise moments, the timpanist tings her triangle, the drummer beats out his rhythm, and the cellos sing their deep-throated song. Each instrument's unique sound blends with the others, combining into a single, soaring sound.

There is no experience like watching and hearing the many members of a master orchestra working as one. Like any skilled orchestra conductor, you are fully aware that a triumphant concert doesn't just happen. It requires hours upon hours of effort from each individual musician. All have a single mission. Not only must each strive to play assigned notes, each must blend with the other players. Precision, accuracy, and focused attention on every detail of the score mark each player's collaboration.

In the classroom, you can prepare your students to work together to turn their project-based learning experience into an equally peak performance. For this, you take on the conductor's role as you lead the students in creating a collaborative learning environment. Like orchestra members, students will work together for a maximum effect that benefits all. Just as the conductor prepares the orchestra's members for their symphonic performances, you will prepare the students to reach their highest achievement goals by working as an integrated unit.

When all students in a classroom commit to making a conscious, consistent, and collaborative effort to accomplish a single goal—a goal of helping each other master the grade-level standards or producing a high-quality product—a learning community emerges. At times, cracks may appear. Discord and disagreement may sidetrack students from their shared goal. However, if the students—guided by you—work together to put the distraction aside, the community will return to its primary goal. Guided by your skilled baton, your students will bond more tightly as the learning community faces each new challenge.

What Tools Create a Collaborative Culture?

In the modern workplace, collaboration is increased when the tech workers use electronic tools, such as the following, to complete their assignments:

- Blogs
- Chat rooms
- Concept maps
- Content management systems
- Data conferences
- E-calendars
- Email
- Extranet
- Faxes
- Internet
- Moodle
- Podcasts
- Project management systems
- Social networks
- Text messages
- Twitter
- Videoconferences
- Voicemail
- Voiceover Internet Protocol (Skype)
- Whiteboards
- Wikis
- Workflow systems

With email, they talk with each other or with a collection of colleagues; with videoconferences and data conferences, they discuss critical issues and solve common problems, even though the collaborators are countries part; with content management systems such as Bitrix and Documentum, they work together to manage website design and use.

Today, more and more teachers are learning that many of the same e-tools used in the modern workplace can enrich their students' learning experiences, especially in the enriched learning project model. Unlike projects in the workplace that focus on an end product, such as a new piece of software, projects in the classroom are designed primarily to improve students' attainment, to develop their knowledge and skill goals, and to help them advance their creative thinking when designing new products. Many e-tools help students with tasks that end with shared learning outcomes. Although some may disagree, the products of projects, no matter how interesting or unique, are secondary in value to the learning outcomes that enrich students' learning experiences.

New Research on Cooperative Learning

The terms *cooperative* and *collaborative* learning are often used synonymously, with some definitions reserving the term *cooperative* for more structured approaches with greater teacher involvement and more traditional content (Rockwood, 1995a, 1995b). However, cooperative learning in the context of collaborative schoolwork applies equally well to *collaboration*, as we use that term in the three *C*s.

Cooperative learning is a well-researched instructional strategy familiar to most veteran teachers. Like a good wine, a teacher's skilled use of cooperative learning grows better with age. The cooperative learning strategy is a high-yield collection of tactics that fine tune students' collaborative work. These tactics prepare students who are not used to working together to learn together.

Technology-supported cooperative learning tends to increase achievement, positive attitudes toward technology and cooperation, cognitive development, learning control, social competencies, positive relationships with team members, including social presence, and innovation in groupware and hardware. Cooperative learning and technology-supported instruction have complementary strengths. The computer, for example, can control the flow of work, monitor accuracy, give electronic feedback, and do calculations. Cooperative learning provides a sense of belonging, the opportunity to explain and summarize what is being learned, shared mental models, social models, respect and approval for efforts to achieve, encouragement of divergent thinking, and interpersonal feedback on academic learning and the use of the technology. The use of cooperative learning with technology-assisted instruction allows for argumentation (or constructive controversy) to be part of lessons utilizing technology. Cooperative learning is an important part of enhancing the effectiveness of interaction around and through computers—using local networks, email, videogames and simulations, and adventure learning, as well as electronic pedagogical agents (Johnson & Johnson, 2008).

Roseth, Johnson, and Johnson (2008) completed a meta-analysis of more than five hundred studies of cooperative learning. The studies included seventeen thousand early adolescents from eleven countries. From the data reviewed, they concluded that when a classroom is dominated by a goal structure that promotes positive interdependence, achievement exceeds that of classrooms with individualistic or competitive goals.

Since the late 1970s, Roger Johnson, David Johnson, Robert Slavin, and other researchers have studied the effects of cooperative learning in the classroom. Johnson and Johnson have produced several meta-analyses of this strategy's impact on learning, classroom behavior, and other factors. They have advocated the establishment of a common learning goal, interpersonal interdependence, individual accountability, development of team social skills, and assessment of group performance as required determinants of a successful cooperative team. Most of the tactics that they espouse (such as jigsaw and three questions in one) have classroom research that shows their effectiveness as cooperative learning tactics (Roseth, Johnson, & Johnson, 2008).

In 1991, Robert Marzano, Debra Pickering, and Jane Pollock (2001) conducted a meta-analysis of the research data on cooperative learning and other instructional strategies. Cooperative learning was one of nine strategies that Marzano and his colleagues identified in this study as having the most impact on improving student achievement. Within each strategy grouping, Marzano identified a number of tactics that were especially effective in developing cooperation. Among these tactics in the cooperative learning strategy were formal groups, think-pair-share, and team use of graphic organizers.

For any teacher wanting to raise achievement scores, use of cooperative learning is one of the most powerful strategies for increasing learning performance. The supporting research is exceptionally strong in reinforcing the teacher's role in structuring a cooperative goal structure. When developing 21st century skills, it seems only natural to select cooperative and collaborative learning as primary tools. The addition of technology tools as a second tactic for developing mutual interdependence can only further enrich the learning experiences.

The Teacher's Role in a Collaborative Culture

What is your role in a classroom that you elect to build into a high-functioning collaborative learning community? Given what the studies indicate, you—like an orchestra conductor—have the responsibility to set the mission, determine the shared goal, select the strategy and tactics, and facilitate the development of the necessary classroom cohesion. You select the score the musicians will play; you encourage, direct, interpret, cajole, assess, set tempo, and keep everyone focused on the shared goal of an outstanding performance; and you signal who stands and takes bows for their special contributions. Following your lead, the students make the music.

What are some specific ways that you can increase collaboration to build community and enrich students' learning? Here are seven suggestions that Roseth, Johnson, and Johnson's (2008) meta analysis supports:

1. Identify e-tools and structure e-tasks that enable students to collaborate to reach a single, shared goal. The tasks and e-tools, by their nature, will require more than one set of hands.
2. Structure thinking tasks that allow students to benefit from each others' ideas.
3. Arrange the room so that students can communicate easily with each other.
4. Structure the learning phases so that the tasks of gathering information, making sense, and communicating results are more complex than a single student can complete in the time you allot.
5. Encourage students to find ways to help each other.
6. Identify, guide, and coach students in pairs and trios in the development of the social skills that enhance the interpersonal communication, trust, and positive interactions necessary for the students to bond with each other for achieving their shared goal.
7. Encourage student teams to strengthen connections with the other classes and team members to build an environment that mediates positive social interactions with the mission of constructing an inclusive, high-achieving workplace.

A Learning Activity for Turning Groups Into Teams

This is a cooperative learning activity that you can use intentionally to increase the bonding among your students, improve their teamwork, and increase their task achievement. By using the activity as a purposeful tactic, you transform it from being a fun activity into being a productive strategy.

1. Form teams of three. Place each team at a computer station.
2. Explain the shared goal: "To improve each team's interdependence."
3. Have each team decide on each member's role: group facilitator, computer operator, checker. Encourage each team to define the roles.
4. Using a slideshow application, instruct each team to design a presentation that will include an agreed-upon team: (a) name, (b) symbol, (c) slogan, and (d) cheer.
5. Allow one class period for the teams to complete these steps and practice their presentation delivery. Encourage creative thinking, especially brainstorming.

6. Share the following criteria: (a) make the slideshow as visually appealing as possible, (b) make sure the presentation will not offend and is governed by good taste, (c) make sure all team members have a part in the presentation, (d) prepare the presentation so that other teams may view it via the projection screen, and (e) make sure the presentation does not exceed two minutes.

When you are trying to enrich learning in a project, you can best enhance your students' achievement by purposefully embedding specific learning tactics. This not only increases the odds that you will raise their achievement for this task, but also enables you to build the learning community. Whenever possible, you want to include hardware, software, and Internet sites as the base tools to which you attach cooperative learning tactics.

Sample Lesson Using Collaboration and Communication as Outcomes and Tactics

Title: The Radio Project

Teacher: Danielle Johnson, City Arts and Tech High School, San Francisco

Driving question: Does History Repeat Itself?

Have you ever been interested in being on the radio? In this workshop you will have the opportunity to express your own opinions and be heard. Through writing and recording an audio commentary, you will answer the question: does history repeat itself? You will examine the roles of up-standers [people involved in saving Jews] and bystanders during the Holocaust and relate them to another historical or present-day event, such as the Palestine/Israeli conflict; post-9/11 internment; Japanese internment during WWII; the Civil War in Central America; genocide in Armenia, Cambodia, Rwanda, and Darfur (Sudan); immigration issues; racial profiling; or another related issue that interests you. In addition, you will create a unique visual art piece related to your commentary. Your recordings and visual pieces will be broadcast and displayed on the night of the exhibition. You might even have the opportunity to have your commentary aired on a local radio station.

Subject area(s): Social studies

Teaching days to complete: Two weeks

Keywords: Holocaust, genocide, radio commentary

Outcomes: 21st century leadership skills—communicate effectively and persuasively, manage projects effectively, think critically, solve problems resourcefully, express creatively, collaborate productively

Project launch: Oftentimes when studying history, one is presented with the question of whether history repeats itself. Over the next two weeks, you will explore how you will answer this question.

continued →

Commentary writing: First, we will listen to sample radio commentaries from Youth Radio. You will generate a list of the purpose of commentaries.

Recording commentaries: Before recording, you will practice in front of peers and receive peer feedback on your rehearsals. In pairs, you will be divided into three panel groups. All of the commentaries of a particular group will be played and then each panel will give feedback.

Radio Project reflection: After the completion of the Radio Project and the exhibition, you will write reflections about the process and product.

Adapted with permission of Danielle Johnson, Envision Schools, www.envisionprojects.org.

The Five Stages of Development in a Learning Community

According to Peter Senge, quoted in the epigraph to this chapter, the intentional development of a learning community passes through five stages. Each phase is important not only for setting the conditions that invite students to learn, but also for developing the interpersonal skills that will provide them with the tools to work together and communicate most effectively in their projects. Figure 7.2 demonstrates these five stages of a learning community's development.

Yes, students can work in projects without the support of cooperative conditions and tools. However, there is no need to have students work in a sweatshop atmosphere where unnecessary competition, selfish individualism, and the inability to resolve conflicts slow down a project's completion. Nor is it sensible to ask students to use Stone Age tools to complete their projects when they can take advantage of collaboration-inducing tactics such as pairs and trios, as well as electronic tools that will make their project work more effective and efficient. As students become familiar with collaborative tactics and e-tools, bolstered with sharpened interpersonal communication and teamwork skills, you will find them producing a higher level product and learning more effectively from their "doing" (Roseth, Johnson, & Johnson, 2008).

To obtain optimal learning from all students, the classroom community is an essential starting place. The stronger the collaborative climate, the more forcefully the community drives students to higher achievement. By building the community from the ground up, you can create conditions that will bring your students closer to achieving the best thinking and learning they can possibly do.

Each of the stage descriptions that follow contain goals, timelines, key strategies, and sample tactics that you can use in your own plan to develop a classroom learning community that will encourage your students to do their best learning.

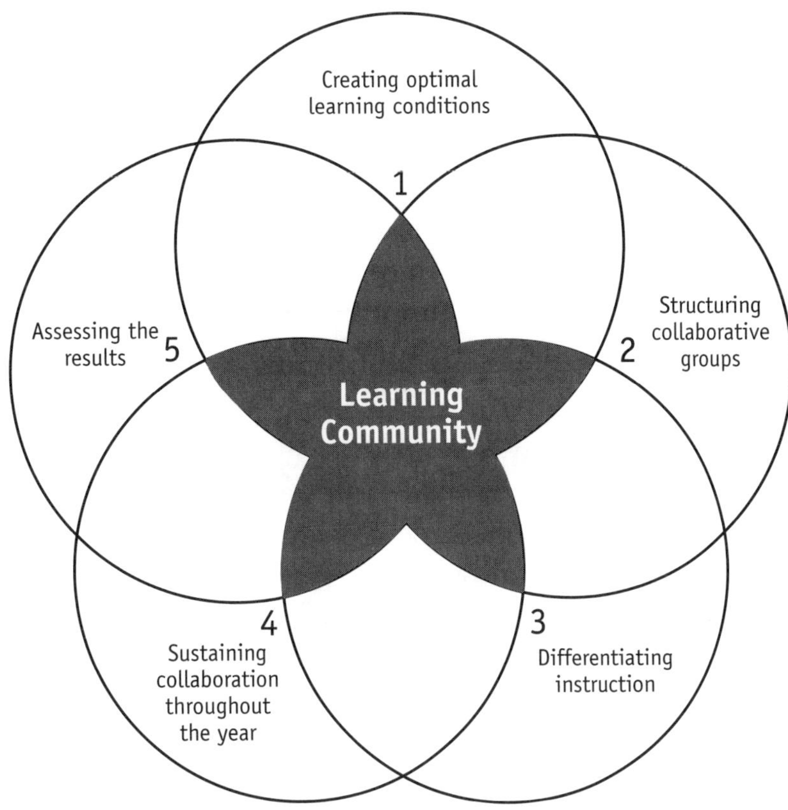

Figure 7.2: Five stages of a learning community's development.

Stage One: Create Optimal Learning Conditions

The Goal—To establish those conditions that will most enable students to achieve the highest learning expectations in a supportive learning community

Timeline—The first two weeks of the school year

Two strategies for creating optimal learning conditions are presented: communicate expectations and awaken knowledge of teamwork.

Strategy One: Communicate Expectations

High expectations are more than a set of words. High, but reasonable, expectations create a sense of urgency. They also serve as a weathervane pointing the students in the right direction. High expectations are especially helpful for those students who are not used to learning from doing. These students have built-in low expectations that teachers will tell them what and how to learn as "solo" flyers. These students come to a project-centered classroom with expectations for passive learning by themselves. By changing the expectations up front, project-based learning teachers say directly, "I expect you to work together and to be an active generator of your learning." To help students achieve this expectation, your first step is to integrate selected community-building tactics into the initial class time in the school year.

Start by choosing one or more collaborative tactics to make your high expectations visible as you intentionally build a community of active learners. Select tactics like the following that are most age appropriate for your students and adapt them as you see fit.

- **Networked whiteboards and slideshows:** On the first day of class, assign groups of three to each computer station. Set up the whiteboards or slide presentations on their screens with the following—
  - ☐ Pictures of sports teams, wagon teams, orchestras, and other images that show collaborative effort
  - ☐ A tagline extolling the principle of collaboration (such as "We sink or swim together" or "All for one and one for all")
  - ☐ Quotes from historic figures who extolled the importance of collaboration (for example, Washington, Lincoln, Rosa Parks); use your browser to find "collaboration quotes"

  Invite the teams to discuss the connections they see among these items and what they suggest in regard to working with their assigned peers as a team. After five minutes of discussion, ask the teams to agree on their answers to the two questions and post them on the class blog. (Remember that you may have to review your procedures and guidelines for blog work in your classroom.)

- **Blog guidelines for collaborative work:** Use an acronym that identifies the core social skills students are expected to use when working on collaborative project tasks. Post these on the class blog. Discuss and review these on a weekly basis or ask students to write a reflection in their e-journals. Following is a sample acronym for working together.

  U=Use positive comments.

  N=No put-downs or disrespect to each other.

  I=Individuals are responsible for their own work.

  T=Team has no "I" in it.

  E=Energize each other.

  Ask students to think about sports teams in which players have assigned positions (for example, the point guard in basketball). Ask why the positions are assigned. What are some of the responsibilities of other team positions students like? After identifying several examples, note that well-functioning work-and-learn teams also benefit from roles. As an illustration, randomly assign students to groups of three. Target the roles of task guide, recorder, and timekeeper. Assign a fun task, such as making a list of favorite singers or songs whose last names begin with the same letter. Brainstorm with the class what the job responsibilities are for each of the roles assigned. Give a time limit. When the task is done, ask the task guide to report on the team's list, saying how many names were found and giving two examples. When this task is done, ask random students to describe the job they held and how they performed. Finally, summarize the value of roles in a team, and plan to use roles in future tasks.

Strategy Two: Awaken Knowledge of Teamwork

Before they arrived at your classroom door, it is likely that most of your students experienced some aspect of collaboration through sports, work, or another class. You can awaken this prior knowledge by conducting a fifteen-minute mini-activity in the first week of class that focuses on what students already know about collaboration. You can use such prior knowledge tactics as the KWL, the parachute, or the question web (available online at **go.solution-tree.com/instruction**).

Start by choosing one or more collaborative tactics to make your high expectations visible to build a community of active learners. Select the tactics that are most age appropriate for your students, and adapt them as you see fit.

- **Interviews/slideshows:** Divide the class into three teams in three corners of the room with the labels collaborative, competitive, and individual. Each of the three teams will divide into subgroups of three. Define each of the three words for the groups:

    1. *Collaborative*—All members of the team work together for a single goal.
    2. *Competitive*—Everyone has the same goal. Each person has a goal that he or she can obtain only by outperforming the other individuals in order to get to the goal first.
    3. *Individualistic*—Each person has his or her own goal.

    Each subgroup will make up five questions to ask three persons outside the classroom about the major word assigned to their team: *collaborative*, *competitive*, or *individualistic.*

    Questions may not be a search for facts. They must solicit opinions that will either justify this way of learning or explain why it should not be used in the classroom. After teams have gathered information from their targeted interviewees, the members will combine their responses and then create a visual representation of the responses using a slideshow to create a presentation. Each team will have five minutes to make its presentation and explain its answers to another team. All members of the team must participate in the team's explanation.

- **A team-building blog:** As soon as all students are seated on the first day of class, welcome them and tell them that the first order of business will be a team-building activity. Explain its purpose (working together), and then begin immediately. When the activity is finished, connect what they learned and did in the activity with your learning community goal.

Team-Building Activity

Purpose: To introduce students to a start-up tactic for building collaboration in a learning community

Materials Needed: Computer access for each team, blogs, Twitter

Appropriate Age: Middle and secondary

Approximate Time: One class period

Products: Blog entries, Twitter statements (tweets)

How to Proceed:

1. Match students in pairs with a computer terminal.
2. Ask students if they have ever played or studied in a team. Seek multiple responses as they identify what they were doing on that team and how the coaches or teachers promoted teamwork.
3. Explain the purpose of this activity and how it will proceed ("to work together").
4. Instruct the pairs to introduce themselves and share why they think teamwork is or is not important.
5. Show the students how to post their ideas on the classroom blog. Review your guidelines for proper entries.
6. When teams have completed their discussions, have the students take turns filling in the blog.
7. When the entries are complete, invite each team to review the entries. Afterward, show them how to make a tweet that completes the sentence "Teamwork helps when . . ." in less than 140 words.
8. If time allows, call on random groups to share their statements aloud with the class.

These strategies and tactics will help you introduce your students to the values and skills inherent in your expectation that they learn together and form a community of support. Select those tactics that fit into your vision of a learning community and allow time in the first two weeks of school to set your plans in motion. Although it may seem like you are eating up valuable instruction time by taking time to make your community expectations concrete, you will find that it was time worth taking as your students become more and more skilled at working together in an atmosphere where teamwork is the byword and collaborative tools are the bonus.

Stage Two: Structure Long-Term Collaboration

The Goal—To develop the skill of collaboration among your students in order to ensure a higher degree of success of your project-based learning experiences

Timeline—The first two months of the school year

This stage has two strategies: cooperative learning teams and work spaces for collaboration.

Strategy One: Collaborative Learning Teams

After introducing students to your expectations in stage one, structure informal and formal groups. And to assure that your student teams develop and work effectively together, take the time early in the school year to introduce and assess the early development stages of cooperative and collaborative learning. As students proceed in your projects, you can determine which tactics most suit your students and which you could develop further for establishing a highly functioning classroom learning community.

Informal Collaborative Groups

An informal pairing of students is the easiest way to stimulate collaboration. It requires a minimum amount of classroom management and matches easily with most collaborative e-tools. An informal pairing simply requires you to match each student with a partner and give the task instructions. By providing a single goal that the pair must work together to complete, you initiate the essence of teamwork. Choose your selection of informal cooperation tactics from the following examples. Use each as often as you like so that students become automatically familiar with the procedures (visit **go.solution-tree.com/instruction** to find additional tactics online).

- **Turn-to-a-partner:** Ask a thought-provoking question about an e-task (such as "Explain why you think . . ." or "What do you think might happen if . . ."). Have student pairs at their computer stations engage students at adjacent stations.
- **Think-pair-share:** Ask each student to think about a response to a question you pose on the blog. Use silent wait time to allow for ample individual reflection. Instruct the students to describe answers with a partner before making their entry. When the entries are finished, ask each pair to make a summary entry on the blog: "What makes the most sense from these ideas is . . ."

Formal Collaborative Groups

Prior to the start of your first project and after you have observed students working together easily with your informal collaborative tasks, introduce the first formal workgroups. The formal groups have the following characteristics:

- An explicitly stated common academic goal is articulated and shared by a heterogeneous group of three or more—"Learn how to make a blog entry," "Understand the difference between Internet and extranet," or "Complete three word problems."
- A checklist like the following encourages team members to assess their own collaborative social skills—

☐ Listened to each other	☐ Made contribution
☐ Helped each other	☐ Asked clarifying question
☐ Did own job	☐ Took turns

- Each group member is assigned his or her roles and responsibilities. These include a reader, who will read the assigned material aloud to the group; a recorder, who will take notes on the discussion; a timekeeper, who will keep the group on task within the time limits; and a scribe, who will make entries on the computer.
- A challenge is given for the group to work together to produce a single product.
- An assessment of the group's collaborative process is entered into a team assessment e-file folder. Here are some sample e-file assessment questions—
    - ☐ "What did our team do well today?"
    - ☐ "How could we improve our teamwork?"
    - ☐ "What help do we need?"

Prior to the start of a learning task, divide the class into heterogeneous groups of three. You may make the selections on the basis of ability differences, gender differences, talent differences, or other differences. Whatever criteria you use, each formal group should have a mix of those differences.

To make the mix, start with your class list. Work out the best mix according to your criteria that will work with the students you have. Use a spreadsheet to mark who is in which group, assign roles in the group, and leave columns for test scores, quizzes, and so on. Give each group a color so that you can mark their work location.

For the first mix, it will help if you rearrange the chairs in groups of three at each station before the students come into the class. Place index cards with students' names at each station.

Strategy Two: Work Spaces for Collaboration

Most American schools look like boxes piled on boxes. They reflect the work model of the late 19th-century factory plan. Walk down a hallway in the typical high school, and you are walled in by banks of lockers interspersed with classroom doors. Enter the door, and you most likely see the same arrangement that visitors seventy years ago saw—five or six rows of chair-desks headed by a teacher's desk in the front and chalkboards on two or three sides. These square classrooms are configured for frontal instruction with teachers talking to or occasionally questioning the students.

For a brief spell in the 1960s and 1970s, innovative teachers and principals tried to break down the school walls with open spaces, adding tables and chairs or placing chairs in a circle.

In the late 1970s, alternative schools entered the scene. Some were set up in church basements or storefronts. Others were schools-within-a school occupying several classrooms or a large study hall. At New Trier East's Center for Self-Directed Learning in Winnetka, Illinois, the school-within-a-school occupied a first-floor study hall and two adjacent classrooms. The five faculty members and 125 upper grade students designed the space to facilitate multiple types of teacher–student and student–student interactions.

One center classroom was subdivided into six workspaces by portable dividers. These work areas were reserved by study and lab groups to complete projects and hold small group discussions. The second classroom was saved for "noisy activity" such as musical instrument practices, play rehearsals, debates, and other activities whose volume might distract others. The large room was multipurpose. Once a week, when the entire community met, students rolled back the movable dividers so all could sit or stand in a giant circle. The community also used this semi-open space when project presentations were made to large groups of guests, including parents. When this open space was broken into small sections, students and teachers conferred, worked on projects in pairs or trios, planned experiments, tutored, or conducted conferences. Sometimes, a student sat alone reading or studying. Against the back wall, the five faculty members maintained office spaces where they conferenced with students and parents, reviewed student work, or maintained required records.

The center's flexible workspace was not unique among the alternative programs. The new space arrangements allowed for the comings and goings of students to their off-campus apprenticeships, internships, or group projects with local artists, scientists, doctors, florists, and craftspeople. Because the center was constructing a community of learners, the once-a-month community meeting gathered the students to discuss and make community decisions, to talk with guest experts, to interact about critical social issues of the day, and to network with their peers.

Students met weekly in groups of twelve to fifteen with their teacher-advisors to review academic progress, get alternate input about their field projects, interact with their support group members, and socialize.

Alternative schools that pursued more diverse, personal, and individualized learning experiences while attempting to build a community of learners emerged across North America. Secondary schools across the continent attempted to break the mold. Although a few survived into the 21st century, most gave way to the pressures of measurable accountability and other Tayloresque beliefs that returned under the Reagan administration.

In the late 1990s, after departments of education first allowed charter schools to set aside many mandates, a new school model emerged. High Tech High School, a private charter in San Diego (and now in other locations), was one such model. It was created to reflect the high-tech work environment with large open spaces, small private spaces, expansive display walls, the latest in collaborative technology tools, and other features that promote interdisciplinary, differentiated, and collaborative work. In this environment, students are learning as they will be working in the future. They, and their teachers, must learn how to adjust to a life without thirty seats in five rows (sometimes still bolted to the floor), a teacher lecturing in front of the room, bells sounding every fifty-three minutes, and the quiet noise of snores.

Not all communities have the resources or the opportunity to develop such a high-tech environment. The lack of an expansive and expensive physical environment such as that found in the growing number of High Tech schools may hinder 21st century learning in an ideal space, but this shortfall cannot be an excuse for failing to build collaborative work teams or a more collaborative learning community. When teachers restructure their traditional classrooms so they may build learning communities, they are well on their way to creating an enriched learning environment that facilitates learning by the enriched learning project model of instruction.

To make space for collaborative teams in a classroom learning community, use a collaborative classroom floor plan as shown in figure 7.3.

If you are a teacher who is limited by the box design of your school and its squared classrooms, there are several considerations that will help you adjust your classrooms in preparation for community building "inside the box."

- If you are in a science lab, decide on groups of three or four based on the lab stations' arrangement. At each position on the lab table, use four colors of tape to indicate role stations. Set up a computer station at each table with at least one computer and one printer. To build your class into a community, change group membership after each major experiment.

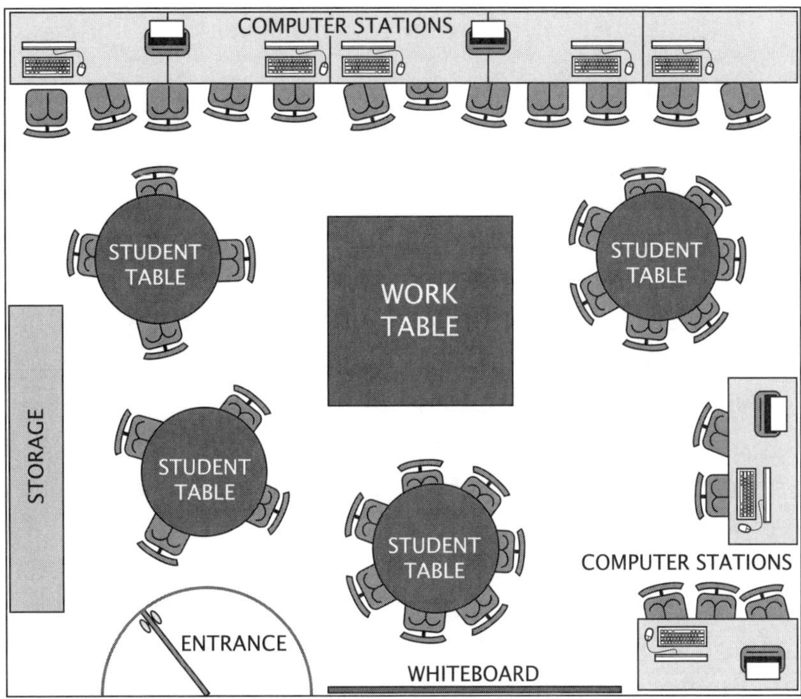

Figure 7.3: Sample collaborative classroom floor plan.

- If you are in a regular classroom, arrange your desks into groups of three around a U.
- If your class doesn't divide into an even number of threes, form two groups of four to go with the trios. If you are forced to return desks to specific spots at the end of the period, post a map and assign students the desk-moving tasks at the start and end of the period. When possible, set up printer stations on the perimeter so that those stations don't have to move.
- If you don't have your own classroom and must move each period, organize your computer equipment on one or two carts. Each week assign different students to move the carts with you.
- If your students' families can afford to buy a laptop, encourage it. Find local businesses to fund printers and help with the higher expenses of high-speed Internet service. Push for wireless.

Your primary responsibility is to enable students to master the academic content of your course. Learning strategies and collaborative e-tools can help students meet your academic goals more efficiently. Once you have prepared students with the "how to" work in task groups with e-tools, you are ready to move your instruction forward into the third stage.

Stage Three: Differentiate Instruction

The Goal—To use a variety of goal structures and strategies to differentiate instruction to fit individual needs, styles, and pace of learning while continuing to maintain a bonded community in which individuals respect and support differences

Timelines—Two to five weeks

When organizing a class for enriched learning projects, you have several recipes that will help you differentiate instruction as you build community. When you mix formal groups whose membership you rotate for each project, informal collaborative learning tasks, and e-tools that allow teams to decide who does what in the assignment, you help students develop the trust as well as the problem-solving, decision-making, and learning skills that build the teams and the entire community. At the same time that you are building the community, you want to allow students oportunities to work alone, to work in homogenous groups by interest, talent, or motivation, or to work in mixed-ability groups. Here are three possible strategies for differentiating at the same time as you are strengthening the learning community: jigsaw, role differentiation, and email multilevel questions.

Strategy One: Jigsaw

All teams work on a single project with each team being given one part to work on. As if it were a jigsaw puzzle, the teacher divides up the parts of the assignment. Each team completes one part. Each group then reports on its part, and the jigsaw is put back together, so that all the parts give a complete picture. To heighten differentiation, further split each team's task into pieces, one per student.

Again, in research you may assign one article per student per group. When all are finished with their research tasks, the group puts the jigsaw together. If each group has a different set of articles to read, the task of reading five to ten articles may take only one class period. If you have carefully laid out the format for reporting on what was read, the assembly task will take no more than a second class period. By any count, that is a lot of research in two hours!

When dividing tasks among teams and individuals, take note of students' reading levels, their interest in the topic, and the level of sophistication of the materials. You may set up teams that are alike in ability or motivation and distribute the assignments accordingly. When jigsawing, many teachers think only of reading tasks, but it is easy to jigsaw lab experiments, blog newsletters, roles in a group, and so on. Examples of jigsawed groups include the following:

- **Lab jigsaw**—Group A: the skeleton; group B: the organs; group C: the soft tissue

- **Blog newsletter**—Group A: the editorial; group B: cartoons; group C: ads
- **Different e-products**—Group A: shareware; group B: web page; group C: graphics

Here are some examples of roles in a jigsawed group:

- **Making-a-product roles**—designer, digital picture maker, layout
- **Presentation roles**—emcee, explainer, question responder
- **Product exhibition roles**—brochure, booth design, video display

The jigsaw tactic takes many forms. Whatever form it takes, it is important that the teacher structure the jigsaw so that students do their differentiated tasks in alignment with the team goal. Using the common launch question to start a project provides each individual with a focal point.

Strategy Two: Role Differentiation Within Each Team

When there is a clear difference among students in reading or mathematical ability, assign roles to match. For instance, assign the strongest reader the task in a group to read the material. Assign a second student to manage the materials. Pick a third to record answers to the questions or to report the group's results to the class.

Using Launch Questions

1. **How can we best protect the most endangered animal species in our state?**

   Differentiated Team Assignments: Each team selects one species to research per the research template. Each team also selects its presentation media. The entire class uses a graphic to answer the launch question with a vote.

   Benefits: A small-team effort is achieved, while all teams also contribute to the final class decision. Differentiation occurs because each team selected its own medium.

   Shared Question: Each team works on its response to the same launch question and makes its own final product.

2. **What is a novel?**

   Differentiated Team Assignments: Each team prepares a research report that defines the term *novel* and distinguishes the novel from other literary genres. Each individual may select one novel from the required list. Teams work together on a multimedia presentation to be networked to the class.

   Benefits: Similar launch questions enable students to compare responses.

   Shared Question: Each team uses the same question with a different novel.

continued →

3. **What are the ways we can depict the ravages of the Vietnam War on the different societies involved?**

   Differentiated Team Assignments: Form groups of three. Start with a jigsaw of readings on the Internet about countries that were affected by this war. Provide the groups with lists of sites about the war that have articles, streamed video, and audio of different levels of difficulty. Allow students to self-select the specific "ravages" they want to research. They will each use their own research results to help the team form its conclusions in response to the question.

   After the teams have finished their research and assembled their ideas, let each team select its online or offline presentation method. Each person on a team must contribute to the preparation and participate in the presentation. Each team will decide the appropriate roles for its members, based on members' talents and interests.

   Benefits: Differentiation within the team occurs, with a final product made by all team members. Everyone in class discusses different ways to depict the answer with various e-tools.

   Shared Question: Each team uses the same question with different information from diverse sources.

Strategy Three: Email Multilevel Questions

Assign all group reading material from their text or other resources you provide (such as a poem, a news article, or a speech). After reviewing the roles, rules, and other procedures, use your projector or whiteboard to show three questions: a factual question, a comparison question, and a predictive question for the content they read.

1. **Factual:** Who stabbed Caesar?
2. **Comparative:** How were Caesar and Brutus alike?
3. **Predictive:** What would happen if someone murdered a U.S. senator?

Instruct the team members to divide and answer the questions. When finished, ask the group to agree on an answer for each question. They can then send their responses to you via email or use a whiteboard.

The heart of differentiated instruction is the group arrangements that you make. The mix of choices like those above allows you to take advantage of the research that supports heterogeneously mixed groups to promote the highest achievement by all in the group. Within the group, you can differentiate tasks by using different tactics and content for each student. You can also add homogeneous groups that have a shared goal but different tasks. Here is one sample of a tactic for informal collaborative learning that demonstrates the integration of informal or formal task groups into all projects.

Tactic for Integration of Task Groups

Title: Cell Division

Date: October 12 **Class Periods:** One

Selected Tactic: Turn to a Partner

What I Want to Happen: On a daily basis, I want students to talk with each other to summarize key points in our discussion of photosynthesis. Each day they will work with a different partner who sits nearby.

Materials Needed: Students' notes

Allotted Time: Three minutes, once per class period

Student Products: Verbal summaries of key points in the discussion

How Will I Know It Is Working? I will make random checks after each time they talk. I will call on different students to share their partner's points.

Notes: I had to back up and show the students how to make a summary. That took a little longer. I think I will start the next time just with an "I learned" or "One key point today was" stem. 10/13

The summaries are improving. I hear more examples related to a key point. I am thinking of moving to a write-pair-share with this class. I feel ready to start my other classes, but this time I will wait on the summary and just do a think-pair-share with a stem starter. 10/16

Stage Four: Sustain Collaboration

The Goal—To enable students to become self directed in their use of collaborative learning to maintain the classroom's collaborative culture

Timeline—Through the school year

With care, you can sustain collaboration through the school year if you integrate e-tools into every project. You can advance the collaboration by increasing the challenge level of the e-tools students must use. For instance, with the first project of the year, you may ask student pairs to email their summary responses to the launch question to another pair for feedback. In a later project, you may ask the pairs to set up a blog so they can share the summaries with all other teams and the teams can provide feedback. In a like manner, you can increase the challenge level of media presentations moving from simple shareware presentations to audio and video streaming or podcasts. As a result, you will increase the collaborations by level of difficulty, the numbers of students involved, and the development of new skills with new e-tools.

You can also sustain the collaboration by being careful to have students, individually and in teams, review the skills they are developing in your classroom. At the start of each project, review students' prior experiences with collaborative guidelines and team roles. Interject a quick checkup each week that reminds students to assess the quality of their work together. You can make these three-minute checkups online by instructing students to respond in their e-journals with a tweet statement (using the 140 character limit) the creation of a banner ad, or a simple role checklist.

Perhaps, once per quarter, you can make the time for a team-building task that will advance the trust and cohesion in your learning community. If you use your browser to call up teamwork or team performance, you will find Internet sites that provide tips, tactics, and techniques for strengthening your teams. Mind Tools (www.mindtools.com) is a free site that will show you how to develop team roles, manage time, create balanced teams, and use a variety of team building skills. Wilderdom (www.wilderdom.com) provides a comprehensive list of engaging motivational tasks for team building and problem solving used in the business world. All are adaptable to your classroom and usable in less than one class period.

As you work to sustain the collaborative community through the school year, follow these practices on a weekly basis.

1. Continue use of the collaborative learning tactics that students learned in the earlier stages. Use informal and formal learning groups with opportunities for differentiation.
2. Give feedback on students' growing self direction in use of learning tactics and development of collaborative skills.
3. Use journals with stems, a plus-minus-interesting chart (PMI), and other organizers for peer-peer feedback, self-assessment and teacher-student feedback on contributions to the classroom culture

Stage Five: Assess Collaboration

The Goal—To evaluate the quality of student performance as member-contributors to the continual collaborative culture

Timeline—One day at the end of each marking period

How well students work together in your classroom and contribute to the development of collaborative effort is important for you to assess. As with the assessment of content mastery and critical thinking, your formative and summative assessment of collaboration will benefit your students' performance and the cohesion of your classroom learning community. These guidelines will remind you to assess collaboration.

Start by sharing a rubric with the students. Post it online or on the classroom wall. You can build a strong rubric with Johnson and Johnson's heavily researched attributes for cooperative activities. These five attributes can guide all interactions in your projects, with and without technology (Johnson & Johnson, 1983).

1. Positive interdependence is fostered by each interaction between two or more persons (including you!). Learning is primarily in small, face-to-face arrangements. Whenever possible, large community meetings also foster face-to-face talk. Have students sit at computer stations so they can dialogue face to face as well as computer to computer.
2. Individual accountability is emphasized. You have a way of checking each student's responsibilities in a team including roles, project goal tasks, and interactions.
3. Social skills, specifically interpersonal skills, are developed by students.
4. Group processing is cultivated because the project allows time and enables students to assess their own team development. Schedule activities using research validation tactics to assess students' cooperative and collaborative performance. Using blogs, have students complete a weekly self-assessment with stems or open-ended questions (see page 162, for example). You may construct a checklist with one or more of the attributes from our rubric (pages 35–37 and online at **go.solution-tree.com/instruction**). Send these by email to students at scattered times.
5. Walk about the classroom when students are working on their projects. Use note cards containing a short checklist to record your observations.

At the end of a project or a quarter, use the rubric to structure a more complete assessment. Ask students to self-assess and assess their peers' collaboration in the project work teams. Use the data you have collected during the project to make your final assessment. Tactics can include checklists and rubrics that focus on a student's individual performance as a contributing member of the culture. Provide the students with your assessment in a conference or online. Highlight your recommendations for improvement.

Have the students do a think-pair-share classroom assessment culminating in a concept map that shows individual contributions to the classroom culture. Using a rubric based on the five attributes of cooperative learning, individuals should assess the classroom climate before proceeding to a pair-discussion and the final scoring of the rubric by class consensus.

Summary

The 21st century skills framework calls for students to develop collaboration skills. Some suggest that the best way is to give students the e-tools that promote collaboration and let the students work together with no interference from you. Such an idealistic approach, advocated by educators who consider themselves pure constructivists, does not always work, especially in classrooms that are on pressurized curriculum schedules. On the surface, this approach suggests that students will do this naturally without any mediation by you. All students will have to do is develop their collaboration abilities for using e-tools. In practice, your mediation of the collaborative skills will speed the development of these skills in the teams. As you facilitate the development of a community with a common goal, you will see how guided work in small teams will advance students' communication skills and achievement.

However beneficial the use of e-tools may be for developing collaboration, they will be insufficient for advancing the quality of interpersonal communication skills students will require to stand out in their future jobs. For this, you must add the intentional development and mediation of their abilities to talk face to face and through technology, so they are highly effective with their interpersonal communications.

When you purposefully help students develop collaborative learning skills, you not only help them improve their interpersonal skills, but you also help teams accomplish project tasks more effectively and raise each student's achievement level. At your beck and call, you have learning strategies with which you can enrich students' learning from working together on a project and build a strong, supportive learning community. Together, these strategies, tactics, and structures increase the chances of your students' success. You will be preparing them for a work world that has changed dramatically since the end of the 20th century.

Creating Your Tactical Plan for Collaborative Learning

Title:
Date:
Class Periods:
Selected Tactic:
Informal Tactic:
Formal Tactic:
What I Want to Happen:
Materials Needed:
Allotted Time:
Student Products:
How Will I Know the Plan Is Working?
Notes:

Chapter 8

Assessing Enriched Projects

"Nothin'!"

—An anonymous student,
asked what he learned that day

The purpose of this chapter is to illustrate how to make students responsible for the assessment of project-based learning. Assessment is a dual process. First, standards are a guiding light to help students assess their enriched learning in a project. Second, using this light, students decide what will improve their performance. The person most responsible for a learning assessment is the student. The teacher's job is to provide constructive and expert feedback so that students can see and decide about making improvements. In this chapter, you will review the rationale and methods for facilitating assessments that enrich students' learning experiences in a project.

I Had to Figure It Out

"Hi, Anna," Mary Jo greeted her daughter as she had done every day since Anna entered preschool fourteen years prior. "What did you learn today?"

"I don't know," mumbled Anna as she opened the refrigerator door.

"You don't know?" Her mother smiled. "Another day as a zombie, I guess!"

"There's nothing to eat in here," Anna grumbled.

"Well, zombies never get hungry."

"Moooom . . . you're not funny," complained the teenager.

"So what did you do in social studies today?" Mary Jo asked. "That's still your favorite subject, isn't it?"

"We wrote in our journals about our projects," Anna said, pulling a bottle of water out.

"I bet Mr. Wilson asked you to tell what you learned . . . like he always does."

Anna sighed as she unscrewed the bottle cap. "Yeah."

"Anything not a secret?" her mother asked.

continued →

"No. I had to write a summary about the research I was doing on John Adams. Me and Mindy are going to write his biography."

"That sounds interesting."

"It is . . . kinda. Did you know he hated being vice president?"

"No, I didn't," Mary Jo responded with serious attention. "Why?"

Anna perked up. "He said it was a useless job. He didn't have anything to do."

"Really?" her mother asked. "How did you find that out?"

"We have to read some original documents in our project. I read some of his letters."

"Did he just come out and say that he hated the job."

"No way," Anna said. "I had to figure it out from a lot of things he was saying."

"Sounds like you really did a lot of learning today."

"I guess." Anna sighed again.

Who Is Responsible?

Many students fail to assume responsibility for their own learning, especially if their classroom experiences have been limited to the "pour and store" method of teaching. Many students believe grades are something that teachers give out. Some students see learning, evaluating, and how they receive a grade as something that is done to them. This sense of "not my responsibility" leads to a habit of coming home each day and answering "nothin'" to the parental inquiry, "What did you learn today?"

Projects give you an opportunity to shift the primary responsibility for learning and its assessment onto the students' shoulders. Although not a quick and easy task, this shift is possible and desirable. Making the shift so that students take the lead in assessing what and how they are learning enables you to enrich their learning.

It is important to note, at this point, the distinction between assessing and grading. *Assessing* is the process of making judgments about how well a student understands a concept or developing a skill and providing instructive feedback that will instigate improvement. *Grading* is the process of assigning a number or letter that indicates a judgment about how well a student has learned a concept or mastered a skill. Many minds, starting with the students', can participate in assessment; grades are the teacher's obligation.

Classroom practices often obscure this distinction and lead to students' mistaken belief that both processes are your obligation. The heavy emphasis on teacher accountability for implementation of the standards and the failure of many educators to distinguish grading from assessing are two of the factors that lead to this confusion in students' minds.

A well-designed enriched learning project can help eliminate this confusion. As a result, students can better understand that the process of assessment begins with them, not with you. You can inform your students about what progress they are making toward the project content goals, use of e-tool and thinking skills, or collaboration.

For students to develop self-direction, it is important that you enrich their learning know-how by teaching them how to weigh the information you supply and what they are going to do as a result of their judgments. It is equally important that you help students learn how to assess their own performance, as well as to gather assessment data from their project partners.

As part of your role in helping students learn more effectively from project tasks, you can select assessment tactics that will help students move from passive acceptance of your feedback to active generation of their own learning. The first mark of the active generator is the students' willingness to accept feedback from you and others about what will improve their learning.

The most practical assessment tactics for your role as assessment facilitator are those that invite students to reflect about the content they are learning, the thinking that they are doing, and the ways they are collaborating. In the 21st century classroom, students do not have to have special lessons or courses to develop their assessment skills. Your projects can be their learning lab.

When your assessment tactics engage your students in reflection and help them better grasp the meaning of their enriched study, it is more likely that they will hold themselves to higher standards of personal accountability. This accountability will grow to include learning the required content (which may sometimes not interest them, but is mandated by your state's standards) and developing the cooperative and critical thinking skills they will need in the 21st century advanced learning and work worlds.

Depending on the meaning you highlight for students to take from a project, their answers to your tactics will reinforce the understanding that their learning is the raison d'être for the project. Whenever you provide a formative rubric, guide, or checklist prior to starting the project or during the project, you reinforce their understanding that the most important reason for doing projects is to learn.

The enriched learning project model of instruction provides you with a wide range of opportunities to integrate assessment tactics into daily and weekly schedules. With your guidance, students can assess their daily learning experiences in all three dimensions: content mastery, critical thinking, and collaboration. An especially effective tool for enabling self-assessment is the completion of stem statements in journals, such as "Today, I learned . . ." "Today, I fostered my ability to challenge assumptions when . . ." or "Today, I used my conflict-management skill to . . ."

Occasionally, in order to encourage collaborative cohesion, you can call on students to share their journal entries either with their teams or the entire class. At the end of the project, you can also invite students to create a one-page summary of their self-assessments or include those assessments with the other feedback from you and their peers. The following journal entries demonstrate how students can use the three Cs of assessment:

- Content mastery—"*What did I learn?*" "John F. Kennedy and Abraham Lincoln were assassinated. There were many similarities in the reasons for each murder; there were also many differences. . . ."
- Critical thinking—"*How did I use my critical thinking in learning this information?*" "I needed to see similarities and differences in several dimensions: the events, the people involved, the political agenda.
- Collaboration—"*What did collaboration do to expand my learning?*" "Our team used a jigsaw for gathering the information. We agreed on what each of us would look for as we read. I worked alone to find out about the social context. The jigsaw saved us time, but also helped us gather more information to consider. . . ."

Aligning Assessment With Standards

In the current educational climate, you can never ignore the presence of the standards or the pressure they exert. However, any given course of study is likely to have more content standards than you can teach well. This is true even of the Common Core standards being developed by the National Governors Association and the Council of Chief of State School Officers (Common Core State Standards Initiative, n.d.). If you follow a "less is more" guideline, you may find it more helpful to select those content standards that you deem most important for the project at hand. (If it is an interdisciplinary project, include all the relevant subject-area standards.) One practical way to select the most appropriate standards for your project is to identify what concepts most often appear on the state's standardized tests for your subject. Another is to identify your students' learning needs (that is, which concepts have given your students the most difficulty in past years). A third way is to begin with your students' pronounced interests and match these with the content standards. A fourth is to select those standards that attach a 21st century thinking process to the content.

Selecting Appropriate Standards

Content Area: Algebra

Identify Most Common Concepts Tested: Fractions, integers, rational and irrational numbers, value

Identify Students' Learning Needs: Irrational numbers and integers

Identify Students' Interests: Tips and discounts

Identify Thinking Attachment: Estimate, distinguish, compare

Many who advocate for learning projects argue that students' interests are the best starting point. Yes, it is likely that their interests will provide the best chance for starting the project with high student motivation. However, until standards change and are aligned with student interests, using their interests is not always in their best interest (no pun intended!). In an essential skill such as algebra, it may be easier for a teacher to design the project to ensure that the learning needs and tested concepts for this topic, such as integers or place value, are included. However, when this is not the case, you may have to design a project that is built around what your students need to learn for the test in a format that builds their interest.

In whatever way you select the content standards around which you will build a project, the standards are only the starting point for your assessment. Consider the eighth-grade math standard from Pennsylvania with its detailed benchmarks (see also www.pde.state.pa.us for ten additional standards for grade 10, each equally detailed):

> Pennsylvania's public schools shall teach, challenge, and support every student to realize his or her maximum potential and to acquire the knowledge and skills needed to:
>
> A. Complete calculations by applying the order of operations.
> B. Add, subtract, multiply, and divide different kinds and forms of rational numbers including integers, decimal fractions, percents, and proper and improper fractions.
> C. Estimate the value of irrational numbers.
> D. Estimate amount of tips and discounts using ratios, proportions, and percents.
> E. Determine the appropriateness of overestimating or underestimating in computation.
> F. Identify the difference between exact value and approximation and determine which is appropriate for a given situation. (Pennsylvania Department of Education, n.d.)

To give priority to this standard, teachers at an urban high school surveyed the tenth-grade math test data. This data indicated the difficulty the current tenth graders were having with estimation (C, D, E). The data confirmed their prior experiences with previous classes. After a one-week unit review of the order of operations (benchmark A) with applications to the various kinds and forms of rational numbers (benchmark B), the tenth-grade teachers planned a four-week project that would enable students to match successfully with the estimations benchmarks.

Applying Assessment to Projects

Many teachers, when they think of assessment, think about evaluating the content they are teaching. They want to know, "Do my students know the information?" "Do they know the materials in the three pigs' homes? "Do they know who discovered America?" "Do they know the causes of the Civil War?" "Do they know the reasons Lady Macbeth gave to her husband as justification for killing Duncan?" "Do they know why the larch doesn't keep its needles, even though it is a conifer?" This model of assessment, which judges what students do or do not know, fits well with the common understanding that learning is about gathering and recalling information—nothing more. As a result, teachers need only to measure the percentage of information recalled by each student. In the math project described earlier, it means that students will meet the standard if all the benchmarks are recall tasks on a test of knowledge.

In a project-centered classroom, the definition of learning is more complex. With projects, teachers are asking students to construct new knowledge. Thus, students not only must gather information, they must also use their thinking skills, their operating minds, to understand the information so they form their own concepts and then show, in a problem solution, an answer to a question or a new design of their own making.

When helping students construct and communicate their new understandings, project-facilitating teachers work with their students at several levels. First, they help the students complete each phase of the learning process: gathering information, making sense, and communicating the results. Second, to help the students complete these phases more effectively (so they capture the meaning of what they are studying) and more efficiently (so that each learning experience becomes richer and deeper), teachers help students develop their thinking skills. To do this in the project format, teachers facilitate thinking-skill development primarily by establishing collaborative work situations.

If assessment does truly drive instruction, then it is imperative that teachers assume an additional responsibility: the assessment of all the elements that contribute to successful project-based learning experiences. This means that teachers not only assess the information the students gather, but assess how they progress in their thinking skills as they work through each of the three critical phases, and how well they learn to collaborate and communicate with their learning team. Thus, assessment in the paradigm of project-based learning must look not only at understanding of the content and the development of content-embedded skills, but also the development of the students' thinking, problem-solving, collaboration, and communication skills.

In the project model of learning, teachers do the most help when they balance assessment of student performance to include each of the three Cs: content mastery, critical thinking, and collaboration.

The Three Cs in Assessment

In traditional instruction, you focus on one learning objective at a time in each lesson. For instance, when you want the students to learn about the food families, you start with a lesson that will enable them to identify the characteristics of a single food family, such as dairy. They will learn all the information about dairy before going on to learn about vegetables, fruits, and so on. In an enriched learning project, one of these three does not have to precede the other. You can integrate them, using content mastery, critical thinking, and collaboration to make students more effective. That is, the three Cs are not used sequentially—they are intermingled, with each helping the others. Like three tributaries flowing into a river, they combine to become a powerful flow of water.

When you combine the three Cs in a single project, you increase its power, so that students have an optimal chance to achieve highly; and you increase that power when you have students examine how well they have developed each of these elements and integrated them into a single learning experience.

When it comes time for you to assess a project, give a balanced assessment that includes all three elements. You can assess each one separately or combine them into one assessment. To start, concentrate on one item at a time, making sure that you assess all the others at some point.

Content Mastery

When assessing the content that students come to understand better as a result of their project work, you may find yourself using familiar tactics. First, you give a pretest so students and you can see their level of content knowledge and skill. As students complete ministudies in the project, use quizzes and observation checklists so you and your students can check how much new knowledge they are gaining. As the project progresses, observe with a checklist how students are faring at using new content skills (such as numerical operations or reading a compass), and listen to how well they can identify the differences identified in the targeted content standard. All of these checks for students' understanding of the content help you determine progress being made at the formative stages of learning. At the end of the project, you can then assign a test or an essay that matches a content rubric to tell you what knowledge each student has gained.

Critical Thinking

In addition to assessing the first C, content mastery, you can plan for students to assess the second C, critical thinking. Here you would focus on thinking skills such as analysis of bias or estimation, as called for in the benchmarks you selected. At the project's end, you would use a rubric to guide students in self-assessment or perhaps in a peer assessment of the product. The rubric assesses the degree of success students had in results that reflected their estimates.

Collaboration

For the third C, collaboration, shift teams would complete checklists related to how students helped each other apply the estimation skills. In addition, shift managers would evaluate each team member once per week on four collaborative criteria. See page 166 (and online at **go.solution-tree.com/instruction**) for the reproducible Shift Cooperation Checklist.

Using Assessments as Learning Guides

The most helpful project assessments encourage students to use multiple tools to complete their self-assessments and peer assessments. These assessments provide students with information about the progress they have made in understanding the core concepts they are studying and in applying thinking skills such as estimating.

The same assessments can also encourage students to think about what is most important to learn from a project. When a teacher presents assessment criteria aligned with a project's outcomes at the start of the project, the teacher increases the value and the power of the assessment process. When students are told not only the outcomes, but the criteria that will mark the quality of performance in reaching these outcomes, they find it far easier to keep focus on what is most important to learn from each of the three Cs.

In project assessments, you can secure multiple snapshots of how students are learning and engaging with their peers. You do this, as in any instructional model, when you quiz or test students' knowledge, when you ask questions and probe their responses for deeper thought, or when you watch how they interact in a team. However, because students spend more time in work teams when they are working on projects, you spend less time providing frontal information. The time you have to observe and give feedback during their project work time increases dramatically.

Although you still can gather information formally from written tests on the content, you now have increased time to walk among the students to observe, ask questions, and note responses. You may stop next to a randomly selected team and ask, "What do you understand?" You can take time for a "learning dump" assessment. In this assessment activity, enabled when students have become self-directed in their collaborative and cooperative work, you ask them to tell all they have learned about a topic, ask follow-up questions to clarify fuzzy thinking, probe for depth of understanding, and coach with corrective feedback that fills in important blanks in their grasp of the problem, issue, or topic. Then you move on to observe another team.

In addition, you have time to use checklists and action guides to help students assess their application of key concepts and development of the two other Cs, critical thinking and collaboration. As you wander around, use the prepared lists and guides to note what students are doing. You may ask probing questions that help you decide on the quality of the "doing." Most important, provide students with feedback on what you have seen and heard. Use of the guides and checklists makes it easier for you to focus students on the project's standards-based objectives. At set times, you may schedule individual or group conferences so that you can review your observations and provide the high-quality feedback that research shows is most important to student achievement (Marzano, Pickering, & Pollock, 2001; Roseth, Johnson, & Johnson, 2008).

When using a triple C project with intertwined content mastery, critical thinking, and collaboration, it is important to remember that students' level of concern—an important element for motivation—is driven by what you say you will assess. Thus, it is important for you to schedule both formative and summative assessments. To encourage self-direction, some of the mix should include students' self-assessments of each C. To encourage collaboration, include more peer-to-peer assessments. Depending on your students' need to develop one or the other of these highly valuable 21st century traits, you are the decider.

You can capture many of the assessment tools you need from online sites. With these e-tools, you can organize the assessment process so you have a system that makes it easier for your students to track their progress. When you are systematic in the way you ask students to assess their own "know and do" (for example, when you instruct students to use a tagged section of their e-journals, with dated entries and scoring rubrics), you can more easily select times and places to read and provide written feedback. For example, you can decide to read five entries sent to your blog each week and either give feedback for each student to include in his or her e-file folder or tabulate scores for grading purposes. This system also will make it easier for students to review their entries, the feedback they received from peers, and your feedback before they draw conclusions about what they have done well and what they need to improve.

You can also use criteria checklists to help students communicate to their parents what they are learning. For instance, if your project includes teaching students how to estimate, you could print out a checklist of the benchmarks, send it home with students to share with their parents, and explain what they are doing with each benchmark. In the last ten minutes of the class period, discuss with the students the examples they can share with their parents: "I am learning to estimate in math. I can do percents of . . ."

Peers can share the feedback responsibility, especially when collaboration is the issue. By providing a standardized rubric, action guide, or checklist, you can encourage students to give each other feedback based on these criteria. As they give feedback to each other, you need to stress honesty tempered by respect and mutual trust to make the feedback constructive and specific. If your students are not used to giving and receiving feedback, early in your course would be the best time to spend several class periods teaching them how. Use stems such as "I liked the way you . . ." or "It helped me when you . . ."

At times, especially when students' project work takes them outside school walls, you may want to require feedback from the other adults with whom the students are engaged. If students are working with adults in the community or completing an internship, you can ask the adults to complete written feedback related to one or more of the three Cs.

Adult Feedback on Jonas's Project

Name: Jonas Hammer **Date:** April 13

Jonas has been learning to carve a human figure out of granite. He is halfway through the project. What I like about his work is his care in sketching the figure he wants to make, the way he surveyed and marked the stone, and the care he takes with his tools. He stops and thinks about what he is doing and asks a lot of questions. He does need to be a little more adventuresome, though.

Maria Steele
876–980–9087

You, peers, and other adults provide specific feedback to students about what and how they are learning. Each day should include five minutes of feedback time. At least once per week, your schedule should allot at least ten minutes for students to review the feedback and assess its worth. Use the following three easy questions to structure their entries. Each week you can dictate which of the three Cs you prefer the students to highlight: content mastery, critical thinking, or collaboration.

- "What did I learn well this week?" (content mastery)
- "How can I improve what and how I am learning? (critical thinking)
- "What help do I need?" (collaboration)

Finally, as the teacher, you prepare the summative evaluation of each student's performance in the project. As with any other instructional model, you gather from the students the feedback information you have asked them to present. You first give the students the opportunity to analyze the data and summarize its value. It is most helpful if you give your conclusions in a written summary during an oral conference. A good time to hold these conferences occurs when the teams are preparing their final presentations.

Selecting Assessment Tools

So that you and the students don't become inundated with paper and so they receive helpful feedback during the project along with practical information for making improvements in their future enriched learning experiences, it helps to keep project assessments simple. Less is more. On the other hand, it is helpful when you build your toolbox to include a variety of strategies. The more tools you keep in that toolbox, the more likely it is that you will be able to meet individual needs in different learning situations.

First, set up your assessment system. In the students' project journals, invite them to mark off a section that will focus on achievement. Have the students keep their journals in their personal file folder online. Restrict access to yourself and the student. It is even better if the journal contains a section to hold blank assessment forms that students can easily copy and paste. Instruct students to date every entry and keep them in date sequence. If you are using the three Cs, you may ask them to use one tag for content mastery assessments, a second tag for critical thinking assessments, and a third for collaboration assessments. It is their responsibility to keep their assessments organized by these categories.

A Paper-and-Pencil System

If you use an offline system, give the students file folders or journals. The most useful pen-and-paper journals are either three-ring binders or spiral-bound notebooks that students can divide with permanent tabs. Both the binder and the spiral notebook make it possible for the student to lay the pages flat for double-page work. In addition, it is helpful if the covers have inside pockets to store index cards, charts, and so on.

Have students write their names and your name on the notebook. They may also wish to decorate the covers. If you are using study teams that will work together throughout the project, you may want to schedule a class period for students to decorate their covers as a team.

Discuss how you want students to use the journal. Invite them to tab each of the three Cs with a different color. You may want them to save a section for note taking and another for information gathering. They may want to use another section for weekly reflections and assessments. You can also use a double-entry format (students write on one side of the page, and you write on the other so that you can have a dialogue).

Rubrics

Rubrics are assessment tools that are especially helpful in evaluating projects. Rubrics are helpful in two ways: (1) they announce the terms of assessment for the project, and (2) they guide the assessment at its end. By announcing the criteria or benchmarks for the assessment, rubrics help students to more easily learn the priorities in a task or project as applied to the three Cs. For standards-aligned content, you can easily transform a standard with benchmarks into the criteria for the assessment. You may send each student a set of the rubrics at the start of the project in a slideshow using a spreadsheet for them to save in their project folders.

To use downloadable rubrics, templates, and tutorials, browse the teaching and learning services section for the University of New Castle (Australia) and find the "Rubric Templates for Student Assessment" (www.newcastle.edu.au). If you are knowledgeable about what a rubric is, why they are important, and how to use one, you can jump to "A Rubric for Rubrics" and the checklist "Before You Use Your Rubric." The key steps section will provide you with what you need to know for creating your rubrics. The exemplary column makes very clear the criteria that mark a rubric for the most enriching project learning experience. Another helpful site is located at www.rubystar.com. You can explore this site to select from a multitude of options that fit the subjects, types, and grade levels that will most help you.

Checklists

Checklists provide lists of tasks or procedures needed to complete a task or develop a skill. Checklists serve a double function. First, they guide you and the students in remembering the procedures or important points that a task involves. Second, you and the students can review a checklist to determine what has been done or not done in a project task.

Feedback Cards

Using index cards or emails, provide students with feedback related to the project goals. Make feedback constructive and specific. Ask students to keep these in their journal pockets so you can review them later. You can also ask students on teams to give feedback to teammates.

Teacher Feedback on Stanley's Project

Name: Stanley Paulson

Date: November 5, 2008

Topic: Estimating Coins

Stanley: When I was listening to you make estimates on the amount of change needed each day, I was pleased to hear how specific you were in determining each type of coin you wanted. I was also pleased to hear how you checked to make sure each team member understood what you were saying. I have one suggestion: use more than one mode; that is, explain in both percentages and dollar amounts.

Self-Reflections

At least once per week, allow time for students to complete assessment reflections in their journals. Use stems or probes to help students start their reflections. It also helps if the reflections tie to project, team, or individual student goals. By alternating the probes pointed to content mastery goals, critical thinking goals, or collaboration goals, you make it easier for students to get started with the writing.

If time allows on the day that you ask for the self-reflections, you may ask a random selection of students (different each week) to share their reflections without feedback or commentary from anyone. At the end of the writing or the sharing, you can tell students what the focus of the next self-reflection will be. At the end of a project, you may ask students to select one of their personal goals and summarize their attainment in a paragraph or two. For instance, students may include critical thinking and impulse control as goals:

> October 12
>
> Will I ever slow down? This past four weeks, I have tried. I did it by stopping to think about what I wanted to accomplish in my role as shift manager. I gave myself weekly goals and I wrote out my weekly strategy. I also talked to my team so they could remind me when I was pressing. Every Thursday, I reviewed how I did and gave myself a grade. I ended up with a B-. I guess I am slowing down, but I could do more.

Quizzes and Tests

For each of the benchmarks, you can check student knowledge with a quiz. At the end of the project, your best assessment of knowledge will come from a summary test.

Sample Summary Test

Name: ________________________________ **Date:** ______________

What is the total amount of change you have for each of the following:

1. 1 nickel, 2 dimes, 1 quarter, and 3 pennies ________
2. .05, .40, .50, .13 ________
3. 6 pennies, 5 quarters, 4 dimes, 2 nickels, and a dollar bill ________
4. How much change is due to a person who gives you a two-dollar bill for a charge of $1.38? ________

continued →

5. Express this in the types/amount of coins: ____ pennies ____ dimes ____ quarters
6. If you don't have any dimes, how many nickels will you give in change? _________
7. If you don't have any quarters, how many nickels will you give in change? _________
8. If the price of the coffee is $15.98 per bag, how much will two bags cost? _________
9. If the customer gives you two twenty-dollar bills, how much change will be due when the tax is $1.20 per bag? _________
10. If the customer wants you to give the change from the coffee purchase to his two children in equal amounts, how much change will you give each child? _________

Essays

Formal, multiple-paragraph expository essays are an often-overlooked tool for assessing student learning of content, development of critical thinking skills, or increased ability to collaborate. By making the due date the first Monday of the project's final week, you give students ample time to prepare an essay. You also give yourself ample time to review what they have written and, if time allows, discuss what they have learned. Ultimately, it gives you another product to use to assess what they have learned in one of the three C domains, combined with a rubric that focuses on the content with a strong introduction, a detailed middle, and a summary conclusion. You may use emails to send the feedback to students for inclusion in their file folders or e-portfolios.

Sample Essay Questions for the Three Cs

Content Mastery:

- Explain why it is important to know how to give change.
- Identify three forms of rational numbers, and give examples of each.
- Tell your parents the differences between rational and irrational numbers with examples.
- Distinguish between exact value and approximation, and describe the advantages of each for a person giving change to a customer in a story.

Critical Thinking:

- Define the term *estimation,* and give three examples of appropriate use.
- Summarize the various ways that you have made estimates in and out of the classroom this month.
- Evaluate your ability to make estimates when calculating distance.

Collaboration:

- Summarize what you have learned about being a team member in a study group, and apply that learning to one out-of-school situation.
- Predict what would happen to you in and out of this classroom if you used your collaborative skills well.
- Explain the value of collaboration in the work world.

Blogs

As indicated, e-journals, or blogs, are one of the easiest ways to organize assessments in a project. Each week, you can make assignments for journal entries—what you want the students to enter as well as how, why, and when. A systematic plan for making entries, reviewing those entries, and grading the entries will simplify your assessment process.

A major function of a project journal is to help students reflect on what and how they are learning. In addition, a journal is a tool that helps students gather important information by taking notes, completing graphic organizers, or making sketches. In this way, you can align students' reflections on what and how they are learning with the standards you have selected.

When you and your students have classroom, school lab, or home computer access, you can use e-journals, also known as blogs, in place of the paper journal. Your students have likely used blogs outside of the classroom. Some may have created their own. All the ways for using paper journals with projects transfer easily to blogs. There are, however, some differences.

- Blogs motivate students who don't like to write or who struggle with grammar, spelling, and syntax. Students can see their writings develop more quickly on a blog. They overcome the pain of writing words by hand. They can more easily make changes in their writing and incorporate items readily from Internet sources.
- Blogs can lead to very serious consequences. This happens when students start engaging with inappropriate content on the Internet or violating Internet etiquette. It is very important that you put controls on the use of the Internet and any blogs that go outside your classroom network.

Set your blog up before the project starts. If you do an Internet search for "blogger," you will find instructions for setting up a classroom blog. If you use some of the blogs for educators (http://edublogs.org or http://classblogmeister.com), you maintain control and security. Make sure to do the following:

- Get parent and principal approval.
- Review school policies regarding the Internet.

- Lock your classroom network, and allow only individual student PINs to open the blog.
- Discuss appropriate blogging content.
- Lay down strict guidelines and consequences for violating Internet etiquette (especially in what students say about fellow students in and out of your class and how they address and respond to each other online).
- Keep all student names and other individual identifiers off the blogs.
- Block sending of personal information.
- Insist on respect for all.

If you set up blogs as student journals, determine whether you want all project blogging done in class or if students may also blog outside of class. Make it clear to students you will have access to their blogs and that you will be reviewing and assessing entries (just as you would with paper journals). Use a PIN-safe blog that restricts entry. Only you and the student should have access.

When you are ready to engage students with the blog, pair those with experience with those who have little or no experience. In the first week of use, allow class time for everyone to come up to speed on making blog entries, discuss the dos and don'ts, and then make the first assignment.

On a daily or weekly basis, you can schedule five minutes at the end of each work session for students to complete reflective stems in the journal. For example: "In my project work today,

- I learned . . ."
- I discovered . . ."
- I expanded my ideas by . . ."
- I completed . . ."
- I noticed . . ."
- I am pleased that I . . ."
- I wondered why . . ."

If you ask students to make daily entries, you can use one day each week for them to summarize what they are learning or how they are thinking. After teaching them how to make a good summary, they will have ample time in a multiweek project to develop at least one type of summary each week, such as one of the following:

- Summary of stem statements
- Summary of key steps or procedures completed

- Summary of progress made
- Summary of new insights
- Summary of new questions to ask
- Summary of fact analysis
- Summary of conclusions

Sample Progress Summary

This week we completed our project plan. As the first step, we will design the hospital for treatment of refugees in a camp in Darfur. We then will have to create plans to staff the hospital, equip its treatment rooms, and deal with emergencies. Finally, we will have to determine how to pay for all of this.

Making Journals Work Well

At the end of the first day give students a starter stem, such as "Today, I learned . . ." After two minutes or so for writing, use a wrap-around to hear the entries. Start with a volunteer, and then hear every student in that row or at that table. Move to each succeeding row until all have shared or passed.

Review your guidelines for journal use. Before the first assessment, share several examples with the entire class via the video projector or posted newsprint. Point out the positive characteristics. Conclude this task by presenting the rubrics you will use for assessing weekly entries and the rubric or checklist for the assessment of the complete project journal.

Tweets from Twitter are a perfect tool for having students send their completed stem statements to you. If you can set up Twitter on your system, you can also encourage students to send question tweets to you anytime they don't understand an idea or become confused in a task. If your students have their own laptops, they can tweet you from home regarding homework issues.

Finally, let students know about your journal reading procedure. To prevent turning yourself into a late-night reader, set up a schedule for random collection of a fifth of the journals each week (if you teach multiple classes, schedule the pickups on different days). Read the entries and select one that strikes you for feedback and commentary. Toward the end of a project, you may ask students to compare an early assessment with a current one.

Electronic Portfolios

If your project will produce a number of different artifacts, you may want to have teams maintain electronic portfolios. The emphasis here is on *team* portfolios. This emphasis not only assists in building teamwork, it saves you time when you set up a system so that each team will have a table of contents that highlights categories of tasks completed.

In this way, your teams can group the e-journals and other artifacts from each member in a section of the portfolio. With each student grouped by team, you can review products such as graphic organizers, plans, sketches, photographs of a mural made by the team, or other multimedia products more quickly. If students complete offline products such as a sculpture, a painting, or a dance, you may encourage students to store photographs in the e-portfolio along with their comments. To access the many sites that provide information, tutorials, and free services, browse e-portfolios.

Grading Projects

Connecting back to the standards that are governing a project, you can create a project rubric. This rubric will show students the learning priorities you have set for the entire project. The rubric will enable students to chart their own path to the final know-and-do results. Lastly, the project rubric will help you review all assessments completed through the project into an orderly finale.

In addition to the multimedia project rubric, you can access free project rubrics at several sites. At the Microsoft Office website (www.office.microsoft.com), you can download templates that will make the task of preparing the rubrics along with aligned performance checklists and tests easy. The project template will assist you in scoring your students on projects. The template considers four aspects of students' performance—content, conventions (spelling, grammar, vocabulary), organization, and presentation—and defines the achievement required in each aspect to merit a score from 1 (lowest) to 4 (highest). For an enriched learning project, you will have to add critical thinking and collaboration aspects. The site also provides instructions for you to use Word or Excel to create rubrics for other project activities.

At the University of Kansas site (www.4teachers.org), you will find RubiStar 4 Teachers. At this free site, funded by the U.S. Department of Education, you can use an electronic template to make your own rubric or select a rubric to duplicate from over five hundred examples for specific types of projects. As with most other sites that show rubrics, you will have to select carefully. Most are very specific to traditional skills. You will have to add benchmarks for critical thinking, collaborating, and using e-tools to most of the examples, so that your rubric will reflect the enriched learning qualities.

After assessing all of the elements that differentiate an enriched learning project, your rubric will let you tally the final project grade for each student. This grade will come from assessments completed in the project; end-of-project products such as essays, final tests, presentations, and performances; and all artifacts. You accomplish this by making a summary scoring sheet that draws results from the various rubrics you may have used in the project. The reproducible Project Report for use at the end of a project is provided on page 167 and online at **go.solution-tree.com/instruction**.

Summary

First and foremost, assessment of learning is the student's responsibility. It is the teacher's responsibility to develop students' skills by creating the formative opportunities throughout a project and by providing the students with feedback that enriches students' self assessments. As students work through the phases of learning, it is they who must first ask, "What am I doing well?" "How can I learn more effectively?" and "What help do I need?" Students benefit from a deepening understanding of what and how they are learning throughout the project, how they are answering the essential question, how they are achieving the standards-aligned outcomes, and how they are challenged to review their performances as knowers, thinkers, and collaborators. Yes, they do listen carefully to their teacher's feedback, but it is the students who must learn to judge and evaluate the quality of what they are accomplishing as they complete each phase of the project. Ultimately, their teachers may evaluate projects with final grades, but these are mere summations of the more essential assessments that the students make as they grow in wisdom and knowledge.

Shift Collaboration Checklist

Name: ______________________________ Date: ______________

Manager: ______________________________ Shift #: ______________

	Not at all	Sometimes	Mostly	Always
How well did this employee problem solve this week?				
Cooperate with other team members?				
Cooperate with manager?				
Communicate with other team members?				

Total Score __________ Signature ______________________________

Project Report

Name: ______________________________ Class: __________

Project: ______________________________ Date: __________

Key: 1 Not yet

2 Some

3 A large amount

4 Exceeded expectations

You have shown mastery of the content standards for this project.

1 ______ 2 ______ 3 ______ 4 ______

You have shown development of the following targeted thinking skills: ______________

____

1 ______ 2 ______ 3 ______ 4 ______

You have shown an increased ability to work in a team.

1 ______ 2 ______ 3 ______ 4 ______

Your final product, ______________________, reflects application of the required knowledge and skill.

1 ______ 2 ______ 3 ______ 4 ______

My Final Comments:

Chapter 9

An Enriched Project Sampler

> The necessary processes are more like bringing a healthy garden along.
>
> —John Goodlad

This chapter's purpose is to show samples of enriched learning project plans. It presents four sample project plans, along with instructions for following the enriched learning project rubric to plan your project.

We've Got a Lot of Thinking to Do

"Do you think we could really train rats to run the maze?" Dan asked.

His partner, Terry, smiled. Terry thought of himself as the cockeyed, eternal optimist.

"Why not? It's a better hypothesis to test than waiting for butterflies to morph."

"But it's not very original," Dan said.

"No, but it will be a challenge. We have to build our own maze. And we could find our own food."

"This sounds like a repeat of our trying to find a better acid-metal combo for your dad's car battery," moaned Dan.

"Well, we are running out of ideas. Besides, this will let us do better with precision. Mrs. Mangi really hit us hard on that one in the last project," Terry said.

"OK. Then let's do the rats. Get out your planning sheet. We've got a lot of thinking to do if we want a better grade than last time."

Think about how a master gardener works. The gardens he or she cultivates might include a professional botanical garden, a formal English garden, or a simple garden like one you may have admired in your neighborhood. While each garden is distinct, however, certain features make up any distinctive garden.

First, you want to see the big picture. How well does the garden fit into its context? Is there a design or a plan that helps it make the best use of the space, light, or weather conditions? What about the mechanics? How is the garden watered? Fertilized? Weeded? Are you starting from a bare plot of earth, or are you refining what you have already planted?

To answer these questions, this chapter provides you with four sample enriched projects to study. Just as you would visit master gardens to get ideas of your own, you can preview and analyze these project samples to get insights and tips for your own projects.

Each sample is based on the Master Project Planner (pages 194–195 and online at **go.solution-tree.com/instruction**). This template provides the structure or key elements for your projects. By making sure you have those in place, you will know that the decisions you make about strategies, tactics, and content will fit well in your overall plan.

Using the Sample Projects

Like the best gardens, the best projects don't spring from a one-style-fits-all plan. Your challenge comes in filling out the basic structure provided on the template with those specifics that meet your needs. With this in mind, review the template. Make a copy you can take notes on as you read through the text. Then study the following sample projects to see how each teacher created a unique project.

Note also the similarities and differences in each project. See how each project fits with your state standards. Above all, look for the ways that these teachers built in tactics that encouraged students to make the most of the project-based learning experience, including assessment and reflection tactics that encouraged students to learn from their doing.

Although the sample projects show ways for you to enrich students' learning with technology, your students may not have access to the e-tools that would most help them. Don't worry. You can still use nondigital tools. For instance, in place of an e-journal, students can use notebooks and pens to make their entries and complete their reflections. In place of e-portfolios, students can use plain file folders. You can substitute newsprint and markers for groups to record their graphic organizers or to make lists of ideas.

In a like manner, these sample projects do not require you to build a community of learners. If you elect to build your classroom as a community, a strongly urged approach, you will integrate the collaborative and cooperative learning strategies throughout the project and continue their development during the school year. As a start, concentrate on preparing your students to use the learning tactics that you select for this project.

Ultimately, you can use these project samples in a variety of ways. First, you can duplicate the sample in your classrooms with minimum changes relevant to your course standards or the sophistication of your students.

Second, you can replicate the sample, but with more complex adaptations. For instance, in your replication, you can integrate additional technology, tie the project into the development of a learning community, make major switches in content or strategy, or select a different product.

Third, you can use the model to guide the creation of your own completely unique project by adding tactics, tools, and concepts borrowed from your own past experience with the project model of instruction. Your project may contain the elements from the template, but it will have to reflect your own unique ideas.

When you use one of the samples as your model, place it side by side with the Master Project Planner and the project rubric (pages 35–37 and online) so you can visually compare the two more easily.

Three Approaches to Building Projects

1. **Duplicate:** Take the model as it appears and make no changes. Same launch question, same strategies, same standards.
2. **Replicate:** Take the model and make some internal changes. For instance, you may want to change the standards or use different tactics and tools. The rest you leave alone.
3. **Create from scratch:** You use only the elements of the project outline. You decide which of the elements (standards and e-tools) you want to use, and you make the plan with these elements. You use the model to get ideas.

To start using the template, think about the results you want this project to generate: what will students know and be able to do after the project is complete? As you complete each answer, place the answer on the template. For instance, after you think about what you want your students to know or do as a result of this project-based learning experience, you can pick out the exact standards that you want to include. Place these on the template.

While you are thinking about what students will be able to do, it is important to include the skills they will demonstrate in the product(s) they will make during and at the end of the project. For instance, at the end of phase one, you may ask the teams to produce a summary of research they have done in response to the launch question. What skills will this product demonstrate? In phase two, you may ask them to construct a concept map. What evidence of thinking skills will this show? In the final phase, you may require an e-journal to accompany a multimedia presentation that answers the launch question. What skills will the making of these final products show?

One word of caution is appropriate here. Note that the emphasis in the previous paragraph is on *skills and knowledge demonstrated through the making of the products, not on the products themselves.* This means the final assessment of how well students' learning aligns with the projects' standards focuses on the knowledge and skills found in the products and not on the product itself. This distinction is what separates enriched learning projects from those projects that are just the making of a product (for example, a web page, a multimedia presentation, or a book).

Once you have determined the project's know-and-do outcomes, identify the research-strong tactics, e-tools, and other strategies that will enrich your students' learning as they proceed through the project tasks. These are also the means by which you can enrich student learning as they work on their projects. By purposefully selecting instructional strategies that research has shown give you the most chance to advance their knowledge and skill, as well as give them the tools for more efficient, lifetime learning, you deepen the meaning of what they are learning and increase the level of its transfer to other projects.

After you have completed your project plan, you can do a final check with the project-making rubric (pages 35–37). It will give you a way to make a final check of how your project plan will enrich the learning of your students. After this check, your last planning step is to create a blank calendar, save it to your documents, and enter the activity for each day of the project. When allotting days, plan for two extra days per month knowing that plans can change. Nothing remains now except your "doing" and the assessment of your "doing." *Bon voyage!*

Go Green: A Middle Grades Interdisciplinary Project

A middle grades teacher in New York developed this enriched learning project plan for her science class. She collaborated with her middle school house team. This enabled her to sharpen the instruction needed from other disciplines, such as math and science, so that she and her colleagues could ensure that students would have the opportunity to develop the knowledge and skills called for in the New York standards.

Project title: Go Green

Target grade: 7

Target content areas: Interdisciplinary science, social studies, language arts, visual arts, technology

Target type: Teams

Purpose: To engage students in answering a hypothetical question about best ways to take individual responsibility for the care of the environment

Value: This project fosters students' achievement of the New York state standards in multiple subject areas while students learn about taking personal responsibility for the care of their environment as they answer their own hypothetical questions (such as "What would happen that would benefit the environment in our town if all homes switched to natural gas heat?" or "What would happen to the environment in our town if we all rode electrically powered school buses?").

Standards: The project aligns with the following national and New York state standards (National Science Teachers Association, n.d.):

1. National Science Education Standard. Science influences society through its knowledge and worldview. Scientific knowledge and the procedures used by scientists influence the way many individuals in society think about themselves, others, and the environment. The effect of science on society is neither entirely beneficial nor entirely detrimental.
2. NYS Standard 2: The Arts. 5–8. Knowing and Using Arts, Materials, and Resources. Students will be knowledgeable about and make use of the materials and resources available for participation in the arts.
3. NYS Standard 1: Language Arts. 5–8. Students will listen, speak, read, and write for information and understanding. As listeners and readers, students will collect data, facts, and ideas; discover relationships,

concepts, and generalizations; and use knowledge generated from oral, written, and electronically produced texts. As speakers and writers, they will use oral and written language that follows the accepted conventions of the English language.

4. NYS Standard 7: Interdisciplinary Study. 5–8. Students will apply the knowledge and thinking skills of mathematics, science, and technology to address real-life problems and make informed decisions. Students will use mathematical analysis, scientific inquiry, and engineering design, as appropriate, to pose questions, seek answers, and develop solutions.
5. NYS Standard 2: Technology and Tools. Students will use appropriate graphics and electronic tools to process information.

Level of difficulty: x Novice __ Skilled __ Expert x Middle school __ High school

Allotted time: Total time required is eight to nine weeks from Sept. 15 to Nov. 20. Daily time given in science class. Weekly support and bridging in social studies, art, language arts, and math classes.

Cognitive framework: x Hypothesis testing __ Investigating __ Comparing __ Other

Project description: Students work in teams of three to do research that will answer (+ or -) their team's hypothetical question. After students complete the research and establish the validity or invalidity of their idea, they will create a science fair display to share the results of their study. After the fair, presented to the rest of the school and their parents, they will assess all aspects of their study.

Project materials needed: Computer and printer per team, e-journals on class blog, bulletin board materials, tape, video camera and video projector, movie, chart materials and felt markers, PowerPoint masters, model brochures, and one online display with rubric

Instructional Framework for Investigation Process

As an advance organizer, I will use Al Gore's movie, *An Inconvenient Truth*, followed by study teams completing an agree–disagree chart, an all-class brainstorm of research questions, and defining of a hypothesis by each team. I will introduce the project by showing the movie with the idea that they will have to agree or disagree with its key points. They will make their charts in teams and then display them around the room in a carousel. After they have viewed all the charts, I will structure an all-class discussion about what the most important issues are that relate to what they could do to take personal responsibility for care of the environment. We will brainstorm hypothetical launch questions to be posted on the classroom bulletin board.

Estimated time: Three class periods

Phase One—Gathering Information

First, in each team, members will share what ways they have or have not taken responsibility for environmental care and what actions they might take. They will keep the lists for the group in an online team file folder.

I will set up the study teams as formal collaborative groups (trios) with rules and roles. The first task in each group of three will be to select a question to ask. (No more than three groups may select a similar question.) Next, I will review the process of researching including doing research on approved websites in and out of class, set up the guidelines for daily work, and set a schedule for daily work that includes taking notes from print and electronic sources as well as one adult person. I will also ask to write a summary in their e-journals of what they learned that day. At least once a week, I will ask three or four groups to share summaries of their entries with the class.

In their e-journals, students will use the chain of events organizer to schedule the tasks they brainstorm for gathering new data. They will use the concept map or another of their choices as the tool for gathering their data in a pattern. When they do this on newsprint, it will make it easier for me to walk around and monitor their entries.

Each Wednesday, I will present a cognitive function from my list and have students set a goal for the week to work on the tactics for improving that cognitive function in their daily work. I will present a rubric that they can use to set a goal. On the following Wednesday, they will do a self-assessment on how well they worked on the function in the context of their studies (for instance, "How precise and accurate were you in recording your data?" or "What did you do when data from two sources was contradictory?").

Each Friday will be big idea day. I will ask different teams to report their work for the week related to their question and the goal of the project. In this way, I will help them keep a focus on the big idea and the "big think."

In math class, the teacher will initiate a three- to four-week unit on statistical analysis. In the final two weeks, students will learn how to apply this information to the analysis of their science data.

Estimated time: Two weeks

Phase Two—Making Sense

With the data they have gathered, the team must come to a consensus about the answer to their launch question. This means they must allot time to review all data and to make judgments on its reliability, organize their ideas using a concept map or other selected organizer, and make valid conclusions that will stand the test of logic.

Coordination with social studies and math: In math class, the teacher will complete the unit on probability and statistics. She will help students examine their own data from the project and apply the statistical analysis methods they are learning in the math class. In the social studies class, the teacher will focus the students on national and local environmental problems and their relationship to the students' science project.

Estimated time: Two weeks plus coordinating time in other classes

Phase Three—Communicating Results

For this phase, the teams will prepare a science fair display (4 x 4 booth size), a three-fold, black-and-white brochure, and member essays that discuss their team's findings. All items will display the original launch question as a key visual.

After distributing the rubrics for the final products (brochure, essays, journals, and displays), I will show sample brochures and the sample display. Teams will plan their displays and brochures. In arts class, they will work on the visual design of the brochure and build the display. In language arts class, they will learn how to write a scientific report according to the grade-level standards.

Coordination with language arts and visual arts: In addition to time allotted in science class, students will have one week in language arts class to work on the required essay and the written content of the brochure guided by the rubrics supplied for each.

Estimated time: Two weeks plus coordinated time in other classes

How Will I Develop the Learning Community?

This is the first project of the year. I plan to form study teams that will learn how to work together. At the end of the project, we will take one day to assess what they have learned about teamwork. In the next two projects, I will create new study teams and the whole class will work on a single project together.

Targeted issue or big idea: Taking personal responsibility for the environment

Thinking skills to develop: Making thoughtful connections, accepting alternative points of view, comparing, making judgments, and providing logical evidence; the big skill is hypothesizing

Tactics: Questions, think-pair-share, web, graphic organizers, comparison alley, chain of events, fishbone, charts, statistical graphs, goal planning, journal entries and rubrics, summarizing journal entries

Cognitive functions to develop: Impulse control, precision, accuracy, multiple source use

Function method: Multiple sources of information, goal planning

Estimated time: Collaborative study teams—each team, one goal (all days); think-pair-share informal questions (day 1), journal sharing and selected team reports (Wednesdays)

Assessment

What will I assess? _x_ Content mastery _x_ Critical thinking _x_ Collaboration _x_ Products

How will I assess each selected area? _x_ Teacher assessment _x_ Student self-assessment __ Peer assessment _x_ Assessments from other classes

What standards will I assess? National Science Education, NY Language Arts 1, NY Interdisciplinary Study, NY Technology and Tools 2, and NY Arts 2, rubrics-based benchmarks and test scores

What products can I expect? Journal entries, quizzes, booth display with brochure, charts and visuals, final summary of results to match rubrics; rubrics completed by other course teachers in student journals

Time allotted: Five days

Notes: Coordination with the other teachers on our team is important. We are scheduled to meet at our next planning period to chart out each person's role, the alignment of the standards, and the schedules for the project's in-class work. Each student will have a final grade in this project for science. Each will also have grades for work on this project that was completed in other classes.

New People on the Block: A Middle Grades Social Studies Project

This enriched learning project, designed by a sixth-grade social studies teacher for students who were new to the project learning experience, uses a current issue as the big idea to capture student interest. The teacher aligned the project closely with her state's history standards. For the project, she asks students to interview a relative about the family's immigration history. Then they compare their interview with the history of an ethnic group different from their own by going to sources on the Internet and in print. After this comparison, for which the students would have to make judgments about the validity of their sources, they create a product to communicate their new understandings. The teacher would assess those understandings with a rubric based on the standards inherent in the project.

Project title: New People on the Block

Target grade: 6

Target content area: Social studies

Target type: Individual

Purpose: To teach sixth-grade students how to complete a project

Value: Students will learn how to do individual projects. They will also learn about the many issues that America has and is now facing regarding immigration.

Standards: The project aligns with the following California history standards (California State Board of Education, 2009):

1. Students explain how major events are related to one another in time.
2. Students construct various timelines of key events, people, and periods of the historical era they are studying
3. Students frame questions that can be answered by historical study and research.
4. Students distinguish fact from opinion in historical narratives and stories.
5. Students distinguish relevant from irrelevant information, essential from incidental information, and verifiable from unverifiable information in historical narratives and stories.

6. Students assess the credibility of primary and secondary sources and draw sound conclusions from them.
7. Students explain the central issues and problems from the past, placing people and events in a matrix of time and place.

Level of difficulty: x Novice __ Skilled __ Expert

Allotted time: Time required is four weeks from Oct. 1 to Oct. 30

Cognitive framework: __ Hypothesis testing __ Investigating x Comparing

Project description summary: Working within the "big idea" theme of immigration in America and responding to the launch question, "How does my family's immigration history compare to another family's from a culture or nation different from my own?," each student will compare the history of immigration in his or her own family with a young person from another culture or ethnic group. The student will construct his or her own family history by interviews and family records (if available), and will analyze documents and readings to build a history of the family. Students will use a Venn diagram or comparison alley organizer to compare the two histories and draw conclusions about the similarities and differences. Finally, the students will present their findings in one of the following methods: poster, collage, PowerPoint presentation, slideshow, video, or wall mural. I will use a standards-based rubric to evaluate the final product.

Project materials needed: Online graphic organizers, e-journals, newsprint, markers, tape, computers and printers per team, Internet access, and slideshow materials

Instructional strategies I will use: Cooperative learning, nonlinguistic representation, objectives and feedback, questions and cues

Tactics: Graphic organizers, KWL, Venn diagram, comparison alley, chain of event, graphs, timelines, posted goal and rubrics, questions and cues, comparative behaviors chart, and wait time

Instructional Framework for Investigation Process

As an advance organizer, I will invite a local lawyer or other civic official who is familiar with immigration issues in our area. That person will speak to the class about immigration law. I will encourage the class to ask questions with a think-pair-share web.

Estimated time: One class period

Phase One—Gathering Information

Prior knowledge: As a class, we will brainstorm a KWL on immigration. What are the current issues? What could we find out about these issues in our community?

New information: Part 1. Students will interview their parents or an older relative about the history of their family's arrival in the United States. I will provide the class with an interview questionnaire for all to use. Part 2. Students will select an ethnic group different from their own. They will use the Internet, fiction, and nonfiction print materials and, if possible, an interview of a family from that ethnic group. For all, they will use the same interview questionnaire as they used with their own families to determine the history of each family's immigration.

Estimated time: One week in and out of class

Phase Two—Making Sense

All students will use a similar format to draw conclusions from the questionnaire responses. For each source, they will answer the following questions:

- What was difficult about the journey to America?
- Why did the first members come to America?
- When they arrived, what were the requirements for entry?
- How were they received into this country by other groups? Why do you think this happened?
- How long did it take for the persons to be accepted as Americans? Why do you think this was so?
- What are the three most critical differences in these person's immigration experiences; what are the similarities?
- What information is verifiable? Relevant? Accurate?
- How credible are the sources of information?
- How does this information match with the KWL questions?
- What new questions must now be asked?

After completing the questions, the students will make a graphic organizer to compare the results. In groups of four, they will share their organizers. Each group of four will look for the similarities and construct a timeline of events for each family. I will monitor the groups and take notes on the similarities they select and the construction of the timelines.

Estimated time: Four class periods

Phase Three—Communicating Results

After students have completed phase two, they each are expected to select their means of communicating what they discovered via the comparison task. I will post a rubric that lists the criteria I will use for grading the slideshow each makes.

- Does the product show the similarities and differences in the different immigration experiences?
- Is each historic timeline clear, accurate, and precise?
- Are the conclusions about the differences valid?
- Is explanation of significance clear?
- Does the explanation include understanding of the project's title?
- Each student will have five minutes to show his or her product to the class and to explain its significance.
- Assessment: Rubric for product [see pages 35–37] and discussion—observation checklist for cognitive functions.

Estimated time: Five class periods plus out of class work on products

How Will I Develop the Learning Community?

This project focuses on individual accomplishment. However, community development remains important in all my projects.

Targeted issue or big idea: Immigration

Thinking skills to develop: Comparing, drawing conclusions, sequencing events

Cognitive functions to develop: Comparing by questions and graphic organizers, differentiating quality of data, drawing conclusions, using multiple sources of data (interviews, reading, and so on), precision and accuracy

Content areas included: Social studies, technology, language arts

Assessment:

What will I assess? x Content mastery x Critical thinking __ Collaboration x Products

How will I assess each selected area? x Teacher assessment __ Student self-assessment __ Peer assessment

What guidance will the standards provide? How well do the products show that students:

- Can explain how major events in the immigration stories are connected over time?
- Can frame questions that can be answered by their historical study and research?
- Can distinguish fact from opinion in their families' historical stories?
- Can distinguish relevant from irrelevant information, essential from incidental information, and verifiable from unverifiable information in their families' stories?
- Can assess the credibility of primary and secondary sources and draw sound conclusions from them?
- Can explain the central issues and problems from the immigration stories using events in a matrix of time and place?
- Can use e-tools?

What products can I expect? One graphic organizer and one PowerPoint presentation, slideshow, collage, mural, or poster per student

Notes: This is an introductory project for my students. Most have never had a project to do. Thus, I have kept it as simple as possible to allow time to discuss what they are learning as well as to give them responsibility to seek out information rather than wait for me to provide it. In addition, I am developing their ability to work with information and distinguish good information from bad information as described in the California History Standards. In the next project, I will put them into teams and continue working with these same standards in relation to specific periods of American history.

Change: It's About the Law—
A Secondary Grades History Project

In this enriched learning project, an Illinois secondary teacher, Arline Paul, uses the Illinois state goals and standards to prepare her students for a standardized test required for high school graduation. The teacher highlights the state standards in both process and content throughout the project.

Although she does not allot all of their class time to the project, she does allow time each week for the students to work together on the project during the class period.

Project title: Change: It's About the Law

Target grade: 11

Target type: Teams/community in a single-subject course

Purpose: To prepare students for a required test on the Illinois Constitution

Value: Immerses students in a hands-on inquiry study about how laws are made in Illinois so students can better understand that process

Standards: The project aligns with the following Illinois social studies goals and standards (www.isbe.state.il.us):

> STATE GOAL 14: Understand political systems, with an emphasis on the United States. The existence and advancement of a free society depends on the knowledge, skills, and understanding of its citizenry. Through the study of various forms and levels of government and the documents and institutions of the United States, students will develop the skills and knowledge that they need to be contributing citizens, now and in the future.
>
> 14.D.5: Interpret a variety of public policies and issues from the perspectives of different individuals and groups
>
> STATE GOAL 18: Understand social systems, with an emphasis on the United States. Students should know how and why groups and institutions are formed, what roles they play in society, and how individuals and groups interact with and influence institutions.
>
> 18.B.5: Use methods of social science inquiry (pose questions, collect and analyze data, make and support conclusions with evidence, report findings) to study the development and functions of social systems and report conclusions to a larger audience.

NATIONAL EDUCATIONAL TECHNOLOGY STANDARDS (2007): Students will apply digital tools to gather, evaluate, and use information

Level of difficulty: __ Novice _x_ Skilled __ Expert

Allotted time: Six weeks from Jan. 8 to Feb. 28, one to two class periods per week. During the other days, the class will address the Federal Constitution and the balance of the Illinois Constitution required for graduation test.

Cognitive framework: __ Hypothesis testing _x_ Investigating __ Comparing

Project description: To prepare students for the Illinois Constitution test and to meet Illinois Social Studies Goals 14 and 18, students will work in study and action teams to have a law prepared for enactment by the legislature and signed by the governor that will make a change in the Illinois School Code. Teams will have class time one day per week to investigate the process for passing a law, frame their law, and present it in Springfield. A parent-legislator will advise the class in this project. To conclude the project, students will connect what they have learned in this process with the relevant standards and show that they have developed the required skills, as outlined in standards 14.D.5 and 18.B.5, in the creation of a web page and a presentation to the legislature.

Project materials needed: E-journals, computers, email, web page software, and Internet access

Instructional strategies I highlight: Questions, cues, and advance organizers; graphic organizers; hypothesis testing; and summarizing

Instructional Framework for Investigation Process

As an advance organizer, Mr. Kay, our House representative in Springfield will address the class on "Change: It's About the Law." He will outline the process for getting a new law passed and signed by the governor. Questions and answers will follow.

Estimated time: One day

Phase One—Gathering Information

Students will work in collaborative study teams (four and five members) that jigsaw investigating what they must know about the legislative process. After a one-day review of the research process and tools to use, teams will select their area of study. They will have ten days to gather their information. On the second class day, we will review what is happening with their research and solve problems they are encountering. On the third class day, each team will have seven minutes for its report. Team reports will include:

- The House procedures
- The Senate procedures
- How disagreements are resolved
- The governor's role
- The School Code and Illinois Law

Estimated time: Ten days

Phase Two—Making Sense

A steering committee with one member selected from each group will review the gathered information, determine what steps must be taken by the class to frame a law, and carry it through the legislature.

With my assistance, they will form action teams that will have responsibility for carrying out the plan. Teams' responsibilities shall include:

- Writing the law
- Preparing arguments for the House
- Preparing arguments for the Senate
- Presentation to the governor
- Logistics and costs

Estimated time: Three days

Phase Three—Communicating Results

Each team will prepare a PowerPoint presentation for the class detailing the law and the plans for its passage and signing. Teams will present on successive weeks in sequence. After the last presentation, the class will vote on whether to undertake a fundraising campaign and a trip to Springfield. If the idea passes by a 70 percent majority, the next project will focus on the goal of attaining the governor's signature.

Estimated time: Two days

How Will I Develop the Learning Community?

I can't ignore the learning community here. The Constitution itself is about community, and I plan to draw the parallel throughout the project.

Tactics: Collaborative learning study teams, action teams, steering committee, single goal and outcome

Targeted issue or big idea: Investigating via social science inquiry process: "How can alternative school students meet school-code mandated graduation requirements with different ways or methods used to show their knowledge and skill?"

Thinking skills to develop: Hypothesizing, analyzing, comparing, evaluating

Tactics: Posing important questions (question web), analyzing data (data matrix), drawing conclusions (fishbone), supporting conclusions (questions and answers)

Cognitive functions to develop: Considering multiple sources of data, using precise and accurate data, focusing, making logical proofs

Content areas included: Social studies (American history)

Assessment

What will I assess? _x_ Content mastery _x_ Critical thinking _x_ Collaboration _x_ Products

How will I assess each selected area? _x_ Teacher assessment __ Student self-assessment __ Peer assessment

What standards will I assess?

- 14 D.5: Knowledge of levels of government
- 18 B.5: Knowledge of how government institutions are formed and influenced; skill with social studies inquiry process and share conclusions with an audience
- NETS-S 2007: Research with digital tools

What else will I assess? Team collaboration, community collaboration, and students' thinking skills

What products can I expect? Individual e-journals, final Constitution test results, team summary, team action plan, and team website

Notes: It is very hard to cover the material students need to study the Illinois and U.S. Constitutions. I don't have a lot of time to prepare the students for the Constitution tests and cover all of U.S. history. The standards, however, give me a chance to target my priorities. Throughout the Constitution project, I sprinkle mini-lessons on the key concepts and facts that are tested so students can prepare for the test. The project brings up a lot for us to discuss, but also will get the students interested in the legislative process. When I give the departmental test on what they learned about levels of government, how the government operates, and how laws are made, my project students are the top scorers. I also find that they recall more because the project really challenged them. So far, this is the best way I have found to help the students learn how to use the social studies inquiry process.

This project was completed by students with a successful passage of a law by both houses of the Illinois legislature and signature of the governor. Today, the law, which allows for local Illinois school boards to request a change in high school graduation requirements, remains part of the Illinois School Code.

The Play's the Thing—A Secondary Grades Literature Project

A twelfth grade teacher in Montana developed this five-week project aligned with that state's literature standards. The product is a presentation of a play by the entire class.

Project title: The Play's the Thing

Target grade: 12

Target type: All-class project

Purpose: To produce Archibald MacLeish's play, *J.B.*

Value: Enables students to produce a play as the climax of their drama study for the year. Students will experience the play through the eyes of actors, rather than just reading the parts.

Standards: The project aligns with the following Montana state standards for literature (Montana Department of Education, n. d.):

- Content Standard 1: Students construct meaning as they comprehend, interpret, analyze, and respond to literary works.
- Content Standard 2: Students recognize and evaluate how language, literary devices, and elements contribute to the meaning and impact of literary works.
- Content Standard 3: Students reflect upon their literary experiences and purposefully select from a range of works.
- Content Standard 4: Students interact with print and nonprint literary works from various cultures, ethnic groups, and traditional and contemporary viewpoints written by both genders.
- Content Standard 5: Students use literary works to enrich personal experience and to connect to the broader world of ideas, concepts, and issues.

Additional standards:

National Educational Technology Standards-Students (2007): Students will demonstrate creative thinking, construct knowledge, and develop innovative products using technology.

Students will use digital media and environments to communicate and work collaboratively to support individual learning and contribute to the learning of others.

Level of difficulty: __ Novice __ Skilled _x_ Expert

Allotted time: Five weeks plus two days, from May 1 to June 12

Cognitive framework: __ Hypothesis testing __ Investigating _x_ Comparing

Project description: As the last literature piece for the year, students will read and produce the play *J.B.* and compare it to the other plays and novels read in the curriculum. The project will begin with a review of the theme "Heroes and Heroines of History" that unified their literary study for the year. After producing and presenting the play to parents, teachers, and a senior assisted-living home, the students will reflect on their production and assess what they have learned. In the first four weeks of the project, students will work on the production, learn parts, and rehearse three days per week in class. The fifth day each week will be used to discuss the play as it relates to standards 2–5.

Project materials needed: Copies of play, e-journals, newsprint, overhead with markers, blackline masters, markers and tape, costume and staging materials, computers and printers

Instructional Framework for Investigation Process

As an advance organizer, read parts of the story of Job from the Bible. Tell the students the play they are about to study is built on this story and they will be looking to compare the biblical story and the play. Out-of-class reading assignment due for completion and quiz: May 1. Class discussion of *J.B.* using think-pair-share in groups of four and eight: "How is J.B. similar to the other main characters of the plays and novels studied this year as a heroic figure?" Make a matrix for all to see and fill in during the discussion. Introduce journals so that students can copy the matrix and add additional insights through the play's study. Introduce the goal of this play's study: to find the similarities of J.B. with other main characters studied this year.

Estimated time: One class period

Phase One—Gathering Information

Using the overhead, select the actors/actresses for all roles. Change actors each act by drawing names from a hat so that every student can play a role.

Group all students playing the same role. Each student will review his or her lines in the assigned act and analyze the character from what the character says and does or what is said about the character. Use two class periods for each group to chart this information. Post charts so all can do a walkabout and review the character analyses.

Conclude the second walkabout period with journal entries summarizing your character's strengths and weaknesses.

The next day, devote the period to starting the class concept map on the bulletin board. Look for character, setting, plot, and language as major subheadings. Call on students to fill out and expand each of these categories. On succeeding days, any individual may add other important information to the map.

On Friday, allow two-thirds of the period for character groups to discuss how they want to interpret their character and to justify their interpretations. With fifteen minutes left, ask each group to report on conclusions reached.

Estimated time: One week

Phase Two—Making Sense

Begin the second week by asking each student to spend five minutes writing a summary of his or her character's persona in journals. Select students to share a summary of each character. In the second half of the period, assign students to production teams: staging, costumes, lights, marketing, site selection (assisted-living home), and critics panel. Provide a list of duties that begins with each team selecting its manager. Allow time for teams to review duties and present a timeline for completing all duties outside of class time.

Devote days two through four for teams to rehearse their acts with scripts. On day five, add to the concept map and use Montana Reading Standard 2. (Montana Department of Education, n. d.) to frame a discussion of MacLeish's use of language and literacy devices. Use a PMI chart on the board or overhead to assess his language and literary device use. End with a journal entry: "About MacLeish's use of language (or literary devices), I learned . . ."

In weeks three and four, schedule time for each of the following at least once per week: progress reports from production teams, rehearsals, and guided discussion with a Venn diagram comparing this play and its main character to other works read. Use study teams for each discussion and assign each team a different work studied for comparison to *J.B.* End with an "I learned . . ." journal entry.

Devote week five to dress rehearsals of each act and the entire play as well as completion of production tasks, final marketing to parents, and final arrangements with the assisted-living home.

Estimated time: Five days varied time over five weeks

Phase Three—Communicating Results

Present the play as planned and prepared.

Estimated time: Two class periods

How Will I Develop the Learning Community?

Throughout this enriched project, I can weave development of the community by employing various learning tactics that promote 21st century communication and collaboration.

- Assign parts for all production teams.
- Form collaborative study in formal groups.
- Use think-pair-share.

Targeted issue or big idea: The hero's fate: fact or fiction?

Thinking skills to develop: Cognitive connections, alternate points of view, comparing, making judgments

Cognitive functions to develop: Accuracy in analysis of characters, scenes, language, and plot; precision analysis of language and literary devices; impulse control, reflection, and self-assessment

Cognitive tool use to develop: Use of Venn diagram, concept map, matrix

Content areas included: English literature

Assessment

What will I assess? x Content mastery x Critical thinking x Collaboration x Products

How will I assess each selected area? x Teacher assessment x Student self-assessment _ Peer assessment x Expert panel assessment

When will I assess the project?

- E-journal due date: June 12. Students assess their contributions to the production teams using a PMI, their interpretation of the character, and the production as a whole.
- Essay due date: June 12. Students will each compose an essay around the prompt "J.B.'s Fate: Fact or Fiction." The rubric will encourage comparing J.B. to one or more other heroic characters studied this year and to at least one "hero" in a current TV production. The key question to be answered is, "Was J.B. controlled by fate, or did his free will cause his difficulties?" Appropriate citations from the play are required.
- On the final day, students will discuss their comparisons to other literature read and share what they learned by acting and producing scenes from the play.

What products can I expect? Assessment of work teams, e-journals with self-assessments, knowledge quiz of the play, assessment of the production, one summary essay

Notes: I love to end the year with this project. The kids get so excited about what they are doing. Last year's class had only twelve students with only three girls. That didn't make any difference as we spread out the roles and the jobs. It was a lot more intense and so was that last day when they talked about what they had learned. You would think they were on Broadway! I never had a group like that one for bonding together. It was an incredible experience that I can't put into words. I had thought about changing to *Death of a Salesman* for this year, but nixed the idea after the way things went so well. I think it was my peak experience in teaching so far.

Summary

The examples used in this chapter represent only the tip of the iceberg. They are representative of the many mixes and matches you can make as you think about how to integrate enriched learning into your projects. Each of the projects shown here has many possibilities for replication in and out of subject-area classes. Visit **go.solution-tree.com/instruction** for additional project samples.

Whether using the investigation mode to engage students in inquiry of social studies issues, math applications, or science challenges in the local community or around the world; whether setting up hands-on comparisons of current events to historic problems, contrasts of classic literature to popular TV shows, or productions of curriculum-required drama; whether doing role-plays of historic events, or skits lampooning current social foibles; or whether testing hypotheses about the environment, modern family life, or the mysteries of ancient civilizations, students who learn *from* doing projects share many advantages over those who sit at a desk every day as passive receivers of information to memorize.

Master Project Planner

Advance Organizer/Launch Question:
Expected Time:
Standards:
Phase One—Gathering Information
Strategies and Tactics:
Expected Time:
Phase Two—Making Sense
Strategies and Tactics:
Expected Time:
Phase Three—Communicating Results
Strategies and Tactics:
Expected Time:
How Will I Develop the Learning Community?

Targeted Issue or Big Idea:
Thinking Skills to Develop:
Cognitive Functions to Develop:
Cognitive Tool Use to Develop:
Content Areas Included:
Assessment: ▪ What will I assess? __ Content mastery __ Critical thinking __ Collaboration __ Products ▪ How will I assess each selected area? __ Teacher assessment __ Student self-assessment __ Peer assessment __Expert panel assessment ▪ When will I assess the project? ▪ What products can I expect?
My Notes:

Appendix

The Research on Project-Based Learning

Research is what I am doing when I don't know what I am doing.

—Werner Von Braun

This appendix provides a short summary of research that supports the use of project-based learning and its enrichment by the integration of technology tools and high-yield instructional strategies. Following this description is a selection of online and print resources as well as links that may be helpful in creating an enriched learning project.

The Four Primary Areas of Research

Gathering the research on project-based learning is a challenging task. It necessitates the examination of multiple topics, many of which overlap. Most important among these are research on (1) using technology to enrich project-based learning or its components, (2) the project-based learning itself, (3) inquiry and problem-based learning, and (4) classroom strategies that work.

Technology to Enrich Project-Based Learning

The wide variety of rapidly emerging technology tools and their varied application in the classroom have worked against researchers completing meta-analyses like the studies of instructional strategies.

The two most likely conclusions that you might draw from the available studies are: (1) technology usually has a negative effect on achievement when students must use computers and software for drill and practice, and (2) student achievement and higher-order thinking gains are significant when they are encouraged to use digital tools in tasks that require them to think, problem solve in a project format, or create products. A third lesser point is made in several studies about the tendency of schools to use "remediation" software for basic math and reading skills with lower-performing students. In contrast, students perceived as high performing are challenged through technology to engage in higher-order thinking, problem solving, and multimedia projects.

The Cognition and Technology Group at Vanderbilt University (1992) evaluated the effects of a series of video-based adventure simulations. *The Adventures of Jasper Woodbury* encourages collaborative work by students with video simulations of real-world problems. These problems ask students to apply mathematical knowledge and reasoning. Compared with a control group, students who used the Vanderbilt series scored higher in *solving word problems* and in *planning.*

In a study commissioned by the Software and Information Industry Association, Sivin-Kachala and Bialo (2000) reviewed 311 research studies on technology's effectiveness on student achievement. The results included significant, consistent gains in achievement from technology use. The study scanned all grade levels and included students with special needs.

In a study of Enhancing Missouri's Instructional Networked Teaching Strategies (Bickford et al., 2000) program in which schools across the state were included in a technology program, eMINTS students scored higher on the Missouri Assessment Program than non-eMINTS students, including students with special needs.

Results from other studies (Cooper, 2001) suggest that students can benefit from technology-enhanced collaborative learning methods and interactive learning processes.

Research indicates that computer technology can help support learning and is especially useful in developing the higher-order skills of critical thinking, analysis, and scientific inquiry "by engaging students in authentic, complex tasks within collaborative learning contexts" (Roschelle, Pea, Hoadley, Gordin, & Means, 2000). Researchers in Michigan's Freedom to Learn initiative, an effort to provide middle school students with access to wireless laptop computers, have noted improved grades, motivation, and discipline. One school reported that reading proficiency scores on the Michigan Education Assessment Program test administered in January 2005 increased from 29 percent to 41 percent for seventh graders and from 31 to 63 percent for eighth graders (eSchool News Staff and Wire Reports, 2005).

In a five-year study, researchers at SRI International (www.sri.com) found that technology-using students in Challenge 2000 Multimedia Project classrooms outperformed nontechnology-using students in communication skills, teamwork, and problem solving. The Center for Learning in Technology (SRI International, 2009) researchers found increased student engagement, greater responsibility for learning, increased peer collaboration skills, and greater achievement gains when students who had been labeled low achievers use online learning.

A 1999 study by the Center for Research in Educational Policy at the University of Memphis and University of Tennessee at Knoxville found that students using the Co-NECT program improved test scores in all subject areas over a two-year period on the Tennessee Value-Added Assessment System (Ross, Sanders, & Wright, 1999). The Co-NECT schools outperformed control schools by 26 percent due to their use of technology in projects.

In a report, "Does It Compute? The Relationship Between Educational Technology and Student Achievement in Mathematics," Wenglinsky (2000) found that if computers were used for drill or practice, they typically had a negative effect on student achievement. If they were used with real-world applications, such as spreadsheets, or to simulate relationships or changing variables, student achievement increased. Data were drawn from the samples of 6,227 fourth-graders and 7,146 eighth-graders.

In a 1998 report, researchers note that three-fourths of the teachers who participated in a survey reported that project-based instruction increased after the introduction of laptops in their classrooms (Rockman Report, 1998). Among the many reported benefits of this project-based approach to learning are greater student engagement, improved analytic abilities, and a greater likelihood to apply high-order thinking skill.

Many educators express concerns about educational technology's potential to exclude those who may not have access to it or may be unable to use it. Regardless of what research may indicate concerning positive effects of technology on student learning, technology will be of limited use in achieving the goals of NCLB if technology is not available to all students. This is especially true if all students cannot use e-tools in the most effective ways, as suggested by research, to not only raise achievement, but to develop higher-order thinking skills, problem solving, and collaboration.

Schools serving students living in poverty tend to use technology for more traditional memory-based and remedial activities, while schools serving wealthier communities are more likely to focus on communication and expression, according to a nationwide study examining the relationship between socioeconomic status (SES) and teaching practices around technology. The study found that e-tool use in low-SES schools correlated most strongly with using technology for "reinforcement of skills" and "remediation of skills," while teaching in higher-SES schools correlated most with "analyzing information" and "presenting information to an audience" (Becker, 2000).

At the same time, although less studied than other outcomes, demonstration efforts and anecdotal evidence suggest that teaching information and communication technology (ICT) literacy skills (specifically those related to multimedia literacy in web, publishing, and video production) can improve the economic prospects of at-risk youth by giving them marketable skills (Lau & Lazarus, 2002).

Likewise, in teaching English language learners, researchers found that using technology had distinct advantages that relate to language education and to preparing students for an information society. Computer technologies and the Internet are powerful tools for assisting language-teaching, writing with email, and conducting online research (Wang, 2005).

In Oregon secondary schools, online note taking is used to support Hispanic migrant students who speak English as a second language (ESL). As part of the InTime project, ESL students attend regular high school classes along with a bilingual, note-taking/mentoring partner. Note-takers and ESL students communicate using a collaborative word processing and graphics package on wirelessly networked laptop computers. During class presentations, ESL students can read their note-taker's translation of key words, allowing students to build both English and Spanish literacy skills as they advance academically (Knox & Anderson-Inman, 2001).

Universal design for learning (UDL) takes advantage of the opportunity brought by rapidly evolving communication technologies to create flexible teaching methods and curriculum materials that can reach diverse learners and improve student access to the general education curriculum (Rose & Meyer, 2002). UDL assumes that students bring different needs and skills to the task of learning and that the learning environment should be designed to both accommodate, and make use of, these differences (Bowe, 2000; Rose & Meyer, 2002).

Project-Based Learning Resources

Relatively few researchers attended to the direct study of project-based learning until recently. This is likely to have occurred for several reasons:

- The lack of definition for the concept of "project-based learning" or identification of its critical attributes hindered attempts to measure specific outcomes of a common practice.

- Due to pressure from federal and state officials stimulated by the No Child Left Behind legislation, project-based learning went out of favor as an instructional tool. This legislation guided schools to attend more to the study of measurable, basic skills programs in reading and mathematics from the early 1990s. This legislation—paired with a funding emphasis that stressed direct instruction and discouraged models of instruction that promoted the types of skill development now being resurrected in the movement for 21st century skills—dissuaded researchers from examining the more complex outcomes of project-based learning. The Department of Education's use of the gold standard for scientific research on educational practices discouraged researchers from assessing this model of instruction. Project-based learning's multiple components and complex outcomes were not easily measured by government-required evaluation practices instituted after 1990.
- Multiple descriptions with different labels (such as inquiry, investigation, and problem-based) for project-based learning make it difficult to categorize and build a shared database.

John Thomas' *A Review of the Research* (2000) is a comprehensive review of the research on the effectiveness of project-based learning. The author identifies the struggle to find a focal point for gathering the research. This struggle, he notes, is caused by the wide variation in definitions. In his study, Thomas found some evidence that this approach enhanced the quality of student learning compared with other instructional methods. He also cited evidence that project-based learning is effective for teaching processes such as problem solving and decision making.

Please note that because the studies lacked comparisons, the data Thomas gathered failed to meet the standards for scientific research. This methodological weakness does not, however, downgrade the validity or importance of the approach. If anything, the consistency of the results indicates the true value of project-based learning.

A three-year study of two British secondary schools (Boaler, 1999) noted important differences in students' understanding of math achievement data. Boaler, associate professor of education at Stanford University, found that students at a project-based school did better than those at the more traditional school. The comparison showed that project students outperformed their peers in understanding concepts and analyzing math problems by three to one.

Three "expeditionary learning" elementary schools in Dubuque, Iowa, showed significant test-score gains after they adopted the Expeditionary Learning Outward

Bound (ELOB) program. At these three schools, students were challenged to conduct multiple-month learn-by-doing inquiries. After two years in the program, students advanced from "well below average" to "well above the average" on the Iowa Test of Basic Skills. Separate analyses showed similar gains for schools in Denver, Boston, and Portland, Maine (Expeditionary Learning Outward Bound, 1997, 1999a, 1999b).

In their report "Successful School Restructuring," the researchers at Wisconsin's Center for Education Research analyzed project-based learning data from more than 1,500 elementary, middle, and high schools and conducted field studies in forty-four schools in sixteen states between 1990 and 1995. They reported on notable gains made (Newmann & Wehlage, 1995).

Inquiry and Problem-Based Learning

Among the different methods that fall under the project umbrella are "inquiry" and "problem-based learning." Because these methods share most of the attributes of project-based learning, the research into them is important.

The list of educators who have studied these methods is significant. Within their works, you will find bibliographies that contain additional research studies:

Barell, J. (1998). *PBL: An inquiry approach.* Arlington Heights, IL: Skylight.

Bloom, L. Z., & White, E. M. (Eds.). (1993). *Inquiry: A cross-curricular reader.* Englewood Cliffs, NJ: Prentice Hall.

Bransford, J., Brown, A., & Cocking, R. (Eds.). (1999). *How people learn.* Washington, DC: National Research Council, National Academies Press.

Bruner, J. (1987). *Actual minds, possible words.* Cambridge, MA: Harvard University Press.

Gardner, H. (1983). *Frames of mind: The theory of multiple intelligences.* New York: Basic Books.

Gardner, H. (1999). *The disciplined mind.* New York: Simon & Schuster.

Gardner, H. (2006). *Five minds for the future.* Boston: Harvard Business Press.

Joyce, B., Weil, M., & Calhoun, E. (2000). *Models of teaching.* Needham Heights, MA: Allyn & Bacon.

Kilpatrick, W. H. (1918). *The project method.* New York: Teachers College Press.

Polman, J. L. (2000). *Designing project-based science: Connecting learners through guided inquiry.* New York: Teachers College Press.

Classroom Strategies That Work

In their landmark meta-analysis of which instructional strategies had the most significant research showing positive effects on student achievement, a research team from McREL provided educators with a synthesis of best classroom instructional practices. When you purposefully integrate these strategies into a project, you enrich its instruction and students' benefit in the development of many of the key 21st century skills as well as achievement (Marzano, Pickering, & Pollock, 2001).

In educational research, the terms *strategy, tactic,* and *activity* have precise meanings:

- A *strategy* is a generic term applied to more specific, research-supported methods of teaching called tactics that share similar attributes or qualities. If there are sufficient similar methods, they are gathered as a strategy under one name, and their impact on student performance is analyzed as in the meta-analysis *Classroom Strategies That Work* (Marzano, Pickering, & Pollock, 2001).
- A *tactic* is a single method that is part of a strategy group. It is part of a large group of other tactics that have similar attributes. Think-pair-share and groups of four are learning tactics grouped under the strategy cooperative learning.
- An *activity* is a single method that a teacher uses to accomplish a goal. The activity may be a strategy, a tactic, or a way to fill time. An activity becomes a tactic when the teacher, based on research into the activity's effectiveness, places it in the lesson or project as a means of raising student achievement. All tactics are activities, but because many classroom activities are not backed by sufficient achievement research, they are not always referred to as tactics.

Best Print Resources and E-Links

An enriched learning project integrates three components of students' learning: (1) standards-aligned content or subject matter, (2) cognition or the ability to think skillfully, and (3) collaboration or the ability to communicate more skillfully via technology and other means. This learning is enriched when teachers select the appropriate digital tools and instructional strategies as methods to make the students more effective and efficient learners. The following list highlights resources you may find helpful. Links to many of these resources can be found at **go.solution-tree.com/instruction**, the online companion to this book.

Planning Projects

Online Resources

21st Century Partnership (**http://www.21stcenturyskills.org**). White papers describing various positions for national advocacy of 21st century learning skills.

Mind Tools (**http://mindtools.com**). Free descriptions of multiple planning tools.

Print Resources

McTighe, J., & Wiggins, G. (2008). *Understanding by design.* Alexandria, VA: Association for Supervision and Curriculum Development. *The* guide for the backwards planning process.

Technology

Online Resources

Association for Educational Communications and Technology (AECT) (**http://aect.org**). Many resources for planning projects; sponsors of an annual contest for multimedia projects.

International Society for Technology in Education (ISTE) (**http://iste.org**). Provides students, teachers, and administrators with standards for technology use in schools.

Print Resources

Richardson, W. (2008). *Blogs, wikis, podcast.* Thousand Oaks, CA: Corwin Press. A popular and practical resource for guiding teachers' use of emerging technology tools.

Solomon, G., & Schrum, L. (2007). *Web 2.0: New tools, new schools.* Eugene, OR: International Society for Technology in Education. Up-to-date descriptions for using technology in classroom instruction.

About Project-Based Learning

Online Resources

Edutopia (**www.edutopia.org**). Lucas Foundation site that gathers research and promotes best practices for project-based inquiry; essential site for any teacher or school planning to initiate inquiry projects.

Eluminate (**www.eluminate.com**). Home of Fire and Ice international collaboration.

Envision Project Bank (**http://envisionprojects.org**). Free resource bank of projects developed by teachers.

Epals (**www.epals.com**). The place to start for projects that connect students via email projects

Hightech High (**www.hightechhigh.org**). Network of public charter schools, with examples of content area projects for upper grade students.

Just Think (**www.justthink.org**). Media production information for projects.

NewTech High (**www.newtechhigh.edu**). Public schools across the nation that are built to encourage projects as a central instructional tool.

Questia (**www.questia.com**). Online research site from the University of Pennsylvania.

Stay Safe Online (**www.staysafeonline.org**). Online site for teachers and parents providing information about protecting children online.

Think (**www.think.org**). Home of think quest projects; an excellent resource for starting a basic e-project, as well as for access to international project competitions.

Think Quest (**http://thinkquest.org**). Program that holds annual international contest for web projects; a bank of more than 7,000 award-winning projects with free access; especially helpful to teachers of young children or novices at project-based learning; the most up-to-date site and a must-use e-tool.

WestED (**www.wested.org**). A nonprofit site with resources and programs to help low performing schools with innovative solutions.

Print Resources

Pearlman, B. (2009). Making 21st century schools. Education Technology, September-October, 49, 14–19.

Critical Thinking Skills

Online Resources

E-concept Map Maker (**http://cmap.ihmc.us**). Website for constructing free online concept maps.

Freeology (**http://freeology.com**). More free e-tools to promote thinking skills.

International Center for the Enhancement of Learning Potential (ICELP) (**www.icelp.org**). International site for theories, methods programs, and research by cognitive psychologist Reuven Feuerstein.

International Renewal Institute (iRi) (**www.iriinc.us**). Professional development for educators, which includes project-based learning, collaboration and communication, and critical and creative thinking; leading provider of Feuerstein Instrumental Enrichment for K–12 student programs.

Webenglishteacher (**http://webenglishteacher.com**). Internet site loaded with free tutorials, templates, samples for making graphic organizers, and other e-tools that promote critical thinking.

Print Resources

Bellanca, J. (2007). *A guide to graphic organizers: Helping students organize and process content for deeper learning.* Thousand Oaks, CA: Corwin Press. Describes twenty-eight graphic organizers with samples linked to various content areas. Includes instructions for using organizers in cooperative teams and for critical thinking.

Bellanca, J., & Rodriguez, E. R. (2006). *What is it about me that you can't teach?* Thousand Oaks, CA: Corwin Press. Discusses challenges faced by urban students, examines research that supports "high expectations" instruction, and provides practical strategies for all grade levels.

Feuerstein, R. (2002). *Theory and applied systems: A reader.* Jerusalem: International Center for the Enhancement of Learning Potential Press. For educators and researchers interested in Mediated Learning Experience (MLE), Learning Propensity Assessment Device (LPAD), and Instrumental Enrichment (IE); provides a comprehensive look at the main theoretical and applied topics of Feuerstein's theory presented from different angles—historical, theoretical, and applied.

Feuerstein, R., Falik, L., Rand, Y., & Feuerstein, R. S. (2006). *The Feuerstein instrumental enrichment program: Creating and enhancing cognitive modifiability* (2nd ed.). Jerusalem: International Center for the Enhancement of Learning Potential Press. The revised and elaborated edition of the work first published in the 1980s, with applications and research to different populations (including adult learners, visually impaired students, and others).

McKenzie, J. (2000). *Beyond technology.* Bellingham, WA: FNO Press. A pioneering book that lays out the argument for use of technology as a tool to promote student thinking through research projects.

Mentis, M., Dunn-Bernstein, M. J., & Mentis, M. (2008). *Mediated learning: Teaching, tasks, and tools to unlock cognitive potential* (2nd ed.). Thousand Oaks, CA: Corwin Press. Uses Feuerstein's theory that educators can enhance intelligence and change the way students think with the right kind of intervention; provides practical strategies to help at-risk students develop cognitive skills. The second edition contains an expanded discussion of mediated learning and applications of the cognitive map and structured cognitive modifiability, as well as reflective activities for the educator.

Torp, L., & Sage, S. (1998). *Problems as possibilities: Problem-based learning for K–12 education.* Alexandra, VA: Association for Supervision and Curriculum Development. Looks at how to use problem-based learning to faster creativity and higher-order thinking skills.

Collaborative and Cooperative Learning

Online Resources

A number of sites allow teachers to connect their students with other students around the world. These "tele-collaboration" sites include:

- Global Kids (**http://globalkids.org**)
- Global SchoolNet (**http://globalschoolnet.org**)
- National Writing Project (**http://nwp.org**)
- Schools Linking Network (**www.schoolslinking.org**)

Other sites with resources on collaboration include:

CDA Collaborative Learning Projects (**www.cdainc.com**). Collaborative learning projects for organizations; all projects are field based.

Center for Effective Collaboration and Practice (**http://cecp.air.org**). Focuses on teaching students with special needs the skills of collaboration.

Class Blogs (**http://classblogmeister.com**). Allows teacher maximum control of student blogs.

The Cooperative Learning (**www.co-operation.org**). Site for the publications and programs of Roger and David Johnson on cooperative learning, conflict resolution, and positive negotiations.

Email (**http://gaggle.net**). Free email with high teacher control within a classroom.

Moodle (**http://moodle.org**). Integrates multiple collaborative tools in a single classroom or school.

Teambuilding (**http://wilderdom.com**). Games and activities that can build teamwork.

Wikipedia (**http://en.wikipedia.org**). Lists of free open-source software that can enable different types of collaboration.

Print Resources

Bellanca, J. (2009). *Designing professional development for change: A guide for improving classroom instruction* (2nd ed). Thousand Oaks, CA: Corwin Press. Offers a starting point for cultivating quality professional learning experiences that lead to improved classroom instruction; contains professional development practices that generate systemic change to improve teaching and learning.

Bellanca, J., & Fogarty, R. (2001). *Blueprints for achievement in the cooperative classroom.* Thousand Oaks, CA: Corwin Press. A practical "how to" book for integrating cooperative learning and critical thinking with subject matter, with the goal of improved student achievement.

Johnson, R., & Johnson, D. (1983). *Cooperative learning.* Minneapolis, MN: InterAction Press. Classic study of teacher–student and student–student interaction. Defines the concept of cooperative learning and gives the strong research base behind its effectiveness.

Assessment

Online Resources

Microsoft (**www.microsoft.com/education/teachers**). Free site with tutorials for using spreadsheets to make rubrics.

University of Kansas (**www.rubistar.4teachers.org**). Site for free assessment to templates and tutorials for assessment and other learning tools.

University of New Castle (**www.newcastle.edu.au**). Free site with tutorials, templates, and sample assessment tools including rubrics and checklists.

Print Resources

Burke, K. (2007). *How to assess authentic learning* (5th ed.). Thousand Oaks, CA: Corwin Press. A practical guide that covers the assessment process with practical tools usable in projects.

Feuerstein, R., Falik, L., Rand, Y., & Feuerstein, R. S. (2003). *dynamic assessment of cognitive modifiability.* Jerusalem: International Center for the Enhancement of Learning Potential Press. A revised and extended edition of the original 1979 volume, which includes new chapters on dynamic assessment of young children as applied to Ethiopian immigrants and children with Down syndrome, including case studies.

McTighe, J., & Wiggins, G. (2008). *Understanding by design.* Alexandria, VA: Association for Supervision and Curriculum Development. Uses planning design that starts with a definition of what students should know and do before proceeding to build a systematic plan. This results-first process is especially valuable for developing the assessment of project-based learning.

Standards-Based Learning

To identify the standards for your state and subject area, search "state education standards" plus the state name or the professional organization for your subject area. In order to develop the samples used in this book, the following sites were helpful:

- National Council of Teachers of English (**www.ncte.org**)
- Mid-continent Research on Education and Learning (**www.mcrel.org**)
- National Council of Teachers of Mathematics (**www.nctm.org**)
- National Center for Supercomputing Applications (**www.ncsa.edu**)
- National Science Teachers Association (**www.nsta.org**)
- National Council for the Social Studies (**www.socialstudies.org**)
- International Society for Technology in Education (**www.iste.org**)

In order to show a variety of state samples for this book, the following sites—in particular, the Massachusetts site—were helpful:

- State of Massachusetts Department of Education (**www.doe.mass.edu**)
- State of Pennsylvania Department of Education (**www.pde.state.pa.us**)

- State of Illinois Department of Education (**www.isbe.state.il.us**)
- State of California Department of Education (**www.cde.ca.gov/index.asp**)
- State of New York Department of Education (**www.nysed.gov**)
- State of Maryland Department of Education (**www.marylandpublicschools.org/msde**)
- State of Montana Department of Education (**www.opi.state.mt.us**)
- State of Oregon Department of Education (**www.ode.state.or.us**)

References

Achilles, C. M., & Hoover, S. P. (1996). *Exploring problem-based learning (PBL) in grades 6–12.* Paper presented at the annual meeting of the Mid-South Educational Research Association, Tuscaloosa, AL. (ERIC Document Reproduction Service No. ED406406)

Ausubel, D. (1963). *The psychology of meaningful verbal learning.* Oxford, England: Grune & Stratton.

Barell, J. (1998). *PBL: An inquiry approach.* Arlington Heights, IL: Skylight.

Barr, R., & Parrett, W. (2001). *Saving our students, saving our schools: 50 proven strategies for helping underachieving students and improving schools.* Thousand Oaks, CA: Corwin Press.

Barron, B. J., Schwartz, D., Vye, N., Moore, A., Petrosino, A., Zech, L., et al. (1998). Doing with understanding: Lessons from research on problem- and project-based learning. *Journal of the Learning Sciences, 7,* 271–311.

Becker, H. J. (2000). Who's wired and who's not: Children's access to and use of computer technology. *The Future of Children, 10,* 44–75.

Bellanca, J. (2007a). *Designing professional development for change: A guide for improving classroom instruction* (2nd ed.). Thousand Oaks, CA: Corwin Press.

Bellanca, J. (2007b). *A guide to graphic organizers: Helping students organize and process content for deeper learning.* Thousand Oaks, CA: Corwin Press.

Bellanca, J. (2008). *200+ active learning strategies and projects for engaging students' multiple intelligences.* Thousand Oaks, CA: Corwin Press.

Bellanca, J., & Fogarty, R. (2001). *Blueprints for achievement in cooperative classrooms.* Thousand Oaks, CA: Corwin Press.

Bellanca, J., & Rodriguez, E. R. (2006). *What is it about me that you can't teach?* Thousand Oaks, CA: Corwin Press.

Bereiter, C., & Scardamalia, M. (1999). *Process and product in PBL research.* Toronto, Ontario, Canada: Institute for Studies in Education, University of Toronto.

Berger, R. (1996). *A culture of quality.* Providence, RI: Brown University Annenberg Institute for School Reform.

Bertucci, A., Johnson, D. W., & Johnson, R. (2009, March 1). Teamwork and taskwork. *Newsletter of the Cooperative Learning Institute, 24.*

Bickford, A., Elder, B., Hammer, B., McGinty, P., McKinley, P., & Mitchell, S. (2000). The eMINTS Project: Enhancing Missouri's instructional networked teaching strategies—Promising developments and projected outcomes. In J. Bourdeau & R. Heller (Eds.), *Proceedings of World Conference on Educational Multimedia, Hypermedia and Telecommunications, 2000* (p. 1806). Chesapeake, VA: Association for the Advancement of Computing in Education.

Bloom, B. S. (1956). *Taxonomy of educational objectives.* New York: David McKay.

Bloom, L. Z., & White, E. M. (Eds.). (1993). *Inquiry: A cross-curricular reader.* Englewood Cliffs, NJ: Prentice Hall.

Blumenfeld, P., Krajcik, J. S., Marx, R. W., & Soloway, E. (1994). Lessons learned: How collaboration helped middle grade science teachers learn project-based instruction. *Elementary School Journal, 94*, 539–551.

Blumenfeld, P., Soloway, E., Marx, R., Krajcik, J., Guzdial, M., & Palincsar, A. (1991). Motivating project-based learning: Sustaining the doing, supporting the learning. *Educational Psychologist, 26,* 369–398.

Boaler, J. (1999). Mathematics for the moment or the millennium? What a British study has to say about teaching methods. *Education Week Commentary, 29*(18), 30 & 34.

Bowe, F. G. (2000). *Universal design in education.* Westport, CT: Bergin & Garvey.

Bransford, J., Brown, A., & Cocking, R. (Eds.). (1999). *How people learn.* Washington, DC: National Academies Press.

Bransford, J., Sherwood, R., Hasselbring, T. S., Kinzer, C. K., & Williams, S. M. (1991). *Anchored instruction: Why we need it and how technology can help.* Mahwah, NJ: Lawrence Erlbaum.

Brown, A. (1992). Design experience. *Journal of the Learning Sciences, 2,* 141–178.

Brown, A., & Campoine, J. C. (1996). Psychological theory and innovative learning environments. In L. Shauble & R. Glaser (Eds.), *Innovation in learning* (pp. 289–325). Mahwah, NJ: Lawrence Erlbaum.

Brown, J. S., Collins, A., & Duguid, P. (1989). Situated cognition of learning. *Educational Researcher, 18,* 32–42.

Bruner, J. (1987). *Actual minds, possible words.* Cambridge, MA: Harvard University Press.

Bulgren, J. A., Deshler, D. D., & Schumaker, J. B. (1995). *The concept comparison routine.* Lawrence, KS: Edge Enterprises.

California Department of Education. (2003). *California language arts blueprint.* Accessed at www.cdc.ca.gov/ta.tg/hs/documents/bp/langarts.03.pdf on September 1, 2009.

California Department of Education. (n.d.). *Grade six mathematics.* Accessed at www.dce.ca.gv/ci/ma/im/documents/mathstandmap5.doc on November 9, 2009.

California State Board of Education. (2009). *Content standards.* Accessed at www.cde.ca.gov/be/st/ss on October 1, 2009.

Carter, R. (2000). *Mapping the mind.* Los Angeles: University of California.

Cognition and Technology Group, Learning Technology Center, Peabody College of Vanderbilt University. (1992). *University technology and the design of generative learning environments.* (ERIC Document Reproduction Service No. EJ430232)

Common Core State Standards Initiative. (n.d.). *Core standards.* Accessed at www.corestandards.org/standards/index.htm on December 14, 2009.

Cooper, L. W. (2001, March). A comparison of online and traditional computer applications classes. *Technological Horizons in Education, 28*, 52–58.

Danielson, C. (n.d.). *The framework for teaching.* Accessed at www.danielsongroup.org/theframeteach.htm on May 21, 2009.

Darch, C. B., Carnine, D. W., & Kameenui, E. J. (1986). The role of graphic organizers and social structure in content area instruction. *Journal of Reading Behavior, 18*(4), 275–295.

David, J. (2008). What research says about project based learning. *Educational Leadership, 65*, 80–82.

Dewey, J. (1916). *Democracy and education.* New York: Macmillan.

Dewey, J. (1938). *Experience and education.* New York: Touchstone.

Diehl, W., Grobe, T., Lopez, H., & Cabral, C. (1999). *Project-based learning: A strategy for teaching and learning.* Boston: Center for Youth Development and Education.

Dryden, K. (1983). *The game.* Toronto, Ontario, Canada: Wiley.

Duffy, T., & Jonassen, D. (1992). *Constructivism and the technology of instruction: A conversation.* Hillsdale, NJ: Lawrence Erlbaum.

Edelson, D. C., Gordon, D. N., & Pea, R. D. (1999). Addressing the challenge of inquiry based learning. *Journal of the Learning Sciences, 8*, 392–450.

eSchool News Staff and Wire Reports. (2005, July 11). Michigan laptop program shows early success. *eSchool News.* Accessed at www.eschoolnews.com/news/showStory.cfm?ArticleID=5780 on November 9, 2009.

Expeditionary Learning Outward Bound. (1997). *Evidence of success.* Cambridge, MA: Author.

Expeditionary Learning Outward Bound. (1999a). *A design for comprehensive school reform.* Cambridge, MA: Author.

Expeditionary Learning Outward Bound. (1999b). *Early indicators from schools implementing New American Schools Designs.* Cambridge, MA: Author.

Feuerstein, R. (1980). *Instrumental enrichment: An intervention program for cognitive modifiability.* Baltimore: University Park Press.

Feuerstein, R. (2002). *Feuerstein's theory and applied systems: A reader.* Jerusalem: International Center for the Enhancement of Learning Press.

Feuerstein, R., Falik, L., Rand, Y., & Feuerstein, R. S. (2006a). *The Feuerstein instrumental enrichment program: Creating and enhancing cognitive modifiability* (2nd ed.). Jerusalem: International Center for the Enhancement of Learning Press.

Feuerstein, R., Falik, L., Rand, Y., & Feuerstein, R. S. (2006b). *You love me! Don't accept me as I am* (3rd ed.). Jerusalem: International Center for the Enhancement of Learning Press.

Feuerstein, R., Falik, L., Rand, Y., & Feuerstein, R. S. (2003). *Dynamic assessment of cognitive modifiability.* Jerusalem: International Center for the Enhancement of Learning Press Press.

Feuerstein, R., Rand, J., Haywood, H. C., Hoffman, M., & Jensen, M. R. (1983). *Learning potential assessment device.* Jerusalem: Hadassah-WIZO-Canada Research Institute.

Forest Buddies. (2008). *Forests: Our lifeline.* Accessed at http://library.thinkquest.org/07aug/00720/imptcarboncycle.html on October 30, 2009.

Gardner, H. (1983). *Frames of mind: The theory of multiple intelligences.* New York: Basic Books.

Gardner, H. (1991). *The unschooled mind.* New York: Basic Books.

Gardner, H. (1999). *The disciplined mind.* New York: Simon & Schuster.

Gardner, H. (2006). *Five minds for the future.* Boston: Harvard Business Press.

Glasgow, N. A. (1997). *New curriculum for new times: A guide to student-centered, problem-based learning.* Thousand Oaks, CA: Corwin Press.

Guzdial, M. (1998). Technological support for project based learning. In C. Dede (Ed.), *Learning with technology* (pp. 47–71). Alexandria, VA: Association for Supervision and Curriculum Development.

Herl, H. E., O'Neil, H. F. Jr., Chung, G. K. W. K., & Schacter, J. (1999). Reliability and validity of a computer-based knowledge mapping system to measure content understanding. *Computers in Human Behavior, 15,* 315–333.

Howell, D., Howell, D., & Childress, M. (2006). *Using PowerPoint in the classroom.* Thousand Oaks, CA: Corwin Press.

Hunter, M. (1982). *Mastery teaching.* Thousand Oaks, CA: Corwin Press.

Illinois Department of Education. (1997). *Illinois state standards.* Accessed at www.isbe.state.il.us/ils on October 30, 2009.

International Society for Technology in Education. (n.d.). *National educational technology standards.* Accessed at http://www.iste.org/AM/Template.cfm?Section=NETS on October 8, 2009.

Iowa Department of Education. (n.d.). *Grade 11 reading comprehension.* Accessed at www.iowa.gov/educate/index.php?option=com_docman on October 8, 2009.

Iowa Department of Education. *Iowa state standards.* Accessed at www.iowa.gov/educate/index.php?option=com_content&view=article&id=1350&Itemid=2287#Standards on October 8, 2009.

Jackson, J. (2008). *Modeling instruction: PBL research summary.* Accessed at www.edutopia.org on October 12, 2009.

Johnson, D. W., & Johnson, R. (2002). Ensuring diversity is positive: Cooperative community, constructive conflict, and civic values. In J. Thousand, R. Villa, & A. Nevin (Eds.), *Creativity and collaborative learning: The practical guide to empowering students, teachers, and families* (2nd ed., pp. 197–208). Baltimore: Paul H. Brookes.

Johnson, D. W., & Johnson, R. (2008). Cooperation and the use of technology. In J. M. Spector, M. D. Merill, J. G. Van Merrienboer, & M. P. Driscoll (Eds.), *Handbook of research on educational communications and technology* (3rd ed., pp. 401–423). New York: Lawrence Erlbaum.

Johnson, R., & Johnson, D. (1983). *Learning together and alone.* Minneapolis, MN: InterAction Press.

Joyce, B., Weil, M., & Calhoun, E. (2000). *Models of teaching.* Needham Heights, MA: Allyn & Bacon.

Kilpatrick, W. H. (1918). *The project method.* New York: Teachers College Press.

Knox, C., & Anderson-Inman, L. (2001). Migrant ESL high school students succeed using networked laptops. *Learning and Leading with Technology,* February, 18–22.

Kotter, J. (2005). *Our iceberg is melting.* New York: St. Martin's Press.

Ladewski, B. G., Krajcik, J. S., & Harvey, C. L. (1994). A middle grade science teacher's emerging understanding of project-based instruction. *Elementary School Journal, 94,* 498–515.

Lau, J., & Lazarus, W. (2002). *Pathways to our future: A multimedia training program for youth that works.* Santa Monica, CA: The Children's Partnership.

Lewin-Benham, A. (2006). *Possible schools.* New York: Teachers College Press.

Lewin-Benham, A. (2008). *Powerful children.* New York: Teachers College Press.

Livers, A. (2008). *Using Microsoft Office to enhance student learning.* Thousand Oaks, CA: Corwin Press.

Ljung, E. J., & Blackwell, M. (1996). Project OMEGA: A winning approach for at-risk teens. *Illinois School Research and Development Journal, 33,* 15–17.

Marx, R. W., Blumenfeld, P. C., Krajcik, J. S., Blunk, M., Crawford, B., Kelley, B., et al. (1994). Enacting project-based science: Experiences of four middle grade teachers. *Elementary School Journal, 94,* 517–538.

Marzano, R., Pickering, D., & Pollock, J. E. (2001). *Classroom instruction that works.* Alexandria, VA: Association for Supervision and Curriculum Development.

Massachusetts Department of Elementary and Secondary Education. *Massachusetts curriculum frameworks.* (n.d.). Accessed at www.doemass.org/frameworks/current.html on November 3, 2009.

McTighe, J., & Wiggins, G. (2008). *Understanding by design.* Alexandria, VA: Association for Supervision and Curriculum Development.

Montana Department of Education. (n.d.). *Montana state standards for literature.* Accessed at www.opi.mt.gov/pdf/Standards/ContStds-Literature.pdf on October 9, 2009.

Murray, C., & Herrnstein, R. (1994). *The bell curve.* Mankato, MN: The Free Press.

National Academies Press. (1996). *National science education standards.* Accessed at www.nap.edu/openbook.php?record_id=4962&pagebook on November 9, 2009.

National Council of Teachers of Mathematics. (n.d.). *Principles and standards for school mathematics.* Accessed at www.standards.nctm.org/document/chapter5/alg.htm on October 24, 2009.

National Science Teachers Association. (n.d.). *National science education standards.* Accessed at www.nsta.org/publications/nses.aspx on November 9, 2009.

Nelson, C. A., & Thomas, K. (2006). *The neuroscience of cognitive development.* Hoboken, NJ: John Wiley & Sons.

New York State Academy for Teaching and Learning. (n.d.). *New York state learning standards.* Accessed at www.nysatl.nysed.gov/standards.html on October 8, 2009.

New York State Education Department. (n.d.). *Learning standards of New York State.* Accessed at www.emsc.nysed.gov/ciai/standards.html on December 12, 2009.

Newmann, R. M., & Wehlage, G. G. (1995). *Successful school restructuring: A report of the public and educators by the Center on Organization and Restructuring of Schools.* Madison, WI: Center on Organization and Restructuring of Schools.

November, A. (2008). *Web literacy for educators.* Thousand Oaks, CA: Corwin Press.

Ogle, D. (1987). K-W-L-Plus: A strategy for comprehension and summarization. *Journal of Reading, 30,* 626–663.

Oregon Department of Education. (n.d.). *Oregon content standards.* Accessed at www.ode.state.or.us/search/results/?id=53 on November 9, 2009.

Pennsylvania Department of Education. (n.d.). *Pennsylvania state standards.* Accessed at www.pde.state.pa.us/state board_ed/lib/stateboard.html on December 10, 2009.

Penuel, W. R., & Means, B. (1999, July). *Observing classroom processes in project-based learning using multimedia: A tool for evaluators.* Paper presented at the Secretary of Education's National Conference on Educational Technology, Washington, DC. Accessed at www.ed.gov/Technology/TechConf/1999/whitepapers/paper3.html on October 8, 2009.

Perkins, D., Fogarty, R., & Barell, J. (1991). *How to teach for transfer.* Palatine, IL: IRI/Skylight Publishing.

Piaget, J. (1974). *La prise de conscience.* Paris: University of Paris.

Pohlmann, J., & Pea, R. D. (1997). *Transformative communication in project science learning discourse.* Paper presented to the American Educational Research Association, Chicago.

Polaman, J. L. (2000). *Designing project-based science: Connecting learners through guided inquiry.* New York: Teachers College Press.

Pritchard, A. (2008). *Effective teaching with Internet technologies.* Thousand Oaks, CA: Corwin Press.

Rockman Report. (1998). *Powerful tools for schooling: Schoolbook laptop projects.* Beaufort County (SC) School District. Accessed at www.beaufort.k12.sc.us/district/ltopeval.html on October 8, 2009.

Rockwood, H. S., III. (1995a). Cooperative and collaborative learning. *The National Teaching & Learning Forum, 4*(6), 8–9.

Rockwood, H. S., III. (1995b). Cooperative and collaborative learning. *The National Teaching & Learning Forum, 5*(4), 8–10.

Roschelle, J. M., Pea, R. D., Hoadley, C. M., Gordin, D. N., & Means, B. M. (2000). Changing how and what children learn in school with computer-based technologies. *The Future of Children, 10*(2) 76–101.

Rose, D. H., & Meyer, A. (2002). *Teaching every student in the digital age: Universal design for learning.* Alexandria, VA: Association for Supervision and Curriculum Development.

Roseth, C., Johnson, D., & Johnson, R. (2008). Promoting early adolescents' achievement and peer relationships. *Psychological Bulletin, 134,* 223–246.

Ross, S. M., Sanders, W. L., & Wright, S. P. (1999). *Value-added achievement results for two cohorts of the Co-NECT schools in Memphis: 1995–1999 outcomes.* Memphis, TN: Center for Research in Educational Policy.

Ross, S. M., Wang, L. W., Sanders, W. L., Wright, S. P., & Stringfield, S. (1999). *Two- and three-year achievement results on the Tennessee Value-Added Assessment System for restructuring schools in Memphis.* Memphis, TN: Center for Research in Educational Policy.

Scarmadella, M., & Bereiter, C. (1991). Higher levels of agency for children in knowledge building. *Journal of the Living Sciences, 1,* 37–68.

Sivin-Kachala, J., & Bialo, E. R. (2000). *2000 research report on the effectiveness of technology in schools.* Washington, DC: Software & Information Industry Association.

Slavin, R. (1994). *Essential elements of cooperative learning in classrooms.* (ERIC Document No. ED 370881)

Smith, G. G., Ferguson, D., & Caris, M. (2002). Teaching over the web versus in the classroom: Difference in the instructor experience. *International Journal of Instructional Media, 29,* 61.

SRI International. (2009). *Center for Technology in Learning.* Accessed at http://ctl.sri.com on October 12, 2009.

State Board of Education TEKS Review Committee. (2009). *Texas Essential Knowledge and Skills: Draft of proposed revisions.* Accessed at ritter.tea.state.tx.us/teks/social/WorldGeography073109.pdf on November 9, 2009.

Texas Education Agency. (n.d.). *Texas standards for social studies.* Accessed at http://ritter.tea.state.tx.us/teks/socialstudiesTEKS.html on October 8, 2009.

Thirunarayanan, M. O., & Perez-Prado, A. (2002). Comparing web-based and classroom-based learning: A quantitative study. *Journal of Research on Technology in Education, 34,* 131–137.

Thomas, J. (2000). *A review of research on project based learning.* San Rafael, CA: Autodesk Foundation.

Thomas, J. W., & Mergendollar, J. R. (2000). *Principles from the field.* Paper presented to the American Educational Research Association, New Orleans.

Thomas, J. W., Mergendoller, J. R., & Michaelson, A. (1999). *Project-based learning: A handbook for middle and high school teachers.* San Francisco: The Buck Institute.

Torp, L., & Sage, S. (1998). *Problems as possibilities: Problem based learning for K–12 education.* Alexandria, VA: Association for Supervision and Curriculum Development.

Vygotsky, L. (1979). *Collected works, vols. 1–6.* Cambridge, MA: Harvard University Press.

Wang, L. (2005). The advantages of using technology in second language education: Technology integration in foreign language teaching demonstrates the shift from a behavioral to a constructivist learning approach. *Technological Horizons in Education, 32*(10), 38.

Washington State University. (2006). *Guide to rating integrative and critical thinking.* Accessed at http://wsuctproject.wsu.edu on October 9, 2009.

Wenglinsky, H. (2000). *How teaching matters: Bringing the classroom back into discussions of teacher quality.* Princeton, NJ: Educational Testing Service.

Index